Weidong Kou

Payment Technologies for E-Commerce

With 86 Figures and 4 Tables

 Springer

Weidong Kou

Room G05, TIIB
The University of Hong Kong
Pokfulam Road
Hong Kong, P. R. China
and
National Key Laboratory of ISN
Xidian University
Xi'an, 710071, P. R. China

weidong_kou@hotmail.com

Library of Congress Cataloging-in-Publication Data

Payment technologies for E-commerce/Weidong Kou, editor.
    p. cm.
    Includes bibliographical references and index
    ISBN 3-540-44007-0 (alk.paper)
    1. Computer security. 2. Electronic funds transfers--Security mesures. 3. Electronic
commerce--Security measures. I. Kou, Weidong.

    QA76.9.A25P39 2003
    005.8--dc21
                                                                2002044591

ACM Subject Classification (1998): H.4, K.4.4, J.1

ISBN 3-540-44007-0 Springer-Verlag Berlin Heidelberg New York

Springer-Verlag Berlin Heidelberg New York
is a member of BertelsmannSpringer Science+Business Media GmbH
http://www.springer.de

© Springer-Verlag Berlin Heidelberg 2003
Printed in Germany

Typesetting: Camera-ready by the editor
Cover Design: KünkelLopka, Heidelberg
Printed on acid-free paper   45/3142SR   5 4 3 2 1 0

Payment Technologies for E-Commerce

Springer
Berlin
Heidelberg
New York
Hong Kong
London
Milan
Paris
Tokyo

Table of Contents

1   Introduction to E-Payment:
     An Essential Piece of the E-Commerce Puzzle
     Weidong Kou   1
1.1   Introduction   1
1.2   About This Book   3
1.3   References   6

2   Security Fundamentals
     Fangguo Zhang and Yumin Wang............................   7
2.1   Electronic Commerce Security............................   7
2.2   Introduction to Cryptography.............................   9
2.3   Symmetric Cryptosystems.................................   13
2.4   Public-Key Cryptography..................................   17
2.5   Digital Signatures...   24
2.6   Cryptographic Hash Functions..........................   30
2.7   Cryptographic Random Number Generators   31
2.8   Authentication   32
2.9   Summary...   37
2.10   References...   38

3   Public-Key Infrastructure
     Hui Li and Yumin Wang.....................................   39
3.1   Introduction   39
3.2   X.509..   50
3.3   Credential-Based PKI Systems..........................   61
3.4   Summary...   67
3.5   References...   67

4   Biometrics for Security in E-Commerce
     David Zhang and Li Yu......................................   71
4.1   An Overview of Biometrics..............................   71
4.2   Potential Application Areas...............................   79
4.3   Multiple Authentication Technologies.......................   83

4.4   How to Select a Biometrics System..   86
4.5   Summary..   92
4.6   References...   92

5   Smart Cards and Applications
        Weidong Kou, Simpson Poon, and Edwin M. Knorr........................   95
5.1   Introduction...   95
5.2   Fundamentals of Smart Card Systems...   97
5.3   Java Card...   106
5.4   Smart Card Standards..   109
5.5   Smart Cards and Security..   111
5.6   Smart Card Applications...   114
5.7   A Case Study in Smart Cards: Hong Kong's Octopus Card..............   118
5.8   Summary..   125
5.9   References..   126

6   Wireless Infrastructure
        Weidong Kou..   127
6.1   Introduction...   127
6.2   Wireless Communications Infrastructure.....................................   128
6.3   Wireless Computing Infrastructure..   131
6.4   Wireless Application Protocol...   134
6.5   Wireless Security..   144
6.6   Summary..   145
6.7   Appendix..   146
6.8   References...   147

7   Payment Agents
        Amitabha Das...   149
7.1   Introduction...   149
7.2   Security Implications of Mobile-Agent-Based Systems...................   151
7.3   Security Techniques Protecting Mobile Agents............................   151
7.4   Secure Payment Protocols Using Mobile Agents in an Untrusted Host
        Environment...   156
7.5   Summary..   168
7.6   References...   169

8   Digital Cash
        Yi Mu, Vijay Varadharajan, and Khanh Quoc Nguyen..................   171
8.1   Introduction...   171
8.2   Security Requirements for Digital Cash.....................................   172
8.3   Brands' Digital-Cash Scheme..   173
8.4   One-Response Digital Cash...   175
8.5   Fair Digital Cash..   181
8.6   Summary..   189
8.7   Appendix..   189
8.8   References..   192

9   Digital Checks
        Bo Yang.............   195
9.1   Introduction..   195
9.2   Digital Check Concept..   195
9.3   NetBill...   199
9.4   NetCheque System..   207
9.5   Summary..   209
9.6   References..   209

10   Secure Electronic Transactions:
        Overview, Capabilities, and Current Status
        Gordon Agnew..   211
10.1   Introduction..   211
10.2   Protocol Stack and Capabilities...   212
10.3   SET Overview..   215
10.4   SET Performance..   223
10.5   What Lies Ahead..   225
10.6   Summary..   225
10.7   References..   226

11   Credit Card-Based Secure Online Payment
        Johnny Wong, Lev Mirlas, Weidong Kou, and Xiaodong Lin............   227
11.1   Introduction..   227
11.2   Online Payment by Credit Card..   228

11.3   Trust Problems in Credit Card Payments.................................   230
11.4   Trusted Third Party and a Payment Protocol Using a Trusted Third
       Party...   233
11.5   Summary...   238
11.6   Appendices..   238
11.7   References..   243

12   Micropayments
       Amir Herzberg..   245
12.1   Introduction..   245
12.2   Overview of Micropayment Systems.......................................   246
12.3   Cost Factors for Online Payments..   250
12.4   Disputes and Chargebacks..   252
12.5   Customer Acquiring and Support Costs....................................   262
12.6   Equipment, Processing, and Communication Costs.....................   273
12.7   Summary...   279
12.8   References..   280

13   Industrial E-Payment Systems and Solutions
       Zheng Huang, Dong Zheng, Zichen Li, and Weidong Kou.............   283
13.1   Introduction..   283
13.2   Visa Cash..   283
13.3   iPIN E-Payment..   289
13.4   PayPal..   294
13.5   Summary...   298
13.6   References..   299

14   Challenges and Opportunities in E-Payment
       Weidong Kou..   301
14.1   E-Commerce Challenges: E-Payment Security and Privacy...........   301
14.2   E-Payment Systems Supporting Multiple Payment Methods.........   302
14.3   Smart Cards and Digital Cash...   304
14.4   Micropayment Issues and Solutions.......................................   305
14.5   Summary...   306
14.6   References..   306

Glossary... 309

About the Editor... 323

Contributors... 325

Index 331

1 Introduction to E-Payment:
An Essential Piece of the E-Commerce Puzzle

Weidong Kou

University of Hong Kong
Pokfulam Road, Hong Kong

1.1 Introduction

When we look at the whole picture of e-commerce, there are many pieces in the puzzle, including the Internet communication infrastructure, various web and e-commerce application servers, client browsers, products/services, databases, security and firewalls, electronic payment (or e-payment), and many other components. To make an e-commerce web storefront work, one needs to put all these pieces of the puzzle together. The first thing that happens in cyberspace is that the customer goes through the web storefront, and looks for a product/service that is interesting to him (or her). It is clear that after the customer has searched web storefront and identified products or services, the immediate next step is making the payment for the purchase of the products/services that the customer has selected. Obviously, e-payment is essential to e-commerce transactions. Without a successful e-payment step, the e-commerce picture is not complete, and very often it will not work.

Currently, the most popular method for e-payment over the Internet is credit card based e payment. Credit cards have been widely used for mail ordering and telephone ordering. There are regulations on credit cards established by the Federal Reserve Board, the US federal agency charged with oversight of consumer credit card regulations. According to these regulations, merchants who accept credit card information in a transaction in which the credit card is not present are responsible for unauthorized transactions using the credit card information. Although the rule was developed for the mail order and telephone order context, it applies equally to the context of e-commerce over the Internet. The Federal Reserve Board's credit card regulations also limit consumer liability for unauthorized credit card transaction charges to US $50. This limit applies to all kinds of situations whether the card is used in a face-to-face transaction, a mail order transaction, a telephone order transaction, or an e-commerce transaction over the Internet.

These federal regulations provide a regulatory framework for credit card based payment transactions over the Internet.

Given the regulatory framework, to make credit card payment work over the Internet, a technical framework has to be developed. The technical framework consists of a number of protocols/schemes to implement online credit card payment. There are two notable credit card based e-payment schemes that have been used in most retail online merchant sites. One is the combination of credit cards with the secure sockets layer (SSL) protocol, and the other is the scheme based on the secure electronic transaction (SET). The SSL protocol provides a secure communication channel between the web browser of an online customer and the e-commerce server at an online merchant site. The SSL is based on public-key infrastructure (PKI). The SET is a standard for online credit card payment. Derived from IBM's internet payment protocol (iKP), the SET was developed jointly by Visa and MasterCard in collaboration with major IT companies such as IBM, GTE, Microsoft, SAIC (Science Applications International Corporation), Terisa Systems, and Verisign. The SET standard offers a much higher level of security than the SSL-based scheme by adding much stronger security protection against fraud and unauthorized use of credit card information. The strong security protection comes with the expense of adding more complex cryptographic operations that may require additional computation resources. The additional cryptographic operations can either make the average end user's system slow to respond to the e-payment transaction, which for the end user is not tolerable, or it simply exceeds the processing capacity of the end user's system. These problems together with business issues have contributed a slow adoption of the SET standard. The SSL-based scheme has, on the other hand, become the de facto standard for online credit card payment despite that it only provides minimal security for credit card payment transaction for this over the Internet. The main reasons are that the SSL is relatively simple, the response time of an SSL-based credit card transaction is acceptable to the average user, and the existing regulatory framework of the credit card system supplements the strong protection in the SET standard to make the SSL-based credit card online payment scheme meet the current minimum requirements of online merchants, online customers, and financial institutions [1.1-1.8].

In addition to credit card based online payment, there are other e-payment methods, including digital check, digital cash, e-payment based on debit cards, smart cards, prepaid cards, pay-by-phone service, and micropayments [1.1-1.8]. Some of these e-payment methods are briefly described as below.

- **Digital check:** Digital check is a paper-check-like payment scheme. With a digital check system in place, funds can be transferred from the payer's bank account to the payee's bank account at the time the transaction takes place. Digital check is based on a bank-account debit system. The requirements for digital check systems include the assurance of a high level of security, the capability of handling different volumes (from large to small), digital check processing efficiency, low cost of writing a digital check, and the availability to customers through a variety of service providers.

- **Digital cash:** Digital cash is based on credit and cash-payment systems. A digital cash system usually consists of a client, a merchant, and a bank. The client obtains digital cash from the bank and pays the merchant for the goods or services that he (or she) is purchasing. The properties of digital cash include anonymity, transferability, untraceability, infinite duration, portability, and double-spending protection.

- **Smart cards:** Smart cards are plastic cards with an embedded integrated circuit. When smart cards are used as a payment vehicle, they can be used either as a prepaid card with a fixed monetary value, or as a reloadable card (that is, electronic purse) into which people can reload a monetary value from time to time.

- **Micropayment:** Micropayment deals with a very small payment, typically in the range from one cent to a few dollars. Sometimes, the payment can be even a fraction of one cent. Micropayment is perhaps a new payment method born with e-commerce over the Internet. "Pay per click" for a piece of music or video, or pay for a piece of real-time information related to a particular company or company's stock is a new phenomenon in the Internet age. Traditional credit cards or other payment methods will not work, as there is a minimum charge for processing the payment that could exceed the value of a micropayment transaction.

When we look beyond e-commerce applications in web storefronts, nowadays, transferring business services onto the Web has becomes a trend in various industries, particularly given the recent technological developments in the areas of Web Services and Semantic Web. The idea of virtual communities is becoming a reality, as evidenced by many such communities in cyberspace having been built in the last few years, from educational hubs to virtual shopping centers. The latest technological advances in complex online services have required stronger security and more convenience in online payment over the Internet. The challenge is how to meet this increasing demand to produce new e-payment systems/solutions.

1.2 About This Book

This book is meant to respond to the need for a book that can provide readers with comprehensive information on advances in e-payment technology for e-commerce.

We have invited leading experts across the globe, from North America to the Middle East, from Australia and Singapore to Hong Kong and China, to contribute to this book. Starting with fundamental security, the book covers the major subjects related to e-payment, including public key infrastructure, security based on biometrics, smart cards, wireless infrastructure, payment agents, digital cash, digital checks, a secure online payment protocol using a trusted third party, SET, and micropayment.

The target audience of this book includes e-commerce and e-business developers, business managers, academic researchers, university students, professors, and professional consultants. This book can also be used for e-payment classes and training courses.

The book has been divided into roughly two parts. The first part from Chapter 2 to Chapter 7 covers the infrastructure for secure e-payment over the Internet. The second part from Chapter 8 to Chapter 13 covers a variety of e-payment methods and e-payment systems/solutions.

Security is one of the major emphases of this book. The focus of Chapters 2-4 is on security. The security requirements for e-payment or e-commerce in general, such as message privacy, message integrity, authentication, authorization, non-repudiation, and secure payment, are covered in Chapter 2. In addition, in Chapter 2, the cryptography algorithms and cryptanalysis are also discussed. Chapter 3 is mainly for the discussion of public-key infrastructure (PKI), including certificate authorities (CAs) and the ITU X.509 authentication framework. The authors of Chapter 3 have also covered the recent development of credential-based PKI systems such as simple distributed security infrastructure (SDSI) and simple public-key infrastructure (SPKI). Biometrics, such as fingerprint, retina-scan, facial scan, and voice scan, can be used to strengthen the security. In Chapter 4, a comprehensive overview of biometric technologies is provided. The potential applications of biometrics, including e-commerce applications, are discussed.

Smart cards and applications for security and e-payment are presented in Chapter 5. Smart card topics include fundamentals of smart card systems, Java Card, smart card standards, smart card security, and various smart card applications including e-payment. The Hong Kong Octopus Card, a real-life example of successful smart cards, is presented as a case study of smart cards and related applications.

With the advance of wireless technologies, e-commerce is moving to the wireless world. Wireless payment (or mobile payment) is gaining popularity. Wireless infrastructure is covered in Chapter 6, including wireless communication infrastructure, wireless computing infrastructure, wireless application protocol, and wireless security.

Chapter 7 is devoted to payment agents. A software agent is a software program that acts autonomously on behalf of a person or organization. It is very interesting to know how these software agents can be used for personalization to help us to conduct e-commerce and to make payments online. Chapter 7 covers agent systems for e-commerce and the use of agents for payment. The security implications of mobile-agent-based systems are examined. Various security techniques for protecting mobile agents are also described, followed by a detailed discussion on how to use mobile agents in an untrusted environment to conduct secure payment.

Starting with Chapter 8, the book covers a variety of e-payment methods. The authors of Chapter 8 discuss various digital cash schemes, including Brands' digital cash scheme, one-response digital cash scheme, and fair digital cash scheme. Digital checks are covered in Chapter 9. The subjects include the fundamentals of digital checks and two digital check examples: NetBill and NetCheque. Chapter 10 covers the SET standard with a detailed SET overview. The current status is reported, and the performance issue of the SET standard is discussed. The improvement of the SET standard can be made through the use of alternative PKI systems, such as elliptic curve cryptosystem (ECC). A general introduction to credit-card-based online payment is provided in Chapter 11. In addition, an innovative secure online payment protocol using a trusted third party is also described. This protocol supports privacy protection, as the order information is not released to the third party. A patent application based on this protocol has been filed. Extensive coverage of micro-payment is provided in Chapter 12, including an overview of micro-payment systems, analysis of cost factors for online payments, disputes and charge-backs, customer acquisition and support costs, equipment, and processing and communication costs.

After the discussion of a variety of e-payment methods, in Chapter 13, three systems/solutions of e-payment are introduced, including Visa Cash, iPIN, and PayPal, with descriptions of features, advantages, disadvantages, and security mechanisms.

Finally, the book concludes with Chapter 14, in which challenges and opportunities in e-payment are identified and presented. In particular, we discussed privacy and security issues, multiple payment methods, smart cards and digital cash, and micropayment.

The readers can take advantage of the structure of the book. If they have no background knowledge of security, then they can read chapters of this book sequentially; if they are already familiar with security and PKI, they can escape reading Chapters 2-3; or if they want to focus on payment methods only, they can directly go to Chapter 8, and start their reading from there. Of course, the readers, as they wish, can always select a chapter to read without a particular order.

1.3 References

[1.1]   W. Kou, Y. Yesha (2002) Editorial of special issue on technological chal-
         lenges in electronic commerce. Int J Digit Libr 3: 277–278.
[1.2]   W. Kou, Y. Yesha, C. J. Tan (eds.) (2001) Electronic commerce tech-
         nologies. LNCS 2040. Springer, Berlin Heidelberg New York.
[1.3]   W. Kou, Y. Yesha (eds.) (2000) Electronic commerce technology trends:
         challenges and opportunities. IBM Press, Carlsbad.
[1.4]   W. Kou (1997) Networking security and standards. Kluwer, Boston
         Dordrecht London.
[1.5]   M. H. Sherif (2000) Protocols for secure electronic commerce. CRC
         Press, Boca Raton London New York Washington DC.
[1.6]   M. Shaw, R. Blanning, T. Strader, A. Whinston (2000) Handbook on
         electronic commerce. Springer, Berlin Heidelberg New York.
[1.7]   D. O'Mahony, M. Peirce, H. Tewari (1997) Electronic payment systems.
         Artech House, Boston London.
[1.8]   P. Wayner (1997) Digital cash (2nd ed.). AP Professional, Boston New
         York London.

2 Security Fundamentals

Fangguo Zhang and Yumin Wang

National Key Laboratory of ISN
Xidian University, Xi'an, China

2.1 Electronic Commerce Security

Since the creation of the World Wide Web (WWW), Internet-based electronic commerce has been transformed from a mere idea into reality. The Internet and similar networks provide new infrastructures for communications and commerce. These open networks interconnect computers across many different organizations with dramatically lower communications and distributed-applications development costs. This motivates businesses to transfer commercial activity from closed private networks to open networks like the Internet. Electronic commerce is classified into several forms. Business to business (B2B), business to consumer (B2C), and business to government (B2G) represent the most significant forms in terms of value.

All traditional commercial activities use procedures or occur within contexts designed to generate trust between individuals or between businesses. These trust mechanisms reduce the commercial risks faced by traders and rely on a variety of factors from prior track records, reputations, and the legal context for an exchange. However, unlike discrete face-to-face transactions where some goods are exchanged for cash, electronic commerce creates both opportunities and difficulties for potential traders. Specifically, it opens the opportunity to expand trade at lower costs in a larger marketplace distributed over a wider geographic scope. Indeed, leveraging these new opportunities over an inexpensive global communications infrastructure will be one of the key benefits of electronic commerce.

Open networks like the Internet pose the new requirement of generating trust in an electronic environment. The kernel of electronic commerce is its security, which has been described in many references [2.6-2.8]. We survey the essential requirements for carrying out secure electronic commerce as follows.

- Server security

  Internet commerce requires secure-server computers, computers that serve documents, files, or programs to users. Server computers with critical applications should not be vulnerable to many attacks, such as software viruses, Trojan horses (viruses that are hidden programs or documents to be activated at a later time), and unauthorized access to the network by hackers. The basic way to achieve this is to use firewalls and proxy machines. Proxy and firewall servers intermediate all Internet communications between a firm and its external environment. Every packet and/or file transferred to or from the Internet to a firm's internal machine goes through the proxy or firewall server, where the data is checked to assure that there are no known viruses or other problems.

- Message privacy (also known as confidentiality)

  Message privacy is a key requirement for electronic commerce, it assures that communications between trading parties are not revealed to others as the message traverses an open network, thus, an unauthorized party cannot read or understand the message.

- Message integrity

  Message Integrity is another key requirement for electronic commerce. It is important that the communications between trading parties are not altered by a malicious enemy as they traverse an open network.

- Authentication

  In most contexts, the term authentication on its own is often used to mean *authentication of the sender*, which is the assurance the sender of the message was actually the person they claimed to be. Using the paper-letter analogy, authentication of the sender is primarily provided by the signature at the bottom of the page, but the general look of the document, such as the letterhead and/or watermark on the paper, is usually also taken into consideration. Other contexts in which the term *authentication* is commonly used include

  o *User authentication*, which is the assurance that the user of a computer system is really who they claim to be.

  o *Authentication of the receiver*, which allows the sender to be sure that the party they intend to get the message to is the one who receives it, or at least, is the only one who can understand it.

- Authorization

  Authorization ensures that a party has the authority to make a transaction, or is authorized to access specific information or computer resources. Authorization excludes the risk that employees or others may make transactions that create economic damage or access key information or computational resources of the organization.

- Audit mechanisms and non-repudiation

  Like normal commercial transactions, audit mechanisms for electronic commerce enable the exchange parties to maintain and revisit a history or the sequence of events during a prior transaction. In electronic commerce, these audit trails could include time stamps or records by different computers at different stages of a transaction. In addition, there is a need for confirmations and acknowledgments by the various transacting parties that they have accurately received various messages and made specific commitments. Parties should not be able to repudiate their prior commitments.

- Payments and settlements

  Electronic payment and settlements systems lower transaction costs for trading parties. Secure payment and settlement systems also ensure that the commitments to pay for goods or a service over electronic media are met. They are vital to widespread electronic commerce.

In most cases, authentication and non-repudiation are more important to commerce than confidentiality. The majority of business transactions are not sensitive enough to warrant the sender to pay much effort to prevent their contents from being disclosed to third parties. On the other hand, it is usually vital for the receiver of a message to be certain of the identity (or in some cases, the authority) of the sender of the message and that the message has not been altered in transit. In the event of disputes, it is also important that both the sender and the receiver of a message are able to prove later that the message was indeed sent, and thus, hold both parties to the agreement.

There are a number of ways to meet the above security requirements for secure electronic commerce. Other than server security, all the different mechanisms rely on techniques of cryptography. Cryptographic security mechanisms, including data encryption and digital signature schemes, are often used to provide these security services.

2.2 Introduction to Cryptography

Cryptography is the science of writing in secret code and is an ancient art. The history of cryptography dates back to circa 1900 BC where it was mainly used for military purposes. Classical cryptography is used to protect the contents of a message from being viewed by unauthorized parties. It is the art of transforming the contents of a message from its original form to one that cannot be decoded by un-

authorized parties. This ensures that the message remains incomprehensible to unauthorized eyes, even if it is intercepted. Cryptography is a field that is by no
means new, but until recently, it has largely remained in the hands of the military.
Usage of cryptography for civilian purposes has become more of a mainstream
practice only with the advent of ubiquitous computing and public networks. With
the widespread development of computer communications, many new forms of
cryptography have been proposed. In data and telecommunications, cryptography
is necessary when communicating over any untrusted medium, which includes just
about *any* network, particularly the Internet.

As we move into an information society, the technological means for global
surveillance of millions of individual people are becoming available to major governments. Cryptography has become one of the main tools for privacy, trust, access control, electronic payments, corporate security, and countless other fields.

In the following, we will introduce the basics of modern cryptography. For
more about the concepts and techniques of classical cryptography, we refer the
reader to [2.11, 2.14, 2.16, 2.17].

2.2.1 Basic Concept

In cryptographic terminology, the message is called *plaintext* or *cleartext*. Encoding the contents of the message in a way that hides its contents from outsiders is
called *encryption*. The encrypted message is called the *ciphertext*. The process of
retrieving the plaintext from the ciphertext is called *decryption*. Encryption and
decryption usually make use of a key, and the coding method is such that decryption can be performed only by knowing the proper key.

Cryptology can be broken into two subfields: cryptography and cryptanalysis.
Cryptography is the art or science of keeping messages secret and cryptanalysis is
the art of breaking ciphers, i.e., retrieving the plaintext without knowing the
proper key.

2.2.2 Basic Cryptographic Algorithms

A method of encryption and decryption is called a cipher. Some cryptographic
methods rely on the secrecy of the algorithms; such algorithms are only of histori-
cal interest and are not adequate for real-world needs. Modern algorithms use keys
to control encryption and decryption; a message can be decrypted only if the key
matches the encryption key.

There are two classes of key-based encryption algorithms, symmetric (or secret-key) and asymmetric (or public-key) algorithms. The difference is that symmetric algorithms use the same key for encryption and decryption (or the decryption key is easily derived from the encryption key), whereas asymmetric algorithms use a different key for encryption and decryption, and the decryption key cannot be derived from the encryption key.

Symmetric algorithms can be divided into stream ciphers and block ciphers. Stream ciphers can encrypt a single bit of plaintext at one time, whereas block ciphers take a number of bits and encrypt them as a single unit.

Asymmetric ciphers (also called public-key algorithms or, generally, public-key cryptography) permit the encryption key to be public, allowing anyone to encrypt with the key, whereas only the proper recipient (who knows the decryption key) can decrypt the message. The encryption key is also called the public key and the decryption key is called the private key or secret key.

2.2.3 Cryptanalysis

Cryptanalysis is the art and science of recovering the plaintext of a message without knowing the proper keys. There are many cryptanalytic techniques. Some of the more important ones for a system implementer are described below [2.11, 2.15].

- **Ciphertext-only attack**: This is the situation where an attacker does not know anything about the contents of the message and must work from ciphertext only. In practice, it is quite often possible to make guesses about the plaintext, as many types of messages have fixed format headers. However, this does not work well against modern ciphers.

- **Known-plaintext attack**: The attacker knows or can guess the plaintext for some parts of the ciphertext. The task is to decrypt the rest of the ciphertext blocks using this information. This may be done by determining the key used to encrypt the data, or via some shortcut.

- **Chosen-plaintext attack**: The attacker is able to have any text he likes encrypted with the unknown key. The task is to determine the key used for encryption.

- **Man-in-the-middle attack**: This attack is relevant for cryptographic communication and key exchange protocols. The usual way to prevent the man-in-the-middle attack is to use a public-key cryptosystem capable of providing digital signatures.

- **Correlation**: Correlation between the secret key and the output of the cryptosystem is the main source of information to the cryptanalyst. In the easiest case, the information about the secret key is directly leaked by the cryptosystem. More complicated cases require studying the correlation (basically, any relation that would not be expected on the basis of chance alone) between the observed (or measured) information about the cryptosystem and the guessed key information.

- **Attack against or using the underlying hardware**: In the last few years, as more and more small mobile crypto devices have come into widespread use, a new category of attacks has become relevant which aim directly at the hardware implementation of the cryptosystem.

- **Faults in cryptosystems**: These can lead to cryptanalysis and even to the discovery of the secret key. The interest in cryptographic devices led to the discovery that some algorithms behaved very badly with the introduction of small faults in the internal computation.

- **Quantum computing**: The research on polynomial time factoring and discrete logarithm algorithms with quantum computers has caused growing interest in quantum computing. Quantum computing is a recent field of research that uses quantum mechanics to build computers that are, in theory, more powerful than modern serial computers. The power is derived from the inherent parallelism of quantum mechanics. So instead of doing tasks one at a time, as serial machines do, quantum computers can perform them all at once. Thus, it is hoped that with quantum computers we can solve problems infeasible with serial machines. The recent results of quantum computing research imply that if quantum computers could be implemented effectively, then most of public key cryptography would become history. However, they are much less effective against secret key cryptography. Current states of the art of quantum computing do not appear alarming, as only very small machines have been implemented. The theory of quantum computation show much promise for better performance than serial computers, however, whether it will be realized in practice is an open question.

- **DNA cryptography**: Leonard Adleman, one of the inventors of the well-known RSA Cryptosystem (see Section 2.4), came up with the idea of using DNA as computers. DNA molecules could be viewed as a very large computer capable of parallel execution. This parallel nature could give DNA computers exponential speedup against modern serial computers. There are, unfortunately, problems with DNA computers, one being that the exponential speed-up requires also exponential growth in the volume of the material needed. Thus in practice DNA computers would have limits on their performance. Also, it is not very easy to build one.

There are many other cryptographic attacks and cryptanalysis techniques. However, these are probably the most important ones for an application designer. Anyone contemplating designing a new cryptosystem should have a much deeper understanding of these issues.

2.3 Symmetric Cryptosystems

In *secret key cryptography*, a single key is used for both encryption and decryption. As shown in Fig. 2.1, the sender uses the key to encrypt the plaintext and sends the ciphertext to the receiver. The receiver applies the same key to decrypt the message and recover the plaintext. Because a single key is used for both functions, secret key cryptography is also called *symmetric encryption*.

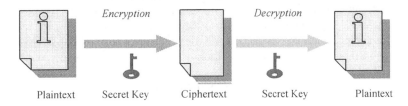

Fig. 2.1   Model of symmetric crytosystems

With this form of cryptography, it is obvious that the key must be known to both the sender and the receiver; that, in fact, is the secret. The biggest difficulty with this approach, of course, is the distribution of the key.

There are several widely used secret key cryptographic schemes, which are generally categorized as being either *block ciphers* or *stream ciphers*. A so called block cipher encrypts more than one block of data at a time; the same plaintext block will always be encrypted into the same ciphertext (when using the same key). Stream ciphers operate on a single bit, byte, or word at a time, and they implement a feedback mechanism so that the same plaintext will yield a different ciphertext every time it is encrypted.

2.3.1 DES and 3DES

The most common secret-key cryptography scheme used is the *data encryption standard* (DES), designed by IBM in the 1970s and adopted by the National Institute for Standards and Technology (NIST) in 1977 for commercial and unclassified government applications. DES is a block-cipher employing a 56-bit key that operates on 64-bit blocks. DES has a complex set of rules and transformations that were designed specifically to yield fast hardware implementations and slow software implementations, although this latter point is becoming less significant today since the speed of computer processors (and, therefore, programs) is several orders of magnitude faster today than twenty years ago. For many years, the US government has insisted that 56-bit DES is secure and virtually unbreakable if appropriate precautions are taken, although the cryptographic community has disagreed. On July 17, 1998, the Electronic Frontier Foundation[1] (EFF) announced the construction of a hardware device that could break DES in an average of 4.5 days. That device cost only about $220,000, including design (it was erroneously and widely reported that subsequent devices could be built for as little as $50,000). The design is scalable, which suggests that an organization could build a DES cracker that could break 56-bit keys in an average of a day for as little as $1,000,000.

Triple DES (3DES) is a minor variation of DES. It is three times slower than regular DES but can be billions of times more secure if used properly. Triple-DES enjoys much wider use than DES because DES is so easy to break with today's rapidly advancing technology. Triple-DES defines three keys, K1, K2, and K3. Generation of the ciphertext, C, from a block of plaintext, P, is accomplished by:

$$C = E_{K3}(D_{K2}(E_{K1}(P)))$$

where $E_K(P)$ and $D_K(P)$ represent DES encryption and decryption, respectively, of some plaintext P using DES key K. (For obvious reasons, this is sometimes referred to as an *encryp-decrypt-encryt mode* operation.)

Decryption of the ciphertext is accomplished by

$$P = D_{K1}(E_{K2}(D_{K3}(C))).$$

The use of three, independent 56-bit keys provides 3DES with an effective key length of 168 bits. The specification also defines the use of two keys where, in the operations above, K3 = K1. This provides an effective key length of 112 bits. Finally, a third keying option is to use a single key, so that K3 = K2 = K1. Given the relatively low cost of key storage and the modest increase in processing due to the use of longer keys, the best recommended practices are that 3DES be employed with three keys.

Triple-DES has been adopted by ANSI as standard X9.52 and is a proposed revision to FIPS 46 as draft FIPS 46-3. NIST suggests that use of 3DES replace DES in all but legacy systems and applications.

---

[1] EFF webside: http://www.eff.org

2.3.2 AES (Rijndael)

The AES is the Advanced Encryption Standard. The AES is the new US government standard to replace the ageing DES. The algorithm of AES is Rijndael, designed by two Belgian cryptographers, Joan Daemen and Vincent Rijmen. To
quote from the NIST press release, Rijndael was selected for its "combination of
security, performance, efficiency, ease of implementation, and flexibility". With
this endorsement Rijndael is quickly finding its way into readily available encryption software. Rijndael has a variable block length and key length. It uses keys
with a length of 128, 192, or 256 bits to encrypt blocks with al length of 128, 192
or 256 bits (all nine combinations of key length and block length are possible).
Both block length and key length can be extended very easily to multiples of 32
bits. In Daemen and Rijmen's book [2.4], they give a detailed description of the
Rijndael algorithm.

Rijndael relies more directly on algebraic constructs than do the other algorithms. Let $GF(2^8)$ be defined by the irreducible polynomial $x^8 + x^4 + x^3 + x + 1$,
and then view the 128 bits = 16 bytes as elements of the field. The data are placed
in a 4×4 array of elements of $GF(2^8)$. Rijndael has ten rounds, each consisting of
four operations: ByteSub, ShiftRow, MixColumn, and AddRoundKey (the last
round skips the MixColumn operation). Let elements in the array be indexed beginning with 0. ByteSub has two steps: (i) each array element is replaced by its
multiplicative inverse in $GF(2^8)$ (0 is mapped to itself), and (ii) the array under-
goes a fixed affine transformation over $GF(2^8)$. Then ShiftRow cyclicly shifts the
elements of the ith row of the array i elements to the right. In MixColumn the columns of the array are considered as polynomials over $GF(2^8)$ (the column $A_i =$
$(a_{0;i}\,;\,a_{1;i}\,;\,a_{2;i};\,a_{3;i})$ is viewed as the polynomial $a_{3;i}\,x^3 + a_{2;i}\,x^2 + a_{1;i}\,x + a_{0;i}$, for
example) and multiplied modulo $x^4 + 1$ by $03x^3 + 01x^2 + 01x + 02$ to give ele-
ments of a new 4×4 array B (thus, $b_{0;i}$ is the zero-th degree term in the product of
$a_{3;i}\,x^3 + a_{2;i}\,x^2 + a_{1;i}\,x + a_{0;i}$ with $03x^3 + 01x^2 + 01x + 02$ modulo $x^4 + 1$, $b_{1;i}$ is the
coefficient of the "x" term, *etc.*). MixColumn diffuses the bits of each array ele-
ment through its column. RoundKey is an XOR of the key (given by the key
schedule) with the elements of the array.

Rijndael admits many possibilities for parallelism: In the ByteSub and Round-
Key operations the bytes can be operated on independently, and in the Shiftrow
and MixColumn operations the rows and columns respectively can be independently manipulated.

The S-box (ByteSub) was designed for resistance to differential and linear
cryptanalysis. It is invertible, and as it has been shown that it minimizes correlation between linear combinations of input bits and linear combinations of the output bits. MixColumn increases diffusion. Let x be a vector, and let A be a linear
transformation. Define the branch number of a linear transformation as:

$$\min\nolimits_{x \neq 0} \mathrm{hwt}(x) + \mathrm{hwt}(A(x)).$$

Since MixColumn works on columns independently, if a state has a single non-zero byte, the output can have at most four nonzero bytes. Hence the maximum branch number is 5. The polynomial $03x^3+01x^2 + 01x + 02$ achieves this maximum.

The key schedule for Rijndael is a simple expansion using XOR and cyclic shift.

2.3.3 IDEA

IDEA is a 64-bit block cipher with a 128-bit key, and has an excellent reputation for quality and strength. It was originally developed in Zurich by Massey and Xuejia Lai in 1990. It was strengthened against Biham and Shamir's differential cryptanalysis attack to become IDEA in 1992.

The same algorithm is used for both encryption and decryption and consists of eight main iterations. It is based on the design concept of "mixing operations from different algebraic groups." The three algebraic groups whose operations are being mixed are: (1) XOR; (2) Addition, ignoring any overflow (addition modulo 2^{16}); and (3) Multiplication, ignoring any overflow (multiplication modulo $2^{16}+1$). IDEA runs much faster in software than DES.

The main drawback of IDEA is that it is patented and requires a license for all but personal non-commercial use, specifically including internal use for normal institutional business.

2.3.4 Other Secret-Key Cryptography Algorithms

There are a number of other secret-key cryptography algorithms that are also in use today.

- *CAST-128* (described in Request for Comments, or RFC, 2144; CAST is not an acronym, rather, its name is derived from the initials of its inventors, Carlisle Adams and Stafford Tavares of Nortel), conceptually similar to DES, a 64-bit block cipher using 128-bit keys. A 256-bit key version has also been described, called CAST-256.

- *RC2 (RC2),* a cipher is named for its inventor Ron Rivest (thus, "RC" is also sometimes expanded as "Ron's Code"). In addition to RC2, there are also RC4, RC5 and RC6. They all are invented by Ron Rivest. RC2 is a 64-bit block cipher using variable-sized keys designed to replace DES. Its code has not been made public although many companies have licensed RC2 for use in their products.

- *RC4*, a stream cipher uses variable-sized keys. It is widely used in commercial cryptography products, although it can only be exported using keys that are 40 bits or less in length.

- *RC5*, a block-cipher supporting a variety of block sizes, key sizes, and number of encryption passes over the data.

- *RC6,* RC6 is based on Feistel rounds but not rounds Feistel operating between the two halves of the block. Instead, the Feistel rounds operate between pairs of quarters of the block, and they are interlocked by the exchange of some data. Circular shifts the extent of which is controlled by data, and a quadratic function applied to 32-bit integers are the nonlinear elements that provide the security of this block cipher.

- *Twofish*, a 128-bit block cipher using 128-, 192-, or 256-bit keys, invented by Bruce Schneier. Designed to be highly secure and highly flexible, well-suited for large microprocessors, 8-bit smart card microprocessors, and dedicated hardware.

2.4 Public-Key Cryptography

In contrast to secret-key cryptography, public-key cryptography is very new. It was first conceived of in 1976 by Diffie and Hellman [2.5], then in 1977 Rivest, Shamir and Adleman invented the RSA Cryptosystem, the first realization of a public-key system. There have since been several proposals for public-key schemes, including the ElGamal Cryptosystem and elliptic-curve cryptosystems.

Each public-key cryptosystem has its own technical nuances, however they all share the same basic property that, given an encryption key, it is computationally infeasible to determine the decryption key (and vice versa). This property lets a user, say Alice, publish her encryption key. Anyone can use that public key to encrypt a message, but only Alice can decipher the ciphertext with her private key.

In practice, computing a public-key cipher takes much longer than encoding the same message with a secret-key system. This has lead to the practice of encrypting messages with a secret-key system such as DES or AES, then encoding the secret key itself with a public-key system such as RSA. We say that the public-key system "transports" the secret key. Since the secret key is usually much shorter than the message, this technique results in significantly faster processing than if public-key cryptography alone were used.

Thus, each securely transmitted message has two components: the message proper (encoded with a secret-key system) and the key used to encode the message (itself encoded using a public-key system). Reading the message is, hence, a two-step process: first decode the secret key, then decode the message. In this chapter, when we say that a person used a public (or private) key to encrypt a message or that a message is encrypted, we are referring to this combined technique. The model of Public-key Cryptosystems (PKC) is shown in Fig 2.2.

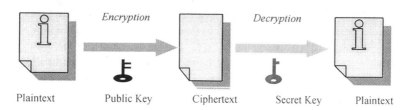

Plaintext   Public Key   Ciphertext   Secret Key   Plaintext

Fig. 2.2   Model of public-key cryptosystems

In a public-key cryptogsystem (PKC), one of the keys is designated the *public key* and may be advertised as widely as the owner wants. The other key is designated the *private key* and is never revealed to another party. It is straight-forward to send messages under this scheme. The sender, for example, encrypts some information using the intended receiver's public key; the receiver decrypts the ciphertext using his own private key. This method could be also used in both directions at the same time. For example, the sender could encrypt the plaintext first with his own private key and then encrypt again with the receiver's public key; this latter scheme might be used where it is important that the sender cannot deny sending the message (*non-repudiation*).

Over the years, many of the proposed public-key cryptographic systems have been broken (that is, proved to be based on an easier problem than first thought), and many others have proved impractical. Today, only three types of systems should be considered both secure and efficient. The systems, classified according to the mathematical problem on which they are based, are: the *integer factorization systems* (of which RSA is the best known example), the *discrete logarithm systems* (such as the U.S. government's DSA), and the *elliptic curve cryptosystem* (also defined as the elliptic curve discrete logarithm system).

2.4.1 RSA

The first, and still most common, PKC implementation is RSA, named for the three MIT mathematicians who developed it, Ronald Rivest, Adi Shamir, and Leonard Adleman [2.13]. RSA is used today in hundreds of software products and can be used for key exchange or encryption (although the latter is relatively rare). RSA uses a variable size encryption block and a variable-size key.

When an entity, say Bob, wants to use RSA cryptosystem. He first chooses two large unique primes, p and q, of roughly equal length. Then, he computes their product $n = pq$, which is called the modulus. The next step is to choose a number, e, less than n and relatively prime to $\phi(n) = (p-1)(q-1)$, which means e and $\phi(n)$ have no common factors except 1. In other words, GCD(e, $\phi(n)$) = 1. Then he finds a number d such that $ed = 1$ mod $\phi(n)$. e and d are called the public and private exponents, respectively. He publishes the public exponent and the modulus, (n, e), and keeps d, p, q private.

Now Alice wants to send a message m to Bob. Alice computes $c = m^e$ mod n, where e and n are Bob's public key. She sends c to Bob.

To decrypt the message c Alice has sent, Bob computes m by $m = c^d$ mod n. The relationship between e and d ensures that Bob correctly recovers m. Because only Bob knows d, only Bob can decrypt c.

The theory behind RSA cryptosystem is that currently there are no efficient algorithms for factoring large numbers. If such algorithms are found, RSA cryptosystem will become useless.

The recommended key size for RSA cryptosystem is 1024 for normal use and 2048 for extreme security.

2.4.2 Diffie-Hellman Public-Key Distribution Scheme

The Diffie - Hellman key agreement protocol was developed by Whitfield Diffie and Martin Hellman in 1976 and published in the ground-breaking paper "New Directions in Cryptography" [2.5]. The protocol allows two users to exchange a secret key over an insecure medium without any prior secrets.

The protocol has two system parameters, p and g. They are both public and may be used by all the users in a system. Parameter p is a prime number and parameter g (usually called a generator) is an integer less than p, with the following property: for every number h between 1 and $p - 1$ inclusive, there is a power k of g such that $h = g^k$ mod p.

Suppose Alice and Bob want to agree on a shared secret key using the Diffie-Hellman key agreement protocol. They proceed as follows: First, Alice generates a random private value a and Bob generates a random private value b. Both a and b are drawn from the set of integers $\{1, ..., p - 2\}$. Then they derive their public values using parameters p and g and their private values. Alice's public value is g^a

mod p and Bob's public value is g^b mod p. They then exchange their public values. Finally, Alice computes $g^{ab} = (g^b)^a$ mod p, and Bob computes $g^{ba} = (g^a)^b$ mod p. Since $g^{ab} = g^{ba} = k$, Alice and Bob now have a shared secret key k.

The protocol depends on the discrete logarithm problem (all of the fast algorithms known for computing discrete logarithms modulo p, where p is a large prime, are forms of the index-calculus algorithm) for its security. It assumes that it is computationally infeasible to calculate the shared secret key $k = g^{ab}$ mod p given the two public values g^a mod p and g^b mod p when the prime p is sufficiently large. Maurer has shown that breaking the Diffie-Hellman protocol is equivalent to computing discrete logarithms under certain assumptions.

2.4.3 ECC

In 1985, Neil Koblitz [2.9] from the University of Washington and Victor Miller [2.12], who was working at IBM at that time, independently proposed the elliptic-curve cryptosystem (ECC), whose security rests on the discrete logarithm problem over the points on an elliptic curve. ECC can be used to provide both a digital signature scheme and an encryption scheme. ECC represents an alternative to older forms of public-key cryptography and offers certain advantages.

To understand what ECC entails, one must understand the arithmetic involved with elliptic curves. Elliptic curves as algebraic/geometric entities have been studied extensively for the past 150 years.

A finite field consists of a finite set of elements together with two operations, addition and multiplication, that satisfy certain arithmetic properties. Finite fields often used in cryptography are F_p; where p is a prime number, and the field F_{2^m}.

An elliptic curve over finite field F_q consists of elements (x, y) satisfying the Weierstrass equation:

$$y^2 + a_1xy + a_3y = x^3 + a_2x^2 + a_4x + a_6$$

When the character of F_q is not equal to 2 and 3, the equation can be simplified into

$$y^2 = x^3 + ax + b$$

If (x, y) satisfies the above equation then $P = (x, y)$ is a point on the elliptic curve. The elliptic curve formula is slightly different for some fields.

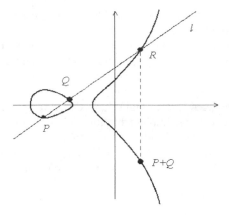

Fig. 2.3   The addition of two points on an elliptic curve

The set of points on an elliptic curve forms a group under addition, where the addition of two points on an elliptic curve is defined according to a set of simple rules. For example, consider the two points P and Q in Fig. 2.3. Point P plus point Q is equal to point $P+Q = (x, -y)$, where $(x, y) = R$ is the third point on the intersection of the elliptic curve and the line l through P and Q.

The *elliptic curve discrete logarithm problem* (ECDLP) can be stated as follows. Given an elliptic curve E defined over F_q, a point $P \in E(F_q)$ of order n, and a point $Q \in E(F_q)$, determine the integer l, $0 \leq l \leq n - 1$, such that $Q = lP$, provided that such an integer exists.

The general conclusion of leading cryptographers is that the ECDLP requires fully exponential time to solve. The security of ECC is dependent on the difficulty of solving the ECDLP.

There are several advantages to ECC [2.10]:

- ECC leads to more efficient implementations than other public-key systems due to its extra strength provided by the difficulty in solving the ECDLP.

- The biggest advantage of ECC is key size. For example, a typical key size for the RSA algorithm is 1024 bits, which would take approximately 10^{11} MIPS years to break. In comparison, an ECC key size is 160 bits and offers the same level of security.

- Computational efficiencies are achieved with ECC. ECC does not require processing of prime numbers to achieve encryption, unlike other public-key cryptosystems. ECC is roughly 10 times faster than either RSA or DSA.

- ECC offers considerable bandwidth savings over the other types of public-key cryptosystems when being used to transform short messages, such as the typical implementation of ECDSA. Bandwidth savings are about the same as other public-key cryptosystems when transforming long messages.

- These advantages lead to higher speeds, lower power consumption, and code-size reductions. Implementations of ECC are particularly beneficial in applications where bandwidth, processing capacity, power availability, or storage is constrained. Such applications include wireless transactions, handheld computing, broadcast, and smart card applications.

2.4.4 Other Public-Key Algorithms

Knapsack Cryptosystem

The Chor-Rivest knapsack cryptosystem was first published in 1984, followed by a revised version in 1988 [2.3]. It was the only knapsack-like cryptosystem that did not use modular multiplication. It was also the only knapsack-like cryptosystem that was secure for any extended period of time. Eventually, Schnorr and Hörner developed an attack on the Chor-Rivest cryptosystem using improved lattice reduction which reduced to hours the amount of time needed to crack the cryptosystem for certain parameter values (though not for those recommended by Chor and Rivest). They also showed how the attack could be extended to attack Damgård's knapsack hash function.

McEliece Cryptosystem

The McEliece cryptosystem is based on a class of error-correcting codes, known as Goppa codes. It was developed by R.J. McEliece in 1978. The idea behind this algorithm is to first select a particular code for which an efficient decoding algorithm is known, and then to disguise the code as a general linear code, using the fact that the problem of decoding an arbitrary linear code is NP-hard. There were no successful cryptanalytic results against the system. The system was the first public-key encryption scheme to use randomization in the encryption process. Also, the system is very efficient. But it has received little attention in practice because of some problems: the public key is enormous. The data expansion is large, and the ciphertext is twice as long as the plaintext.

NTRU

The NTRU is a public-key cryptosystem based on the hard mathematical problem of finding very short vectors in lattices of very high dimension. It was developed by J. Hoffstein and J.H. Silverman in 1996. The process of solving this problem is called "lattice reduction", and the general study of small vectors in lattices goes by the name "geometry of numbers". The NTRU Cryptosystem is parameterized by three values, N, p, and q. All objects are univariate polynomials of degree N, which are multiplied using the convolution product rule. p and q are moduli, i.e., multiplications and additions are generally followed by reduction mod p or mod q. The most time-consuming operations in the NTRU cryptosystem are the convolution multiplications. This tutorial describes ways to speed up those multiplications.

Braid Groups Cryptosystem

The braid groups are infinite noncommutative groups naturally arisen from geometric braids. The word problem of braid groups is easy, but the generalized conjugacy search problem of braid groups is difficult. It was developed by six inventors: K.H. Ko, S.J. Lee, J.H. Cheon, J.W. Han, J.S. Kang , C.S. Park in 2000. The underlying problem of this public key cryptosystem is the generalized conjugacy search problem in the braid group and the underlying mathematical structure is the infinite noncommutative braid group B_n.

Lucas Cryptosystem

Lucas sequences can be used for encryption and signature systems in a manner similar to RSA, but using Lucas sequences modulo a composite number instead of exponentiation. It was developed by P.J. Smith of New Zealand in 1993. It has roughly the same security as RSA for the same size key but is about twice as slow. It also has message-dependent keys. Its underlying mathematical structure is the ring of integers of the quadratic field modulo a prime p.

Hyperelliptic Curve Cryptosystems (HCC)

Hyperelliptic curves are a special class of algebraic curves and can be viewed as generalizations of elliptic curves. A hyperelliptic curve of genus g = 1 is an elliptic curve. Since 1989, the theory of hyperelliptic curves over finite fields has been applied to construction of cryptosystems. One of the main reasons for researchers interesting in cryptosystems based on elliptic and hyperelliptic curves is that these curves are a source of a tremendous number of finite abelian groups (its Jacobian) having a rich algebraic structure. Again the security depends on our inability to efficiently solve the discrete log problem, the HCDLP. The fact that this simple description of the Jacobian does not hold for curves of genus g>1 has apparently led people to shrink back from HCC. But there are compact ways to represent elements in the Jacobians and efficient algorithms to add and double in these groups.

2.5 Digital Signatures

Digital signatures are one of the most important applications of asymmetric public-key cryptography. They are essentially electronic signatures that can be used to authenticate the identity of the sender of a message or the signer of a document, and possibly to ensure that the original content of the message or document that has been sent is unchanged. Digital signatures are easily transportable, cannot be imitated by someone else, and can be automatically time stamped. It prevents the original signer repudiate his signature later.

A *digital signature* is a cryptographic technique that enables the user to protect digital information (represented as a bit string) from undesirable modification. Since signature cannot just be appended to a digital bit string, more sophisticated methods (also known as signatures schemes) for signing have been developed.

A signature scheme is a pair of efficient functions (*Sig,Ver*) of a key pair (S_A, V_A) and a bit string M, such that

- Anyone who knows the secret key S_A can efficiently compute the signature $C=Sig(P_A,M)$ of any bit string M.
- If $C=Sig(S_A,M)$, then $Ver_{VA}(M,C)$=true.
- For a randomly chosen C, it is intractable for anyone who does *not* know S_A to find a value M such that $Ver_{VA}(M,C)$=true.

Some public-key algorithms can be used to generate digital signatures. A digital signature is a small amount of data that was created using some secret key, and there is a public key that can be used to verify that the signature was really generated using the corresponding private key. The algorithm used to generate the signature must be such that without knowing the secret key, it is not possible to create a signature that would be verified as valid.

Digital signatures are used to verify that a message really comes from the claimed sender (assuming only the sender knows the secret key corresponding to their public key). They can also be used to time stamp documents: a trusted party signs the document and its timestamp with their secret key, thus testifying that the document existed at the stated time.

2.5.1 Some Main Digital Signature Schemes

The RSA Signature Scheme

The RSA cryptosystem can perform authentication, which means it can make sure the message received is authentic, has not been tampered with, and is from the sender claimed in the message. To do that, Alice, the sender, first creates a digital signature s by $s = m^d$ mod n, where d and n are Alice's private key. She then sends m and s to Bob. Upon receiving m and s, Bob can check that the message m is indeed recovered by $m = s^e$ mod n, where e and n are Alice's public key.

The RSA signature scheme is a deterministic digital-signature scheme which provides message recovery. The security of the schemes presented here relies to a large degree on the intractability of the integer-factorization problem.

The Rabin Public-Key Signature Scheme

The Rabin signature scheme is a variant of the RSA signature scheme. It has the advantage over RSA that finding the private key and forgery are both provably as hard as factoring. Verification is faster than signing, as with RSA signatures. In the Rabin scheme, the public key is an integer n where $n = pq$, and p and q are prime numbers that form the private key. The message to be signed must have a square root mod n; otherwise, it has to be modified slightly. Only about 1/4 of all possible messages have square roots mod n.

Signature: $s = m^{1/2}$ mod n, where s is the signature
Verification: $m = s^2$ mod n

The provable security has the side-effect that the prime factors can be recovered under a chosen message attack. This attack can be countered by padding a given message with random bits or by modifying the message randomly, at the loss of provable security.

DSA

In August of 1991, the NIST proposed a digital signature algorithm (DSA). The DSA has become a US Federal Information Processing Standard (FIPS 186), called the *digital signature standard* (DSS). It is the first digital signature scheme recognized by any government. The algorithm is a variant of the ElGamal scheme and is a digital signature scheme with appendix.

The signature mechanism requires a hash function $h: \{0, 1\}^* \to Z_q$ for some integer q. The DSS explicitly requires use of the secure hash algorithm (SHA-1), which we will describe in Section 2.6.1.

Key generation for the DSA [2.11]. Each entity creates a public key and corresponding private key. Each entity A should do the following:

1.   Select a prime number q such that $2^{159} < q < 2^{160}$.
2.   Choose t so that $0 \le t \le 8$, and select a prime number p where $2^{511+64t} < p < 2^{512+64t}$, with the property that q divides $(p - 1)$.
3.   (Select a generator α of the unique cyclic group of order q in Z_p^*.)
3.1   Select an element $g \in Z_p^*$ and compute $\alpha = g^{(p-1)/q} \bmod p$.
3.2   If $\alpha = 1$ then go to step 3.1.
4.   Select a random integer a such that $1 \le a \le q - 1$.
5.   Compute $y = \alpha^a \bmod p$.
6.   A's public key is $(p; q; \alpha; y)$; A's private key is a.

DSA signature generation and verification. In *signature generation*, entity A should do the following:

1.   Select a random secret integer k; $0 < k < q$.
2.   Compute $r = (\alpha^k \bmod p) \bmod q$.
3.   Compute $k^{-1} \bmod q$.
4.   Compute $s = k^{-1}\{h(m) + ar\} \bmod q$.
5.   A's signature for m is the pair $(r; s)$.

To verify A's signature $(r; s)$ on m, B should do the following:

1.   Obtain A's authentic public key $(p; q; \alpha; y)$.
2.   Verify that $0 < r < q$ and $0 < s < q$; if not, then reject the signature.
3.   Compute $w = s^{-1} \bmod q$ and $h(m)$.
4.   Compute $u_1 = wh(m) \bmod q$ and $u_2 = rw \bmod q$.
5.   Compute $v = (\alpha^{u1} y^{u2} \bmod p) \bmod q$.
6.   Accept the signature if and only if $v = r$.

The security of the DSA relies on two distinct but related discrete logarithm problems. One is the logarithm problem in Z_p, where the powerful index-calculus methods apply; the other is the logarithm problem in the cyclic subgroup of order q, where the best current methods run in "square-root" time.

ECDSA

A major application of ECC is ECDSA. ECC applications work extremely well with small amounts of data such as digital signatures. The ECDSA is the elliptic-curve analog of the digital signature algorithm (DSA).

The key generation procedures for ECDSA are as follows [2.9-2.10]:
1. Entity A selects an elliptic curve E defined over F_q. The number of points in $E(F_q)$ should be divisible by a large prime n.
2. Select a point $P = E(F_q)$ of order n.
3. Select a statistically unique and unpredictable integer d in the interval $[1, n - 1]$.
4. Compute $Q = dP$.
5. A's public key is (E, P, n, Q). A's private key is d.

ECDSA signature generation:
1. Entity A selects a statistically unique and unpredictable integer k in $[1, n - 1]$.
2. Compute $kP = (x_1, y_1)$ and $r = x_1 \bmod n$. To avoid a security condition, x_1 should not equal 0.
3. Compute $k^{-1} \bmod n$.
4. Compute $s = k^{-1}(h(m) + dr) \bmod n$. h is the SHA-1.
5. If $s = 0$, then go to Step 1. If $s = 0$, then $s^{-1} \bmod n$ does not exist and s^{-1} is required in the signature verification process.
6. The signature for the message m is the pair of integers (r, s).

ECDSA signature verification:
1. Entity B obtains an authentic copy of entity A's public key (E, P, n, Q).
2. Verify that r and s are integers in the interval $[1, n - 1]$.
3. Compute $w = s^{-1} \bmod n$ and $h(m)$.
4. Compute $u_1 = h(m)w \bmod n$ and $u_2 = rw \bmod n$.
5. Compute $u_1P + u_2Q = (x_0, y_0)$ and $v = x_0 \bmod n$.
6. Entity B accepts the signature if and only if $v = r$.

Instead of choosing to generate his own elliptic curve, the entities can use the same curve E over F_q, and point P of order n. In this situation, an entity's public key consists of just one point Q. This results in smaller public key sizes.

2.5.2 Some types of digital signatures

Blind Digital Signature Schemes

The concept of blind signatures was introduced by Chaum [2.18] to protect the privacy of users in applications such as electronic payment systems. In contrast to regular signature schemes, a blind signature scheme is an interactive two-party protocol between a recipient and a signer. It allows the recipient to obtain a signature of a message in a way that the signer learns neither the message nor the resulting signature. A blind signature should have two requirements: *blindness* (i.e., the signer does not know the content of the message) and *untraceability* (i.e., the signer can not link the message-signature pair after the blind signature has been revealed to the public).

Undeniable Signature Schemes

Undeniable signature schemes are distinct from general digital signatures in that the signature verification protocol requires the cooperation of the signer. It is devised by Chaum and van Antwerpen [2.2], are non-self-authenticating signature schemes, where signatures can only be verified with the signer's consent. However, if a signature is only verifiable with the aid of a signer, a dishonest signer may refuse to authenticate a genuine document. Undeniable signatures solve this problem by adding a new component called the disavowal protocol in addition to the normal components of signature and verification.

Fail-stop Signature Schemes

Fail-stop digital signatures are digital signatures which permit an entity A to prove that a signature purportedly (but not actually) signed by A is a forgery. This is done by showing that the underlying assumption on which the signature mechanism is based has been compromised.

The ability to prove a forgery does not rely on any cryptographic assumption, but may fail with some small probability; this failure probability is independent of the computing power of the forger. Fail-stop signature schemes have the advantage that even if a very powerful adversary can forge a single signature, the forgery can be detected and the signing mechanism no longer used. Hence, the term *fail-then-stop* is also appropriate. A fail-stop signature scheme should have the following properties:

1.   If a signer signs a message according to the mechanism, then a verifier upon checking the signature should accept it.
2.   A forger cannot construct signatures that pass the verification algorithm without doing an exponential amount of work.
3.   If a forger succeeds in constructing a signature that passes the verification test, then with high probability, the true signer can produce a proof of forgery.
4.   A signer cannot construct signatures that are at some later time claimed to be forgeries.

2.5.2.4 Group Signature Schemes

In 1991 Chaum and van Heyst [2.1] put forth the concept of a group-signature scheme. Participants are group members, a membership manager, and a revocation manager. A group signature scheme allows a group member to sign messages anonymously on behalf of the group. More precisely, signatures can be verified with respect to a single public key of the group and do not reveal the identity of the signer.

The membership manager is responsible for the system setup and for adding group members, while the revocation manager has the ability to revoke the anonymity of signatures. A group signature scheme could, for instance, be used by an employee of a large company to sign documents on behalf of the company. In this scenario, it is sufficient for a verifier to know that some representative of the company has signed. Moreover, in contrast to the case when an ordinary signature scheme would be used, the verifier does not need to check whether a particular employee is allowed to sign contracts on behalf of the company, i.e., the verifier needs only to know a single company's public key.

The following informally stated security requirements must hold:

1. *Unforgeability of signatures:* Only group members are able to sign messages. Furthermore, they must only be able to sign in such a way that, when the signature is (later) presented to the revocation manager, he will be able to reveal the identity of the signer.

2. *Anonymity of signatures:* It is not feasible to find out the group member who signed a message without knowing the revocation manager's secret key.

3. *Unlinkability of signatures:* It is infeasible to decide whether two signatures have been issued by the same group member or not.

4. *No framing:* Even if the membership manager, the revocation manager, and some of the group members collude, they cannot sign on behalf of noninvolved group members.

5. *Unforgeability of tracing verification:* The revocation manager cannot falsely accuse a signer of having originated a given signature.

Proxy Signature Schemes

A digital signature protocol allows the signer to give the authority to sign a message to someone else without disclosing their private key.

Proxy signatures allow the signer to designate someone else to verify their signatures. In the absence of a participant, a proxy of the participant can be authorized to sign (analogous to the power of attorney concept) without even disclosing the participant's private key. This is a very strong concept for achieving privacy in a collaborative environment.

The following properties hold for proxy signatures:

- Distinguishability: Proxy signatures are distinguishable from normal signatures by everyone.
- Unforgeabililty: Only the signer and the authorized proxy should be able to sign.
- Verifiability: The verifier should be convinced of the proxy relationship between the participant and proxy.
- Identifiability: The original signer should be able to determine the proxy signer's identity from a proxy signature.
- Undeniability: A proxy/participant cannot deny a message.

2.6 Cryptographic Hash Functions

Cryptographic hash functions are used in various contexts, for example, to compute the message digest when making a digital signature. A hash function compresses the bits of a message to a fixed-size *hash value* in a way that distributes the possible messages evenly among the possible hash values. A cryptographic hash function does this in a way that makes it extremely difficult to come up with a message that would hash to a particular hash value.

Cryptographic hash functions typically produce hash values of *128* or more bits. This number (2^{128}) is vastly larger than the number of different messages likely to ever be exchanged in the world. The reason for requiring more than *128* bits is based on the *birthday paradox*. The birthday paradox roughly states that given a hash function mapping any message to a *128*-bit hash digest, we can expect that the same digest will be computed twice when 2^{64} randomly selected messages have been hashed. As cheaper memory chips for computers become available, it may become necessary to require larger than *128*-bit message digests (such as *160* bits, which has become standard recently).

Hash algorithms are typically used to provide a *digital fingerprint* of a file's contents, and are often used to ensure that the file has not been altered by an intruder or a virus. Hash functions are also commonly employed by many operating systems to encrypt passwords.

2.6.1 SHA-1

The secure hash algorithm also called the *secure hash standard* (SHS) is a crypto-graphic hash algorithm published by the United States Government. It produces a 160-bit hash value from a message of an arbitrary length. It is considered to be very good. The length of the padded message is a multiple of 512 bits. This standard specifies a *secure hash algorithm*, SHA-1, for computing a condensed representation of a message or a data file. When a message of any length $< 2^{64}$ bits is input, the SHA-1 produces a 160-bit output called a message digest. The message digest can then be input to the *digital signature algorithm* (DSA), which generates or verifies the signature for the message. Signing the message digest rather than the message itself often improves the efficiency of the process because the message digest is usually much smaller in size than the message. The same hash algorithm must be used by the verifier of a digital signature as was used by the creator of the digital signature.

SHA-1 is probably the preferred hash function for new applications. Currently, no problems are found from it.

2.6.2 MD5

The *message digest algorithm 5* (MD5) is one of message-digest algorithms developed by Rivest. The other algorithms are MD2 and MD4. MD5 is basically MD4 with "safety-belts". While it is slightly slower than MD4, it is more secure. The algorithm consists of four distinct rounds, with a slightly different design from that of MD4. It can be used to hash an arbitrary length byte string into a 128-bit value.

MD5's ancestor, MD4, has been broken, and there are some concerns about the safety of MD5 as well. In 1996 a collision of the MD5 compression function was found by Hans Dobbertin. Although this result does not directly compromise its security, as a precaution the use of MD5 is not recommended in new applications.

2.7 Cryptographic Random Number Generators

Cryptographic random number generators generate random numbers for cryptographic applications, such as keys. Conventional random number generators available in most programming languages or programming environments are not suitable for use in cryptographic applications (they are designed for statistical randomness, not to resist prediction by cryptanalysts).

In the optimal case, random numbers are based on true physical sources of randomness that cannot be predicted. Such sources may include the noise from a semiconductor device, the least significant bits of an audio input, or the intervals between device interrupts or user keystrokes. The noise obtained from a physical source is then "distilled" by a cryptographic hash function to make every bit depend on every other bit. Quite often, a large pool (several thousand bits) is used to contain randomness, and every bit of the pool is made to depend on every bit of the input noise and every other bit of the pool in a cryptographically strong way.

When true physical randomness is not available, pseudo-random numbers must be used. This situation is undesirable, but often arises on general-purposed computers. It is always desirable to obtain some environmental noise, even from device latencies, resource utilization statistics, network statistics, keyboard interrupts, or whatever. The point is that the data must be unpredictable for any external observer; to achieve this, the random pool must contain at least 128 bits of true entropy.

Cryptographic pseudo-random number generators typically have a large pool ("seed value") containing randomness. Bits are returned from this pool by taking data from the pool, optionally running the data through a cryptographic hash function to avoid revealing the contents of the pool. When more bits are needed, the pool is stirred by encrypting its contents by a suitable cipher with a random key (that may be taken from an unreturned part of the pool) in a mode that makes every bit of the pool depend on every other bit of the pool. New environmental noise should be mixed into the pool before stirring to make prediction of previous or future values even more impossible.

Even though cryptographically strong random number generators are not very difficult to build if designed properly, they are often overlooked. The importance of the random number generator must thus be emphasized, that is, if done badly, it will easily become the weakest point of the system.

2.8 Authentication

In the real world of full competition, those fraudulent of identities are inevitable. One is often asked to prove one's identity. The security of communication and data systems depend to a great extent on whether or not the identities of users can be properly verified. For instance, the *automatic teller machine* (ATM) in a bank can give cash to authorized cardholders, which improves the efficiency of the bank greatly. Access to and use of a computer and confidential data are based on the accurate verification of users' identities. Authentication refers to a process of confirming whether or not the object to be authenticated is exactly what it is claimed to be. The object to be authenticated can be a password, a digital signature, or some physiological characteristic such as a fingerprint, voice, or retina. Authentication is often used in communication to mutually confirm the identities of users so as to guarantee to both sides that the identity of the other side is real and valid. There are many methods to realize authentication.

2.8.1 Authentication Based on Password

Conventional password authentication schemes involve time-invariant passwords, which provide so-called *weak authentication*. The basic idea is as follows. Each user (entity) is associated with a *password*. The user is capable of committing their password to memory. The password is then used as a shared secret between the user and the system. For the user to gain access to a system resource, he inputs a (*user-ID, password*) pair, and explicitly or implicitly specifies a resource. Here *user-ID* is a claim of identity, and *password* is the evidence supporting the claim. The system then authenticates the user by checking the password. The user is authentic and is authorized to access the resource if the password matches the corresponding data held for that *user-ID*.

Password schemes can be divided into many classes according to the means by which information allowing password verification is stored within the system along with the method of verification. Fixed password schemes and one-time password schemes are typical examples.

Authentication schemes based on passwords have some advantages. Many systems, such as UNIX, Windows NT, and NetWare, all support this kind of authentication. They are simple and practical for closed small systems; however, they also have disadvantages [2.11].

Password schemes are only suitable for one-way authentication. That is, the system can authenticate the user, but the user cannot authenticate the system. Hence, the adversary may disguise itself as the system to get a user's password.

To overcome these drawbacks, the system can take measures, such as enciphering the user's password when transmitting, and applying uninvertible encryption to users' password files. However, there are still some ways for the adversary to decipher a user's password or decrypt users' password files.

2.8.2 Double Factor Authentication

In double-factor authentication systems, a user possesses not only a password but also a device-of-access token. When a user enters the system, in addition to a password they need to also input the number showed on their device-of-access token. This number on their device-of-access token changes from time to time and is inherent with the authentication sever.

A double-factor authentication scheme is more difficult for the adversary to attack than a password-based authentication scheme. The adversary cannot pass authentication with only a user's password or access token-device. Changing numbers on the access-token device makes it even harder for the adversary to attack the system. So double-factor authentication is more secure than password-based authentication.

2.8.3 Two-Stage Authentication and Password-Derived Keys

Human users have difficulty remembering secret keys that have sufficient entropy to provide adequate security. Two techniques that address this issue are now described. When tokens are used with offline PIN verification, a common technique is for the PIN to serve to verify the user to the token, while the token contains additional independent information allowing the token to authenticate itself to the system (as a valid token representing a legitimate user). The user is thereby indirectly authenticated to the system by a two-stage process. This requires the users to have possession of the token but only remember a short PIN, while a longer key (containing adequate entropy) provides cryptographic security for authentication over an unsecured link.

The second technique is to map a user's password into a cryptographic key (e.g., a 56-bit DES key) by a one-way hash function. Such password-derived keys are called *passkeys*. The passkey is then used to secure a communication link between the user and a system that also knows the user password. It should be ensured that the entropy of the user's password is sufficiently large that an exhaustive search of the password space is not more efficient than an exhaustive search of the passkey space (i.e., guessing passwords is not easier than guessing 56-bit DES keys).

2.8.4 Challenge-Response Identification (Strong Authentication)

Challenge-response identification is also an important kind of authentication. The idea of cryptographic challenge-response protocols is that one entity (the claimant, or prover) "proves" its identity to another entity (the verifier) by demonstrating knowledge of a secret known to be associated with that entity, without revealing the secret itself to the verifier during the protocol. This is accomplished by answering a time-variant challenge, where the answer is determined by both the prover's secret and the challenge. The *challenge* is typically a random number chosen by one entity secretly at the outset of the protocol. Even if the communica-

tion line is monitored, the response from one execution of the identification protocol should not provide an adversary with useful information for a later authentication, as a later challenge will be different.

The protocols of challenge-response identification fall into three major classes.
They are based on symmetric-key cryptosystems, public-key cryptosystems, and
zero-knowledge proof systems [2.11], respectively.

Challenge-Response by Symmetric-Key Techniques

Challenge-response mechanisms based on symmetric-key techniques require the
claimant and the verifier to share a symmetric key. For closed systems with a
small number of users, each pair of users may share a key in advance. In larger
systems employing symmetric-key techniques, identification protocols often involve the use of a trusted online server. Each party shares a key with the trusted
sever. The trusted sever effectively provides a common session key to two parties
each time one requests authentication with the other.

The Kerberos protocol [2.11] and the Needham-Schroeder shared-key protocol
[2.11] are good examples of authentication protocols that provide entity authentication based on symmetric encryption and involve the use of an online trusted
third party. Kerberos protocol employs a client/server architecture and provides
user-to-server authentication rather than host-to-host authentication. In this model,
security and authentication are based on secret-key technology where every host
on the network has its own secret key. It would clearly be unmanageable if every
host had to know the keys of all other hosts, so a secure, trusted host somewhere
on the network, known as a *key distribution center* (KDC), knows the keys for all
of the hosts (or at least some of the hosts within a portion of the network, called a
realm). In this way, when a new node is brought online, only the KDC and the
new node need to be configured with the node's key (keys can be distributed
physically or by some other secure means).

Challenge-Response by Public-Key Techniques

In such identification protocols, a claimant demonstrates knowledge of its private
key in one of the following two ways:

1.   The claimant decrypts a challenge encrypted under its public key.
2.   The claimant digitally signs a challenge.

Ideally, the public-key pair used in such mechanisms should not be used for
other purposes, since combined usage may compromise security. A second caution
is that the public-key system used should not be susceptible to chosen ciphertext

attacks, as an adversary may attempt to extract information by impersonating a verifier and choosing strategic rather than random challenges.

Challenge-Response by Zero-Knowledge Proof

The verifier learns nothing about the fact being proved (except that it is correct) from the prover that the verifier could not already learn without the prover, even if the verifier does not follow the protocol (as long as the prover does). In a zero-knowledge proof, the verifier cannot even later prove the fact to anyone else. (Not all interactive proofs have this property.)

A typical round in a zero-knowledge proof consists of a "commitment" message from the prover, followed by a challenge from the verifier, and then a response to the challenge from the prover. The protocol may be repeated for many rounds. Based on the prover's responses in all the rounds, the verifier decides whether to accept or reject the proof.

There are few zero-knowledge and interactive proof protocols [2.17] used today as identification schemes. The *Fiat-Shamir protocol* is the first practical zero-knowledge protocol with cryptographic applications and is based on the difficulty of factoring. A more common variation of the Fiat-Shamir protocol is the Feige-Fiat-Shamir scheme. Guillou and Quisquater further improved Fiat-Shamir's protocol in terms of memory requirements and interaction (the number of rounds in the protocol).

2.8.5 Authentication Based on Certificate Authority

The authentication technique based on *certificate authority* (CA) is similar to that of Kerberos. It realizes authentication using a mutually trusted third party. It employs public-key cryptosystems, and its realization is much simpler. The trusted third party here is the so-called CA. The CA is responsible for user identification and issues signed digital certificates for users. The digital certificate is called an X.509 certificate since it follows the format of the X.509 standard. A user possessing such a certificate can access those severs trusting CA. We will describe CA and X.509, in detail in the next Chapter.

When a user asks to access a sever, they are asked to submit their digital certificate. The sever decrypts and verifies the user's certificate. If the certificate is valid, the sever then gets the user's public key. In subsequent communication with the user, the sever can encrypt messages with the user's public key. The authentication mechanism based on an X.509 certificate is applicable to identification in an open-network environment. It has gained wide acceptance. Many network security programs, such as IPSec, SSL, SET, and S/MIME, all use this identification mechanism.

This authentication mechanism employs asymmetric cryptosystem so that the user's certificate and their private key are not transmitted in the network. Hence the security drawbacks of password-based authentication are effectively overcome. Even if the adversary intercepts a user's certificate, they still cannot decrypt the message delivered to the user since they do not know the user's private key.

There are already some authentication organizations on the Internet using the X.509 certificate mechanism. Verisign, US Postal Service, and CommerceNet are examples.

The certificate associates the unique user name with its public key. Whether or not this association is legal is beyond the X.509 standard. X.509 claims that whatever is concerned with semantics and trust relies on the *certification practice statement* (CPS) of CA. This will obviously result in differences in the methods and degree of strictness of identification. Thus, it is necessary to establish a uniform authentication system and related rules all over the world.

2.9 Summary

The promise of electronic commerce is one of the major factors that are contributing to the rapid growth of the Internet as a communications medium. With any commercial activity, it is important to consider the security implications of doing business. It will be especially important to support the use of cryptographic mechanisms for data protection, authentication, and privacy protection in electronic commerce. This chapter introduced the security of electronic commerce and the basics of cryptography. Particularly, it deals with the following themes:

- The essential requirements for carrying out secure electronic commerce.
- A basic introduction to cryptography, include secret-key cryptography, public-key cryptography, digital signature, Hash function, random number generators and authentication techniques.

2.10 References

[2.1]   D. Chaum, E. Heijst (1991) Group signatures. In: Advances in cryptology
         – EUROCRYPT 91, LNCS 547. Springer, Berlin Heidelberg New York,
         pp. 257–265.

[2.2]   D. Chaum, H. Antwerpen (1990) Undeniable signatures. In: Advances in
         cryptology – CRYPTO 89, LNCS 434. Springer, Berlin Heidelberg New
         York, pp. 212–216.

[2.3]   B. Chor, R.L. Rivest (1988) A knapsack-type public-key cryptosystem
         based on arithmetic in finite fields. IEEE Trans Infor Theory 34: 901–
         909.

[2.4]   J. Daemen, V. Rijmen (2002) The design of Rijndael. Springer, Berlin
         Heidelberg New York.

[2.5]   W. Diffie, M. Hellman (1976) New directions in cryptography. IEEE
         Trans Infor Theory 22: 644–654.

[2.6]   W. Ford, M. Baum (1997) Secure electronic commerce: building the in-
         frastructure for digital signatures encryption. Prentice-Hall, Englewood
         Cliffs New York.

[2.7]   S. Garfinkel (1995) PGP: pretty good privacy. O'Reilly, Beijing Cam-
         bridge Farnham Koln Tokyo.

[2.8]   A. Kambil (draft) Trends in electronic commerce security background
         material for discussion on payments and settlements.
         http://www.stern.nyu.edu/~akambil/teaching/cases/secure.pdf.

[2.9]   N. Koblitz (1987) Elliptic curve cryptosystems. Math Comput 48: 203–
         209.

[2.10]   A. J. Menezes (1993) Elliptic curve public key cryptography. Kluwer,
         Boston Dordrecht London.

[2.11]   A. J. Menezes, P.C. Oorschot, S. A. Vanstone (1997) Handbook of ap-
         plied cryptography. CRC Press, Boca Raton.

[2.12]   V. S. Miller (1986) Use of elliptic curves in cryptography. In: Advances
         in cryptology – CRYPTO 85, LNCS 218. Springer, Berlin Heidelberg
         New York, pp. 417–426.

[2.13]   R. L. Rivest, A. Shamir, L. M. Adleman (1978) A method for obtaining
         digital signatures and public-key cryptosystems. Commun ACM 21(2):
         120–126.

[2.14]   G. J. Simmons (ed.) (1992) Contemporary cryptology: the science of in-
         formation integrity. IEEE Press, New York.

[2.15]   SSH - tech corner - introduction to cryptography.
         http://www.ssh.fi/tech/crypto/intro.html.

[2.16]   D. R. Stinson (1995) Cryptography: theory and practice. CRC Press,
         Boca Raton.

[2.17]   W. Stallings (1999) Cryptography and network security: principles and
         practice (2nd ed.). Prentice-Hall, Upper Saddle River.

[2.18]   D. Chaum (1983): Blind signature for untraceable payments. In: Advance
         in cryptology. Plenum Press, New York, pp. 199–203.

3 Public-Key Infrastructure

Hui Li and Yumin Wang

National Key Laboratory of ISN
Xidian University, Xi'an, China

3.1 Introduction

3.1.1 What Is a PKI?

In its most simple form, a *Public-key infrastructure* (PKI) is a system for publishing the public-key values used in public-key cryptography. PKI is the combination of software, encryption technologies, and services that enables enterprises to protect the security of their communications and business transactions on the Internet.

A PKI integrates digital certificates, public-key cryptography, and certificate authorities into a total, enterprise-wide network security architecture. A typical enterprise's PKI encompasses the issuance of digital certificates to individual users and servers; end-user enrollment software; integration with corporate certificate directories; tools for managing, renewing, and revoking certificates; and related services and support.

3.1.2 Why Do You Need PKI

PKI protects your information assets in several essential ways:

- **Authenticate identity.** Digital certificates issued as part of your PKI allow individual users, organizations, and web site operators to confidently validate the identity of each party in an Internet transaction.
- **Verify integrity.** A digital certificate ensures that the message or document the certificate "signs" has not been changed or corrupted in transit online.
- **Ensure privacy.** Digital certificates protect information from interception during Internet transmission.

- **Authorize access.** PKI digital certificates replace easily guessed and frequently lost user IDs and passwords to streamline intranet log-in security and reduce the MIS overhead.
- **Authorize transactions.** With PKI solutions, your enterprises can control access privileges for specified online transactions.
- **Support for non-repudiation.** Digital certificates validate their users' identities, making it nearly impossible to later repudiate a digitally "signed" transaction, such as a purchase made on a web site.

3.1.3 Certificates and Certificate Authorities (CAs)

A *certificate* is a collection of information that has been digitally signed by its issuer (see Fig. 3.1). Such certificates are distinguished by the kind of information they contain. An *identity certificate* is an electronic document used to identify an individual, a server, a company, or some other entity called the certificate *subject* and to associate that subject with a public key. A *credential certificate* describes non-entities, such as a permission or credential. Like a driver's license, a passport, or other commonly used personal IDs, a certificate provides generally recognized proof of a person's identity. Public-key cryptography uses certificates to address the problem of impersonation.

To get a driver's license, you typically apply to a government agency, such as the Department of Motor Vehicles, which verifies your identity, your ability to drive, your address, and other information before issuing the license. To get a student ID, you apply to a school or college, which performs different checks (such as whether you have paid your tuition) before issuing the ID. To get a library card, you may need to provide only your name and a utility bill with your address on it.

Certificates work much the same way as any of these familiar forms of identification. *Certificate authorities* (CAs) are entities that validate identities and issue certificates. They can be either independent third parties or organizations running their own certificate-issuing server software (such as Netscape Certificate Server). The methods used to validate an identity vary depending on the policies of a given CA, that is, just as the methods to validate other forms of identification vary depending on who is issuing the ID and the purpose for which it will be used. In general, before issuing a certificate, the CA must use its published verification procedures for that type of certificate to ensure that an entity requesting a certificate is in fact who it claims to be.

The certificate issued by the CA binds a particular public key to the name of the entity the certificate identifies (such as the name of an employee or a server). Certificates help prevent the use of fake public keys for impersonation. Only the public key certified by the certificate will work with the corresponding private key possessed by the entity identified by the certificate.

In addition to a public key, a certificate always includes the name of the entity it identifies, an expiration date, the name of the CA that issued the certificate, a serial number, and other information. Most importantly, a certificate always includes the digital signature of the issuing CA. The CA's digital signature allows the certificate to function as a "letter of introduction" for users who know and trust the CA but don't know the entity identified by the certificate.

A certificate *user* is an entity who relies upon the information contained in a certificate. The certificate user trusts the issuing authority to issue true certificates, that is, certificates that truly identify the subject and its public key (in the case of identity certificates), or that truly describe a subject's credentials (in the case of credential certificates).

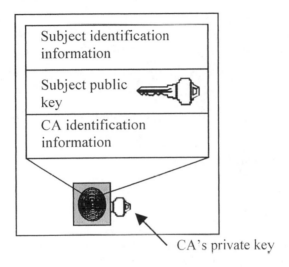

CA's private key

Fig. 3.1   A basic certificate

To help Illustrate these concepts, we present an example using identity certificates. Imagine that Alice wishes to securely communicate with Bob using a public key cryptosystem. Alice needs to know the value of Bob's public encrypting key. Without a PKI, Alice must have direct knowledge of that key, i.e., Bob must communicate it to her via a secure channel.

With a PKI, Alice only needs to have direct knowledge of a CA's public signing key. The CA would issue an identity certificate for each of Bob's public encrypting keys. Then if Alice wishes to communicate with Bob, she can use the appropriate certificate to obtain the correct public key value. In this case, Alice is the certificate user while Bob is the subjects of certificate. See Fig. 3.2.

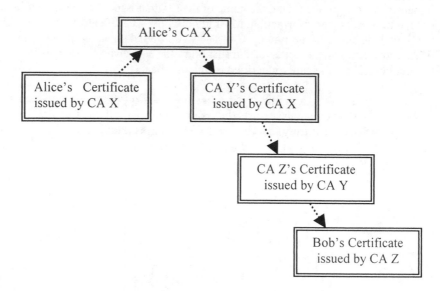

Fig. 3.2   A certification path from Alice to Bob

3.1.4 CA Arrangements

Certificate Hierarchies

In large organizations, it may be appropriate to delegate the responsibility for issuing certificates to several different certificate authorities. For example, the number of certificates required may be too large for a single CA to maintain; different organizational units may have different policy requirements; or it may be important for a CA to be physically located in the same geographic area as the people to whom it is issuing certificates.

It's possible to delegate certificate-issuing responsibilities to subordinate CAs. The X.509 standard includes a model for setting up a hierarchy of CAs like that shown in Fig. 3.3.

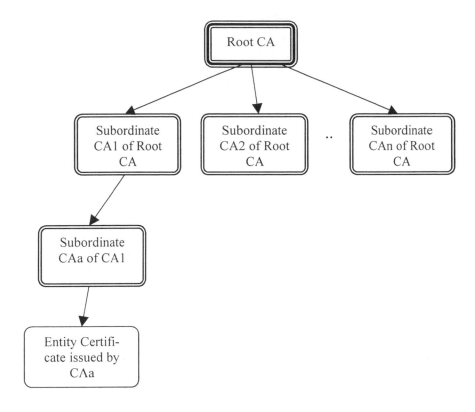

Fig. 3.3   Example of a hierarchy of certificate authorities

In this model, the root CA is at the top of the hierarchy. The root CA's certificate is a *self-signed certificate*, that is, the certificate is digitally signed by the same entity (the root CA) that the certificate identifies. The CAs that are directly subordinate to the root CA have CA certificates signed by the root CA. CAs under the subordinate CAs in the hierarchy have their CA certificates signed by the higher-level subordinate CAs.

Organizations have a great deal of flexibility in terms of the way they set up their CA hierarchies. Fig. 3.3 shows just one example; many other arrangements are possible.

Certificate Chains

CA hierarchies are reflected in certificate chains. A *certificate chain* is series of certificates issued by successive CAs. Fig. 3.4 shows a certificate chain leading from a certificate that identifies some entity through two subordinate CA certificates to the CA certificate for the root CA (based on the CA hierarchy shown in Fig. 3.3).

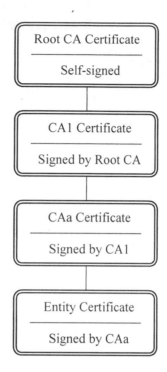

Fig. 3.4   Example of a certificate chain

A certificate chain traces a path of certificates from a branch in the hierarchy to the root of the hierarchy. In a certificate chain, the following occur:

- Each certificate is followed by the certificate of its issuer.
- Each certificate contains the name (DN) of that certificate's issuer, which is the same as the subject name of the next certificate in the chain.

In Fig. 3.4, the CAa certificate contains the DN of the CA1, that issued that certificate. CA1's DN is also the subject name of the next certificate in the chain.

- Each certificate is signed with the private key of its issuer. The signature can be verified with the public key in the issuer's certificate, which is the next certificate in the chain.

In Fig. 3.4, the public key in the certificate for the CA1 can be used to verify the CA1's digital signature on the certificate for the CAa.

3.1.5 Validation

The other basic PKI operation is certificate validation. The information in a certificate can change over time. A certificate user needs to be sure that the certificate's data is true, that is, the user needs to *validate* the certificate. There are two basic methods of certificate validation. A PKI can use either or both methods.

- The user can ask the CA directly about a certificate's validity every time it is used. This is known as *online* validation.

- The CA can include a *validity period* in the certificate – a pair of dates that define a range during which the information in the certificate can be considered as valid. This is known as *offline* validation.

Verify a Certificate Chain

Certificate chain verification is the process of making sure a given certificate chain is well-formed, valid, properly signed, and trustworthy. A PKI usually uses the following procedure for forming and verifying a certificate chain, starting with the certificate being presented for authentication.

1. The certificate validity period is checked against the current time provided by the verifier's system clock.
2. The issuer's certificate is located. The source can be either the verifier's local certificate database (on that client or server) or the certificate chain provided by the subject (for example, over an SSL connection).
3. The certificate signature is verified using the public key in the issuer's certificate.
4. If the issuer's certificate is trusted by the verifier in the verifier's certificate database, verification stops successfully here. Otherwise, the issuer's certificate is checked to make sure it contains the appropriate subordinate CA, and chain verification returns to step 1 to start again, but with this new certificate. Fig. 3.5 presents an example of this process.

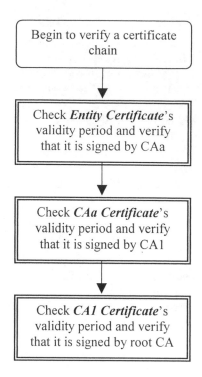

Fig. 3.5   Verifying a certificate chain all the way to the root CA

Certificate Revocation Lists (CRLs)

Closely related to the validation method is certificate *revocation*. Certificate revo-cation is the process of letting users know when the information in a certificate becomes unexpectedly invalid. This can occur when a subject's private key be-comes compromised, or, more benignly, when a certificate's identifying informa-tion changes (e.g. the subject gets a new telephone number).

If a certificate is validated online with the CA every time it is used, then the revocation problem becomes trivial, as the CA can simply state that the certificate is no longer valid. However, when validity periods are employed, the certificate revocation method becomes critical (especially in the case of private-key com-promise).

In the absence of online approaches, the most common revocation method uses *certificate revocation lists* (CRLs). A CRL is a list of revoked certificates that is signed and periodically issued by a CA. It is essential that the user check the latest

CRL during validation to make sure that a certificate she is about to use has not been revoked.

One of the chief concerns with the CRL approach is what happens between the time when a CA receives notification that a certificate should be revoked and when the CA publishes its next CRL. Since the revoked certificate will only appear on the next CRL, any user checking the current CRL will not know of its revocation and will assume that the certificate is still valid. We call this the *CRL time-granularity problem.*

Another concern is the size of the CRL. A CA can be expected to certify thousands, or even hundreds of thousands, of subjects. While the rate of revocations for a given population is generally unpredictable, the CRLs for such CAs can be expected to grow very large. When a CRL is too large it can be difficult to retrieve by users, whose access to the CA may have limited bandwidth. Also, since CRLs are signed, their signatures need to be verified before the CRL can be used, and the time required to verify the signature on a large CRL and process its entries can become significant.

These problems have lead to several refinements of the CRL approach. One is to issue separate CRLs for different revocation reasons and/or for different certificate subjects. For example, the CA could issue one CRL for routine revocations (e.g., a change in a certificate subject's identifying information) and another CRL for revocations due to a security compromise. Similarly, a CA could issue one CRL for its end-user subjects and another for the other CAs it may certify. These measures have the effect of partitioning a large CRL into pieces that can be selectively digested. For example, a user might not be very worried about routine revocations and so would only need to check the security-compromise CRL. Also, when processing a certification path the user need only check the CA CRLs (until reaching the end of the path).

While these steps help reduce CRL sizes, they do little to alleviate the CRL time-granularity problem. Another measure has been proposed to address that problem: *delta CRLs.* A delta-CRL is simply a (CA-signed) list of CRL changes that have occurred since the last full CRL was issued. Delta-CRLs allow revocation notifications to be issued more frequently, and so reduce the probability that a revoked certificate will be falsely validated. Delta-CRLs also help with the CRL size problem. A certificate validating system could start with a full CRL, and then need only process delta-CRLs as they are issued, updating its own copy of the full CRL.

3.1.6 Authentication

Authentication is the process of using a PKI. When a CA certifies an entity and a user then validates that certification, the entity is said to have been *authenticated.*

A certificate can contain entity or nonentity information. When a certificate identifies an entity, it is called an *identity certificate*. Authenticating an identity certificate is called *identity authentication*.

Certificates that contain nonentity information, such as a permission or credential, are called *credential certificates*. Credential certificates identify things such as permissions (e.g., an access computer xyz), credentials (e.g., as a certified stock broker), or other attributes (e.g., as VP Marketing for "ABC Inc."). A credential certificate may or may not identify the entity to which the credential is attached. We call authenticating a credential certificate *credential authentication*.

In the context of network interactions, authentication involves the confident identification of one party by another party. Authentication over networks can take many forms. Certificates are one way of supporting authentication.

Network interactions typically take place between a client, such as browser software running on a personal computer, and a server, such as the software and hardware used to host a web site. *Client authentication* refers to the confident identification of a client by a server (that is, identification of the person assumed to be using the client software). *Server authentication* refers to the confident identification of a server by a client (that is, identification of the organization assumed to be responsible for the server at a particular network address).

Client and server authentication are not the only forms of authentication that certificates support. For example, the digital signature on an email message, combined with the certificate that identifies the sender, provide strong evidence that the person identified by that certificate did indeed send that message. Similarly, a digital signature on an HTML form, combined with a certificate that identifies the signer, can provide evidence, after the fact, that the person identified by that certificate did agree to the contents of the form. In addition to authentication, the digital signature in both cases ensures a degree of non-repudiation, that is, a digital signature makes it difficult for the signer to claim later not to have sent the email or the form.

3.1.7 Limitations of PKI Authentication

Whenever authentication is performed using the PKI, whether online or offline, it is called *in-band authentication*. Authentication performed using more traditional methods, such as over the telephone or physically meeting someone, is called *out-of-band authentication*. The goal of every PKI is to minimize the need for out-of-band authentication.

It is unlikely that out-of-band authentication can ever be completely eliminated. At the very least, a person wishing to use a PKI needs to first have their identity and/or credentials verified by their CA. This initial verification cannot be performed using the PKI, since there is no other CA to vouch for the person's identity/credentials. Thus the bootstrapping process requires out-of-band authentication. Also, different PKIs require different degrees of out-of-band authentication as identity and credential information changes over time and needs to be updated.

The extent to which out-of-band authentication is required in a PKI is partly a result of how much the PKI's designers want to provide *irrefutability*. A signature made by Alice is said to be irrefutable if Alice can not, at a later date, deny that she did in fact make the signature. If the PKI is to be used as the foundation of an electronic replacement for paper-based signatures, then irrefutability is an important consideration. In general, the more out-of-band contact Alice has with her CA, the less she will be able to engage in such fraud.

3.1.8 Registration Authorities

Interactions between entities identified by certificates (sometimes called *end entities*) and CAs are an essential part of certificate management. These interactions include operations, such as registration for certification, certificate retrieval, certificate renewal, certificate revocation, and key backup and recovery. In general, a CA must be able to authenticate the identities of end entities before responding to the requests. In addition, some requests need to be approved by authorized administrators or managers before being serviced.

As previously discussed, the means used by different CAs to verify an identity before issuing a certificate can vary widely, depending on the organization and the purpose for which the certificate will be used. To provide maximum operational flexibility, interactions with end entities can be separated from the other functions of a CA and handled by a separate service called a *registration authority* (RA).

An RA acts as a front end to a CA by receiving end entity requests, authenticating them, and forwarding them to the CA. After receiving a response from the CA, the RA notifies the end entity of the results. RAs can be helpful in scaling a PKI across different departments, geographical areas, or other operational units with varying policies and authentication requirements.

3.1.9 Certificates and the LDAP Directory

The lightweight directory access protocol (LDAP) for accessing directory services supports great flexibility in the management of certificates within an organization. System administrators can store much of the information required to manage certificates in an LDAP-compliant directory. For example, a CA can use information in a directory to pre-populate a certificate with a new employee's legal name and other information. The CA can leverage directory information in other ways to issue certificates one at a time or in bulk, using a range of different identification techniques depending on the security policies of a given organization. Other routine management tasks, such as key management and renewing and revoking, can be partially or fully automated with the aid of the directory.

Information stored in the directory can also be used with certificates to control access to various network resources by different users or groups. Issuing certificates and other certificate management tasks can thus be an integral part of user and group management.

3.1.10 Key Management

Before a certificate can be issued, the public key it contains and the corresponding private key must be generated. Sometimes it may be useful to issue a single person one certificate and key pair for signing operations, and another certificate and key pair for encryption operations. Separate signing and encryption certificates make it possible to keep the private signing key on the local machine only, thus providing maximum non-repudiation, and to back up the private encryption key in some central location where it can be retrieved in case the user loses the original key or leaves the company.

Keys can be generated by client software or generated centrally by the CA and distributed to users via an LDAP directory. There are tradeoffs involved in choosing between local and centralized key generation. For example, local key generation provides maximum non-repudiation, but may involve more participation by the user in the issuing process. Flexible key management capabilities are essential for most organizations.

3.2 X.509

3.2.1 Introduction

X.509 [3.65] is the authentication framework designed to support X.500 directory services [3.64]. Both X.509 and X.500 are part of the X series of international standards proposed by the ISO and ITU. The X.500 standard is designed to provide directory services on large computer networks. X.509 provides a PKI framework for authenticating X.500 services.

The first version of X.509 appeared in 1988, making it the oldest proposal for a worldwide PKI. This, coupled with its ISO/ITU origin, has made X.509 the most widely adapted PKI. There are at least a dozen companies worldwide that produce X.509-based products, and that number is growing. Visa and MasterCard have adapted X.509 as the basis for their secure electronic transaction standard (SET) [3.55]. Netscape's famous World Wide Web software also uses X.509. And there are numerous X.509-based products available from companies, such as Entrust and TimeStep that support corporate intranets. Efforts are currently underway to design an X.509-based PKI that will support a global network such as the Internet. Along with PGP [3.67], X.509 is the only PKI system that has yet to be put into practical use.

3.2.2 The X.509 Standard

X.500

A full understanding of X.509 PKIs requires some basic knowledge of the X.500 directory that X.509 was originally designed for. The X.500 directory[3.64] is very similar to a telephone directory where, given a person's name, one can find auxiliary information about that person. However, X.500 provides more than just a name, address, and phone number. An entry in an X.500 directory can contain a host of attributes, such as the name of the organization the person works for, their job title and their email address, to name a few. An X.500 directory entry can represent any real-world entity, not just people but also computers, printers, companies, governments, and nations. The entry can also contain the certificate specifying the entity's public key.

Distinguished Name

To support looking up entries in the directory, each entry is assigned a globally unique name, called a *distinguished name* or DN. To help ensure their uniqueness, these names are assigned in a very specific fashion. The X.500 directory is arranged in a hierarchical fashion, call the *Directory Information Tree* or DIT (see Fig. 3.6).

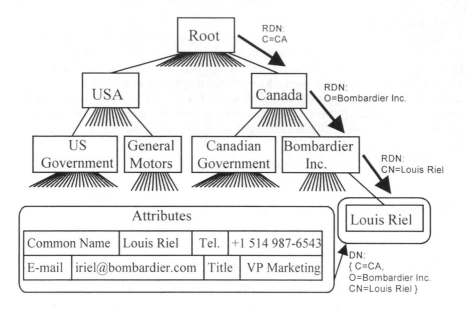

Fig. 3.6   The X.500 directory information tree

Each node, or *vertex*, in the tree has one parent (except the root vertex) and any number of children. Each vertex, except the root, is assigned a *relative distinguished name* (RDN) that is unique among all the vertex's siblings. The RDNs of each of the vertex's ancestors are concatenated with the vertex's own RDN to form the entry's DN. Fig. 3.6 illustrates this process. Under the root vertex there is an entry for each country in the world. These entries are assigned an RDN that is the country's unique two-letter code assigned to it by the ISO. Beneath each country's vertex are entries for all of the country's organizations, such as its government, its states or provinces, and federally-chartered companies. Each of these is assigned a unique RDN that is the name of the organization. Finally, each organization creates entries for all of its employees, and for other entities the organization might control. Each of these is also assigned a unique RDN. In our example, Mr. Louis Riel works for Bombardier, a Canadian company. Bombardier assigns an RDN to Mr. Riel, that is simply his name (specified as his common name, abbreviated as CN in the figure). Bombardier was itself assigned an RDN, Organization = Bombardier by Canada, designating it as the organization named Bombardier, and Canada's RDN is it's two-letter country code, Country = CA. Mr. Riel's DN is thus the concatenation of these RDNs, starting from the root: Country = CA, Organization = Bombardier, CommonName = Louis Riel.

X.509 Version 2 certificate

X.509 was created to support the authentication of the entries in an X.500 directory. The latest version, the third, has evolved beyond its X.500 roots. Currently, version 3 is the official standard. We will first describe X.509v2, before moving on to the extensions added under version 3.

The X.509v2 certificate is illustrated in Fig. 3.7. It contains the following fields.

- Version: The X.509 version that the certificate conforms to.
- Serial number: A unique number assigned to the certificate by its issuing CA.
- CA signature algorithm: An identifier for the algorithm used by the CA to sign the certificate. Identifiers are further discussed below under Object Registration.
- Issuer name: The X.500 name of the issuing CA.
- Validity period: A pair of dates/times between which the certificate is considered valid.
- Subject name: The X.500 name of the entity who holds the private key corresponding to the public key being certified.
- Subject public key information: The value of the subject's public key along with an identifier of the algorithm with which the key is intended to be used.
- Issuer unique identifier (optional, version 2 only): A bit string used to make the X.500 name of the issuing CA unambiguous. It is possible for an X.500 name to be assigned to a particular entity, then de-assigned, then re-assigned to a new entity.[1] The unique identifier fields address this concern. These fields are not widely used, as they have turned out to be difficult to manage and are ignored or omitted in most implementations. The preferred method used to address this problem is to design the RDNs in such a way as to ensure that they are *never* reused. For example, rather than use just the CommonName attribute, a better form of RDN might use both the CommonName and an EmployeeNumber.
- Subject unique identifier (optional, version 2 only): A bit string used to make the X.500 name of the subject unambiguous.

---

[1] For example, in Fig. 3.6, if Mr. Riel changes companies, his DN, in particular the Organization=Bombardier component, is no longer valid and so is de-assigned. Later, if another person named Louis Riel comes to work for Bombardier, he would be assigned the same DN as the first Louis Riel.

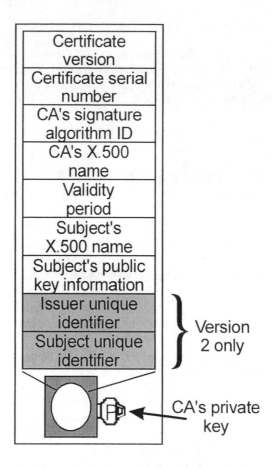

Fig. 3.7   The X.509 version 2 certificate

Because of X.509's close ties with X.500, its CAs are usually arranged in a hierarchy that closely follows the X.500 DIT.

X.509, and X.500, were originally designed in the mid-1980's, before the current explosive growth of the Internet. They were therefore designed to operate in an offline environment, where computers are only intermittently connected to each other. X.509 thus employs CRLs. Versions 1 and 2 of X.509 use very simple CRLs that do not address size issues and the time-granularity problem. Version 3 makes several attempts to solve these problems, with varying success. Fig. 3.8 illustrates the CRL format used in X.509 versions 1 and 2.

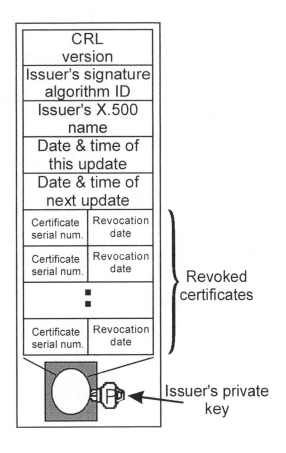

Fig. 3.8   X.509 version 1 CRL format

X.509 Version 3

Version 3 introduced significant changes to the X.509 standard. The fundamental change was to make the certificate and CRL formats extensible. X.509 implementers can now define certificate contents as they see fit. Also, a number of standard extensions were defined to provide key and policy information, subject and issuer attributes, certification path constraints, and enhanced CRL functionality. These extensions are fully described in [3.10] and elsewhere. We concentrate here on those extensions which affect the basic PKI characteristics of X.509.

Version 3 Certificate Extensions

Certificate policies and policy mapping. X.509v3 gives CAs the ability to include with the certificate a list of policies that were followed in creating the certificate. These policies are intended to help users decide if a certificate is suitable for a particular purpose. For example, a policy might indicate that a certified key can be used for casual email messages but not for financial transactions. In general, a certificate policy indicates such things as CA security procedures, subject identification measures, legal disclaimers or provisions, and others. Policy mapping allows a CA to indicate whether one of its policies is equivalent to another CA's policy.

Alternative names. An X.509v3 certificate can contain one or more alternative names for the subject or issuer. This allows X.509 to operate without an underlying X.500 directory. Examples of alternative names include email addresses and World Wide Web universal resource locators. Implementers can also define their own alternative name forms. Alternative names can also be used to identify the issuer of a CRL.

Subject directory attributes. This extension allows any of the subject's X.500 directory entry attribute values to be included in the certificate. This allows the certificate to carry additional identifying information beyond the subject's name(s).

Certification path constraints. These extensions allow CAs to link up their infrastructures in meaningful ways. A CA can restrict the kinds of certification paths that can grow from certificates it issues for other CAs. The CA can state whether or not a certificate's subject is in a fact a CA (to prevent an end user from fraudulently acting as a CA). The CA can also constrict paths growing from the certificate to certificates issued in a particular name space (e.g., within a given Internet domain) and/or to certificates that follow a specific set of certification policies. This is an important extension because it allows CAs to employ a *progressive-constraint* trust model that prevents the formation of infinite certification paths. The concept is illustrated in Fig. 3.9. User a uses D as her certification authority, so she places complete trust in D. D has certified another certification authority, E, for example only trusting E to issue certificates for other CAs (perhaps E performs some kind of national CA registration). Constraint X would then state that D only trusts E to certify other certification authorities.

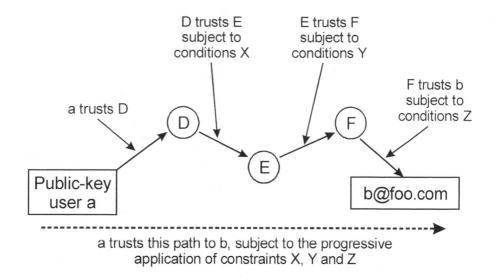

Fig. 3.9   A progressive-constrained trust chain

E has issued a certificate for certification authority F stating that it only trusts F to issue certificates for end users in the domain foo.com. So constraint Y would state that E trusts certificates issued by F only if they certify an end user *and* that user's name is in the foo.com domain. Finally, F issues a certificate for user b, but only trusts b for casual email (as opposed to, say, making financial commitments on F's behalf). So constraint Z states that the certificate issued for b by F should only be used for casual email.

In this way the unlimited trust that a places in D becomes increasingly constrained as the certification path grows. When a obtains a certificate for b she knows that she should only use it for casual email, and she has greater confidence in the strength of the authentication than with, say, PGP's web of trust because she can see how trust has been restricted along the certification path. Given these constraints, she would not accept a certificate issued by E for b (or any other user), nor would she accept any certificates from any certification authority certified by F. If CAs define the tightest practical conditions when they certify other CAs, then as a certification path grows it becomes progressively more constrained until it can grow no longer.

Version 3 CRL Extensions

CRL number and reason codes. Each CRL issued for a given certificate population is assigned a number from a monotonically increasing sequence. This allows users to determine if a CRL was missed. Also, each certificate in a CRL can now have a revocation reason attached to its CRL entry. These two extensions allow for the more sophisticated CRL extensions described below.

CRL distribution points. This extension helps reduce the sizes of CRLs processed by a CA's users. Rather than forcing users to accept the full CRL, the CA can partition the CRL in some way, and issue each partition from a different distribution point. For example, a corporate CA might issue a different CRL for each division of the company. Then when a user wants to verify a certificate for someone from a particular division, they need only check that division's CRL rather than the full CRL. Another way of partitioning the CRL is according to revocation reason. Routine revocations, for example, those due to a name change, can be placed on a different CRL than revocations due to a security compromise. The compromise list can then be updated and checked more frequently without having to also process all the routine revocations that might occur.

Delta-CRLs. This extension provides another method of reducing CRL sizes. Rather than issue a full CRL (or a full partition of a CRL), the CA can simply issue a list of the changes that have occurred since the last time a full CRL was issued. Users that maintain their own CRL database can use a delta-CRL to keep their copies updated without having to download and process all the entries of a full CRL, saving bandwidth and computing time.

Indirect CRLs. This extension allows a CRL to be issued from an entity other than the CA that issued its certificates. This allows for CRL clearing houses that would gather the CRLs from multiple CAs and provide one distribution point for them all.

All of these CRL extensions still do not overcome the fundamental time-granularity problem. Even with partitioned CRLs and frequent delta-CRL issuance, there is still a window of opportunity for a compromised certificate to be used. The X.509v3 framework can be used for online operation, avoiding the need for CRLs altogether. PKIX defines a *online certificate status protocol* [3.48] to do this work.

Object Registration

The extensibility of X.509v3 gives it a tremendous amount of flexibility. However, the way in which that extensibility is provided hampers the widespread application of user-defined extensions for a global PKI.

Every time X.509 needs to identify some object, such as a signature algorithm, certification policy, user-defined alternative name, or a user-defined extension, it uses an internationally defined *object identifier* (OID) mechanism. An OID is a numeric value, composed of a sequence of integers, that is unique with respect to all other OIDs.

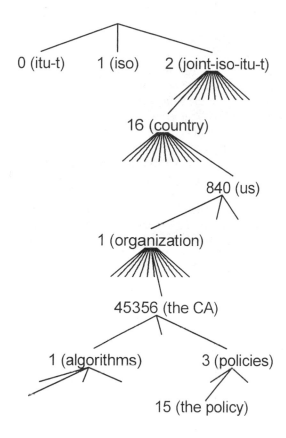

Fig. 3.10   Object registration example

The OIDs are assigned following a hierarchical structure of value-assigning authorities [3.10, 3.64, 3.66]. Essentially, any company or organization can become
a value-assigning authority. The company is itself assigned a value that serves as a
prefix for all the values that it defines. Take, for example, the OID pictured in Fig.
3.10. Imagine a CA operating in the United States. The CA would be assigned an
OID, say 2-16-840-1-45356.[2] This OID would then be the prefix used for the
OIDs of any objects that the CA cares to register. The CA might want to register a

---

[2] The numbers only have meaning within the hierarchy. The leading 2 indicates the branch
   of the hierarchy administered jointly by the ISO and ITU. The 16 is the number assigned
   to the branch used by national registration authorities. 840 is the country code for the
   U.S., whose national registration authority (ANSI) uses 1 as the prefix for all the organizations it registers. The 45356 is simply a number assigned to the CA by ANSI.

particular certification policy to which it has assigned a number, say 15, beneath the policy's branch of its hierarchy (branch number 3, for example). Then the CA's policy could be identified as object number 2-16-840-1-45356-3-15.

This system works well for assigning numbers to objects, and it is used extensively in X.509. For example, if the CA in Fig. 3.10 were to use its policy in a certificate, that policy would be identified solely by its OID. Difficulty arises, however, when OIDs are used without prior agreement as to their meaning. If the CA in our example wants to use their policy in their certificates, they have to ensure that the meaning of the OID identifying their policy is known *a priori* by any entity wishing to use the certificate. Otherwise, when an ignorant entity encounters the value 2-16-840-1-45356-3-15 it will have no idea how to interpret the policy.

Confusion can also arise when the same object is assigned multiple OIDs. For example, imagine that two CAs have each assigned an OID to a particular signature algorithm, such as SHA-with-RSA. As long as the CAs and their users don't interact, there will be no problems. However, if a user from one CA tries to use the other CA's certificate, they won't recognize the second CA's OID for SHA-with-RSA, and might assume that they can't verify the signatures of the certificate's subject even though they may be perfectly capable of doing so. The problem is compounded if the two CAs ever try to link their infrastructures. Then the CAs must either let all their users know that the two OIDs are equivalent, or one CA (or both) has to change its OID and communicate that change to all its users.

The OID problem prevents X.509's extensibility from being used freely on a large scale, since whoever creates a new extension must ensure that the relevant OIDs are known by all parties concerned. There is at present no systematic method for determining the meaning of an OID. They are neither regularly published, nor are they reliably listed in a central registry. The only way you can find out the meaning of an OID is to have the OID's creator tell it to you.

3.2.3 X.509 on the Internet

Privacy Enhanced Mail

Privacy enhanced mail (PEM) was proposed in early 1993 as an Internet standard for cryptography-enhanced email (see [3.34-3.37]). The intention was to endow Internet email with confidentiality, authentication, message integrity assurance, and non-repudiation of origin, using public-key cryptography. To this end, [3.35] proposed an Internet PKI to support PEM. The standard never caught on in the Internet community for various reasons, one of which was that its proposed PKI model proved to be a poor fit to the Internet's peer-based structure.

PKIX

The PKIX working group (WG) was established in the fall of 1995 with the intent of developing Internet standards needed to support an X.509-based PKI. Several informational and standards track documents in support of the original goals of the WG have been approved by the IESG. The first of these standards, RFC 2459 [3.43], profiles the X.509 version 3 certificates and version 2 CRLs for use in the Internet. The certificate management protocol (CMP) (RFC 2510) [3.44], the online certificate status protocol (OCSP) (RFC 2560) [3.48], and the certificate management request format (CRMF) (RFC 2511) [3.45] have been approved, as have profiles for the use of LDAP v2 for certificate and CRL storage (RFC 2587) [3.50] and the use of FTP and HTTP for transport of PKI operations (RFC 2585) [3.49]. RFC 2527 [3.46], an informational RFC on guidelines for certificate policies and practices also has been published, and the IESG has approved publication of an information RFC on use of KEA (RFC 2528) [3.47] and is expected to do the same for ECDSA. Work continues on a second certificate management protocol, CMC, closely aligned with the PKCS publications and with the cryptographic message syntax (CMS) developed for S/MIME. A roadmap, providing a guide to the growing set of PKIX document, is also being developed as an informational RFC.

The working group is now embarking on additional standards work to develop protocols that are either integral to PKI management, or that are otherwise closely related to PKI use. Work is ongoing on alternative certificate revocation methods. There also is work defining conventions for certificate name forms and extension usage for "qualified certificates," certificates designed for use in (legally binding) non-repudiation contexts. Finally, work is underway on protocols for time stamping and data certification. These protocols are designed primarily to support non-repudiation, making use of certificates and CRLs, and are so tightly bound to PKI use that they warrant coverage under this working group.

3.3 Credential-Based PKI Systems

Much recent work has focused on moving away from identity-based PKIs to a more general system based on attributes or credentials. At present, there are two main proposals for this kind of system: the simple distributed security infrastructure (SDSI), and the simple public key infrastructure (SPKI).

3.3.1 Simple Distributed Security Infrastructure (SDSI)

SDSI was created by Ron Rivest and Butler Lampson and is described in [3.54]. SDSI is designed to facilitate the construction of secure systems and provides simple, clear terminology for defining access-control lists and security policies. It is also an attempt to move away from identity-based certification and towards a system based on roles and credentials.

The SDSI system is key-centric. Rather than attach a public key to an identity, SDSI entities are the keys themselves. Specifically, SDSI calls its entities "principals" and defines them to be digital signature verification keys. The idea is that the key is a proxy for the individual who controls its associated private key. Thus SDSI principals are public keys that can make declarations by issuing verifiable signed statements.

3.3.2 SDSI Certificates

Those signed statements come mainly in the form of certificates. SDSI provides for three types of certificates, and any principal can create any kind of certificate. In no particular order, the three certificate types are:

- Identity certificates
- Group-membership certificates
- Name-binding certificates

SDSI identity certificates bind some identifying information to a principal. The main goal of a SDSI identity certificate is to allow a human reader to identify the individual behind a principal. As such, the certificates are designed to be human-friendly, usually containing some free-form text and perhaps a photograph or other information. Machine-readable tags, such as OIDs, are not used, because SDSI's designers believe that determining the identity behind a principal will almost always involve a human anyway.

Identity certificates play a relatively small role in the SDSI system. More important are group-membership certificates, which assert that a principal does or does not belong to some group (more on SDSI groups below), and name-binding certificates, which bind a name to some value (typically, but not necessarily, a principal).

3.3.3 SDSI Names

When a principal creates a certificate binding a name to some value, that name is said to exist in the principal's *local name space*. Each principal can create their own local names which they can use to refer to other principals. The names are arbitrarily chosen – there is no naming system to follow, and no attempt is made make names that are "globally" unique across all local names spaces. Thus some principal that Alice has named bob may be completely different from the principal that Carl calls bob.

SDSI provides a simple method to *link* local name spaces together. If Alice has named a principal Bob, and Bob has named another principal Jim, then Alice can refer to that second principal as Bob's Jim. Alice can refer to any of bob's principals in this way, and the chain can be extended indefinitely, for example, as in bob's jim's mother's doctor. Names can also be "symbolically" defined. For example, Alice's local name bob can denote company's Bob-Smith. If the principal that Alice calls company changes the principal it calls Bob-Smith, then the principal that she calls bob changes as well.

SDSI achieves this name linking because it has an online orientation. Principals that issue certificates are assumed to be able to provide an on-line Internet server to distribute those certificates upon request. Thus for Alice to find the actual principal behind the name bob's jim, she simply connects to bob's server and requests the name-binding certificate that defines the name jim.

SDSI also provides for multiple global name spaces. These are the name spaces defined by a small set of *distinguished root* principals. These principals have special reserved names (that end with !!), which are bound to the *same* principal in *every* name space. SDSI does not describe how this is achieved in any detail. However, it does give SDSI the power to access "standard" name spaces, for example VeriSign!!'s Microsoft's CEO or DNS!!'s com's microsoft's "Bill Gates". Here, the name VeriSign!! evaluates to the *same* principal in *all* name spaces. The name DNS!! also resolves to another, unique principal in all name spaces. Note that this does not mean that all principals have a single, unique global name. Rather, a principal can have multiple global names that start from different distinguished roots (as in our example).

3.3.4 SDSI Groups

SDSI allows its principals to define groups, or sets, of principals. Each group has a name and a set of members. The name is local to some principal, which is the "owner" of the group. Only a group's owner may change its definition. A group can be an explicit list of the group's members (either as a list of principals and/or names of principals), or it can be defined in terms of other groups. Any principal can define his own groups and export them via his servers in much the same way as name bindings. The servers can issue membership certificates based on the groups' definitions.

Groups provide the fundamental mechanism by which SDSI operates. When defining a security policy (for example, specifying who is allowed access to a particular resource), SDSI allows you to define the group of authorized principals, then place the group's name on the resource's access-control list(s). SDSI's naming system allows a person to easily understand security policies created in this way.

3.3.5 SDSI in Action

To better illustrate SDSI's ideas, we now provide a small example of how SDSI would operate in a typical situation. SDSI defines *protocols* in which *messages* are exchanged. Our example, illustrated in Fig. 3.10, shows how the SDSI Membership and Get protocols are used to access an FTP server.

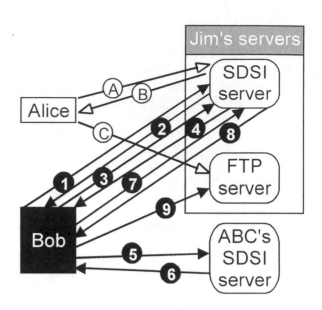

Fig. 3.11   SDSI protocol example

The FTP server is administered by Jim, an employee of ABC Inc. Jim wants to give FTP access to his friends and to other ABC employees. Jim defines a group called ftp-users on his SDSI server. That group contains two entries, the groups named friends and abc's employees, meaning that for a principal to be a member of the ftp-users group it must either be a member of friends or a member of abc's employees (or both). Jim has also defined a group he calls friends on his server, which contains the names alice, stanley and Bob, corresponding to the principals of Jim's friends. Furthermore, Jim has bound the name abc to ABC Inc.'s principal. Finally, ABC Inc. has created a group it calls employees on its SDSI server, which lists all the principals of its employees, including one that they have named BobSmith103456, which is Bob's principal. These group definitions are shown in Fig. 3.11.

We begin our example by illustrating how Jim's friend Alice gains FTP access, then follow with the more complicated example of how Bob gains the same access. The messages sent and received by Alice are depicted in Fig. 3.10 with white-headed arrows, while those involving Bob are shown with black-headed arrows.

To gain access to the FTP server, Alice must show that she is a member of Jim's ftp-users group. She sends a SDSI Membership.Query message (arrow A in Fig. 3.10) to Jim's SDSI server, in which she specifies her principal and the group name ftp-users. The message is a request for a certificate stating the membership status of the given principal for the given group. That status may be one of true (i.e., the principal is a member), false (is not a member) or fail (may or may not be a member, additional credentials are needed for a full determination).

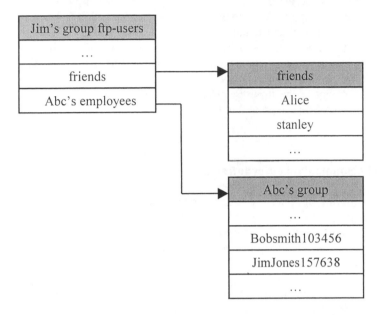

Fig. 3.12   Sample SDSI groups

In Alice's case when Jim's SDSI server performs the membership check it finds that the principal that Jim has named alice matches the principal in the Membership.Query message and is a member of Jim's friends group, which satisfies the membership requirements for the ftp-users group. Jim's SDSI server replies to Alice's query with a true membership certificate for Alice's principal (arrow B). Alice then presents the membership certificate to Jim's FTP server (arrow C) to gain access.

Bob's case is a bit more complicated. Bob is an employee of ABC Inc. but his principal is not a member of Jim's friends group. When Bob sends a Membership.Query to Jim's SDSI server (arrow 1), the reply (arrow 2) is a fail membership certificate along with an indication that if Bob can show membership (or nonmembership) in Jim's abc's employees group it would help in determining his membership in the ftp-users group.

Bob needs to find out which principal Jim has named abc, so he sends a SDSI Get protocol Get.Query message to Jim's SDSI server (arrow 3). The Get protocol is used to retrieve certificates from a server. In this case, Bob requests all of Jim's name-binding certificates that specify the local name abc. Jim's SDSI server replies with a certificate showing that Jim's local name abc corresponds to ABC Inc.'s principal (arrow 4).

Bob now contacts ABC's SDSI server with a Membership.Query message for the employees group (arrow 5). ABC's SDSI server finds that Bob's principal is a member of the group, and returns a true membership certificate (arrow 6). Now Bob can send another ftp-users Membership.Query message (arrow 7) to Jim's SDSI server, this time including the membership certificate he obtained form ABC's SDSI server. Using this new credential, Jim's SDSI server can verify that Bob is a member of the ftp-users group and return a true membership certificate (arrow 8) which Bob can present to the FTP server to gain access (arrow 9).

3.3.6 The Simple Public Key Infrastructure

At the beginning of 1996, just before the publication of the SDSI paper, an Internet working group was formed to propose an alternative PKI to the X.509v3-based PKIX. This new group is called the simple public key infrastructure (SPKI) Working Group. So far, the group has only published a requirements statement, [3.59], and a draft certificate format, [3.58].

There are several similarities between the SPKI and SDSI. In particular, one of the SPKI's requirements is to support, where possible, the SDSI local name space mechanism. SDSI is, and the SPKI will be, key-centric (SDSI speaks of principals" while the SPKI uses the term keyholders"), and both provide a mechanism for attaching credentials (the SPKI calls them attributes) to public key values (SDSI through its groups, the SPKI by issuing certificates).

Although the SPKI will use SDSI names, it considers global naming schemes to be irrelevant. To quote the SPKI requirements document: "A user of a certificate needs to know whether a given keyholder has been granted some attribute and that attribute rarely involves a name." The SPKI recognizes the need to uniquely identify keyholders, and considers the public key value itself (or its hash) adequate for that purpose.

The SPKI will be a credential-based system. Its certificates will carry the minimum attributes necessary to get a job done. This is to protect, as much as possible, the privacy of keyholders. Using monolithic certificates that contain many attributes, most of which are irrelevant in a given situation, would reveal more information about the keyholder than he might like. Also, to discourage keyholders from sharing their private key values, the SPKI will allow a certificate holder to delegate the attributes she acquires from the certificate. Finally, SPKI certificates are to have several validation and revocation mechanisms: validity periods, periodic reconfirmation, CRLs, or some user-defined conditions to be tested online or through other certificates.

3.4 Summary

This chapter introduces the basic concept of PKI. There are several international PKI standards. Among them, X.509 has been widely used around the world. Many companies have released their PKI products for various applications, especially for e-business. Much recent work has focused on moving away from identity-based PKIs, such as X.509, to a more general system based on attributes or credentials. There are two main proposals for this kind of system: the simple distributed security infrastructure (SDSI), and the simple public key infrastructure (SPKI). These two proposals will play an important role in some special enterprise applications.

3.5 References

[3.1]   M. Blaze, J. Feigenbaum, J. Lacy (1996) Decentralized trust management. In: Proceedings of the IEEE Conference on Security and Privacy.

[3.2]   Data Encryption Standard (1993) Federal Information Processing Standards Publication 46-2.

[3.3]   W. Diffie, M. E. Hellman (1976) New directions in cryptography. IEEE Trans Infor Theory 22: 644–654.

[3.4]   C. Liu, P. Albitz (1992) DNS and BIND. O'Reilly, Beijing Cambridge Farnham Koln Tokyo.

[3.5]   T. ElGamal (1985) A public key cryptosystem and a signature scheme based on discrete logarithms. IEEE Trans Infor Theory 31: 469–472.

[3.6]   C. M. Ellison (1996) Generalized certificates.

[3.7]   C. H. Fancher (1996) Smart cards. Scientific American 275(2): 40–45.

[3.8]   W. Ford (1995) Advances in public-key certificate standards. ACM SIGSAC Security Audit & Control Review 13(3).

[3.9]   W. Ford (1995) A public key infrastructure for US government unclassified but sensitive applications. Produced by Nortel and BNR for NIST.

[3.10] W. Ford, M. Baum (1997) Secure electronic commerce: building the infrastructure for digital signatures and encryption. Prentice-Hall, Englewood Cliffs New York.

[3.11] M. Froomkin: The essential role of trusted third parties in electronic commerce.

[3.12] Government of Canada (1995) The challenge of the Information Highway: Final Report of the Information Highway Advisory Council.

[3.13]   M. Branchaud (1997) A survey of public-key infrastructures. Master's degree thesis, McGill University.

[3.14]   N. McBurnett: PGP Web of trust statistics.

[3.15]   N. Negroponte (1995) Being digital. Alfred A. Knopf, New York.

[3.16]   Public Key Infrastructure Study Final Report (1994) Produced by the MITRE Corporation for NIST.

[3.17]   W. Polk (ed.) (1996) Federal public key infrastructure (PKI) technical specifications (version 1) Part A: requirements. NIST PKI Technical Working Group.

[3.18]   N. Nazareno (ed.) (1996) Federal public key infrastructure (PKI) technical specifications (version 1) Part B: technical security policy. NIST PKI Technical Working Group.

[3.19]   W. Burr (ed.) (1995) Federal public key infrastructure (PKI) technical specifications (version 1) Part C: concept of operations. NIST PKI Technical Working Group.

[3.20]   Federal public key infrastructure (PKI) technical specifications (version 1) Part D: interoperability profiles (1995) Produced by CygnaCom Solutions, Inc. for the NIST PKI Technical Working Group.

[3.21]   D. Trcek, B. J. Blazic (1995) Certification infrastructure reference procedures. NIST PKI Technical Working Group (W. Burr, ed), NISTIR 5788, NIST.

[3.22]   M. S. Baum (1994) Certification authority liability and policy. NIST-GCR-94-654, NTIS Doc. No. PB94-191-202. National Technical Information Service, Springfield, VA.

[3.23]   B. S. Jr. Kaliski (1993) An overview of the PKCS standards. RSA Laboratories.

[3.24]   RSA Laboratories (1993) PKCS #10: certification request standard.

[3.25]   RSA Laboratories (1993) PKCS #6: extended-certificate syntax standard.

[3.26]   RSA Laboratories (1993) PKCS #9: selected attribute types.

[3.27]   R. Housley, W. Ford, D. Solo: Internet public key infrastructure, Part I: X.509 certificate and CRL profile (draft). IETF X.509 PKI (PKIX) Working Group.

[3.28]   S. Farrell, C. Adams, W. Ford: Internet public key infrastructure, Part III: certificate management protocols (draft). IETF X.509 PKI (PKIX) Working Group.

[3.29]   M. Stahl (1987) Domain administrators guide. RFC1032.

[3.30]   M. Lottor (1987) Domain administrators operations guide. RFC1033.

[3.31]   P. Mockapteris (1987) Domain names – concepts and facilities. RFC1034.

[3.32]   P. Mockapteris (1987) Domain names – implementation and specification. RFC1035.

[3.33]   R. Rivest (1992) The MD5 message-digest algorithm. RFC1321.

[3.34]   J. Linn (1993) Privacy enhancement for Internet electronic mail, Part I: message encryption and authentication procedures. RFC1421.

[3.35]   S. Kent (1993) Privacy enhancement for Internet electronic mail, Part II: certificate-based key management. RFC1422.

[3.36]   D. Balenson (1993) Privacy enhancement for Internet electronic mail, Part III: algorithms, modes, and identifiers. RFC1423.

[3.37]   B. Kaliski (1993): Privacy enhancement for Internet electronic mail, Part IV: key certification and related services. RFC1424.

[3.38]   J. Kohl, B. C. Neuman (1993) The Kerberos network authentication service (version 5). RFC1510.

[3.39]   C. Malamud, M. Rose (1993) Principles of operation for the TPC.INT subdomain: general principles and policy. RFC1530.

[3.40]   R. Atkinson (1995) Security architecture for the Internet protocol. RFC1825.

[3.41]   J. Galvin, S. Murphy, S. Crocker, N. Freed (1995) Security multiparts for MIME: multipart/signed and multipart/encrypted. RFC1847.

[3.42]   D. Eastlake, C. Kaufman (1997) Domain name system security extensions. RFC2065.

[3.43]   R. Housley, W. Ford, W. Polk, D. Solo (1999) Internet X.509 public key infrastructure certificate and CRL profile. RFC2459.

[3.44]   C. Adams, S. Farrell (1999) Internet X.509 public key infrastructure certificate management protocols. RFC2510.

[3.45]   M. Myers, C. Adams, D. Solo, D. Kemp (1999) Internet X.509 certificate request message format. RFC2511.

[3.46]   S. Chokhani, W. Ford (1999) Internet X.509 public key infrastructure certificate policy and certification practices framework. RFC2527.

[3.47]   R. Housley, W. Polk (1999) Internet X.509 public key infrastructure representation of key exchange algorithm (KEA) keys in Internet X.509 public key infrastructure certificates. RFC2528.

[3.48]   M. Myers, R. Ankney, A. Malpani, S. Galperin, C. Adams (1999) X.509 Internet public key infrastructure online certificate status protocol – OCSP. RFC2560.

[3.49]   R. Housley, P. Hoffman (1999) Internet X.509 public key infrastructure operational protocols: FTP and HTTP. RFC2585.

[3.50]   S. Boeyen, T. Howes, P. Richard (1999) Internet X.509 public key infrastructure LDAPv2 schema. RFC2587.

[3.51]   R. Rivest, A. Shamir, L. Adleman (1978) A method for obtaining digital signatures and public key cryptosystems. Commun ACM 21: 120-126.

[3.52]   M. Saeki (1996) Elliptic curve cryptosystems. M.Sc. thesis, McGill University.

[3.53]   B. Schneier (1996) Applied cryptography (2nd ed). Wiley, New York.

[3.54]   R. Rivest, B. Lampson (1996) SDSI – A simple distributed security infrastructure.

[3.55]   MasterCard and Visa (1996) Secure electronic transaction (SET) specifications.

[3.56]   Secure Hash Standard (1995) Federal information processing standards publication 180-1.

[3.57]   D. R. Stinson (1995) Cryptography: theory and practice. CRC Press, Boca Raton New York.

[3.58]   C. M. Ellison, B. Frantz, B. M. Thomas (1996) Simple Public Key Certificate.
[3.59]   C. M. Ellison (1997) SPKI requirements.
[3.60]   D. Trcek, B. J. Blazic, N. Pavesic (1996) Security policy space definition and structuring. Computer Standards & Interfaces 18(2): 191–195.
[3.61]   D. Trcek, T. Klobucar, B. J. Blazic, F. Bracun (1994) CA-browsing system – A supporting application for global security services. In: ISOC Symposium on Network and Distributed System Security, pp. 123–128.
[3.62]   ITU/ISO (1988) Recommendation X.208. Specification of abstract syntax notation one (ASN.1).
[3.63]   ITU/ISO (1998) Recommendation X.209. Specification of basic encoding rules for abstract syntax notation one (ASN.1).
[3.64]   ITU/ISO (1993) Recommendation X.500. Information technology – open systems interconnection – the directory: overview of concepts, models, and services.
[3.65]   ITU/ISO (1993) Recommendation X.509. Information technology – open systems interconnection – the directory: authentication framework.
[3.66]   ITU/ISO (1996) Final text of draft amendments to X.500/9594 for certificate extensions.
[3.67]   P. Zimmermann: PGP user's guide vol. 1 and 2.

4 Biometrics for Security in E-Commerce

David Zhang[1] and Li Yu[2]

[1] Department of Computing
Hong Kong Polytechnic University, Hong Kong

[2] Department of Computer Science and Technology
Harbin Institute of Technology, China

4.1 An Overview of Biometrics

The advance of technology is always inspired by the practical applications, and the emergence of automatic biometrics technology is rooted in the requirement for real-world security applications. Whether this new technology can last for a long time will be decided by how well it can solve security problems. Although biometric technology is at the development stage, it has been implemented in various applications and some of them work well. Along with the widespread application of biometrics technology, more funds and more attention are being given to this ascending technology [4.1-4.4, 4.20-4.22, 4.24, 4.32, 4.34].

Biometrics refers to the automatic identification of a person based on his/her physiological or behavioral characteristics [4.19]. Today a variety of biometric technologies are used, each with its own strengths to make it more appropriate than others for certain types of applications. Fig. 4.1 shows the major biometric technologies:

- Finger-scan
- Hand-scan, aka, hand geometry
- Retina-scan
- Iris-scan
- Facial-scan, aka, facial geometry
- Signature-scan, aka, dynamic signature verification
- Voice-scan, aka, voice or speaker verification

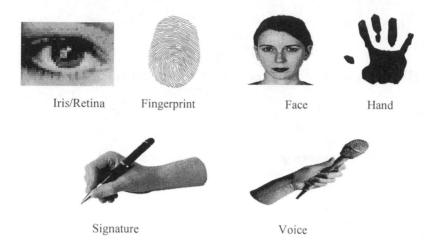

Iris/Retina   Fingerprint   Face   Hand

Signature   Voice

Fig. 4.1   Biometrics technologies

Biometric is the most secure and convenient authentication tool. It cannot be borrowed, stolen, or forgotten, and forging one is practically impossible. Common physical biometrics includes fingerprints, hand or palm geometry, retina, iris, and facial characteristics. Behavioral characteristics include a person's signature, voice (which also has a physical component), keystroke pattern, and gait. Technologies for signature and voice are the most developed for the behavioral biometrics [4.30-4.33, 4.35].

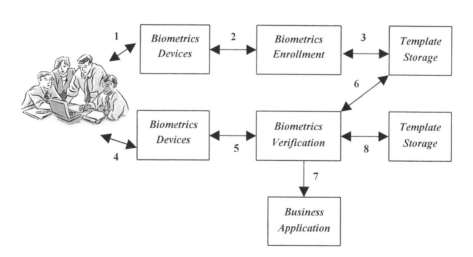

Fig. 4.2   How a biometric system works

In Fig. 4.2 the process involved in using a biometric system is described. The text descriptions of these processes are as follows:

(1) Capture the chosen biometric data.
(2) Process the biometric data, extract it and enroll it to form a biometric template.
(3) Store the template in a local repository, a central repository, or a portable token such as a smart card.
(4) Live-scan the chosen biometric.
(5) Process the biometric data and extract features to form a biometric template.
(6) Match the new template against stored templates.
(7) Calculate a matching score for the business application.
(8) Record a secure audit trail with respect to system use.

4.1.1 Finger-Scan Technology

Finger-scan biometrics is based on the distinctive characteristics of the human fingerprint. A fingerprint image is read from a capture device, features are extracted from the image, and a template is created. If appropriate precautions are followed, the result is a very accurate means of authentication [4.2-4.4, 4.6-4.8, 4.23, 4.27].

Fingerprint matching techniques can be placed into two categories: minutiae-based and correlation-based [4.25]. Minutiae-based techniques first find minutiae points and then map their relative placement on the finger. However, there are some difficulties for this approach when the fingerprint is of such low quality such that accurate extraction of minutiae points is difficult. Also, this method does not take into account the global pattern of ridges and furrows. In contrast, the correlation-based method is able to overcome the problems of the minutiae-based approach. However, correlation-based techniques require the precise location of a registration point and are affected by image translation and rotation.

The most widely used methods of controlling access to computers and data are passwords and PINs. While passwords and PINs are easy to use, they provide weak proof of identity. They are rarely changed, frequently shared, often used in plain sight, and easily defeated using widely available hacker programs. Implementing fingerprint authentication and replacing passwords and PINs makes access to corporate information more efficient and secure. Fingerprint verification may be a good choice for in-house systems that operate in a controlled environment where you can give users adequate explanation and training. A fingerprint authentication solution can provide secure online banking transactions, secure customer financial information, new online services, and non-repudiation. The benefits include fraud protection, customer confidence and retention, time/cost efficiencies, and the ability to extend services to non-local customers.

4.1.2 Hand-Scan Technology

This approach uses the geometric shape of the hand for authentication. Authentication of identity using hand geometry is challenging work, as hand features are not very descriptive. The problem can be tackled by combining various individual features to attain robust verification [4.2-4.4].

Hand-scan is occasionally misunderstood as "palm reading," as the placement of the hand palm-down on the reader can be confusing to those unfamiliar with the technology.

Hand-scan is a relatively accurate technology, but does not draw on as rich a data set as finger-, face-, or iris-scans. A decent measure of the distinctiveness of a biometric technology is its ability to perform one-to-many searches, that is, the ability to identify a user without the user first claiming an identity. Hand-scan does not perform one-to-many identification very well, as similarities between hands are not uncommon. It has an advantage in failure-to-enroll (FTE) rates, which measures the likelihood that a user is incapable of enrolling in the system. In contrast, finger-scan is prone to FTEs in the case of poor-quality fingerprints, and facial-scan requires consistent lighting to properly enroll a user. Since nearly all users will have the dexterity to use hand-scan technology, only a few employees and visitors will need to be processed outside the biometric.

Organizations use hand-geometry readers in various scenarios, including time and attendance recording, where they have proved extremely popular. Hand-scan technology offers the following benefits:

(1) Cards and associated administration costs can be eliminated.
(2) "Buddy-punching" is impossible; this is particularly rated by leading time and attendance software systems.
(3) True-time clock functionality including department transfers, supervisor override, and time restrictions.

Various applications, such as credit card and ATM transactions, check cashing, and even picking up a child from daycare, benefit from this technology.

The benefits of hand-geometry scanning in personal identification are:

(1) High user acceptance, non-intrusive technology.
(2) Fast and easy enrollment use.
(3) Low false reject rate equates to a positive user experience.

Ease of integration into other systems and processes, coupled with ease of use, makes hand-geometry scanning an obvious first step for many biometric projects.

4.1.3 Retina-Scan Technology

Along with iris recognition technology, retina scan is perhaps the most accurate and reliable biometric technology. However, it is difficult to use and is perceived as being moderately to highly intrusive. In films, portrayals of retina-scan devices reading at an arm's length, with a non-stationary subject, are false. Retina-scan biometrics requires a cooperative, well-trained, patient audience, or else performance will fall dramatically [4.2, 4.4-4.5].

Even when those unfamiliar with the rudimentary anatomy of the eye are reminded that all vision is based upon light passing through the pupil to the retina, there is still notable resistance to retina-scan technology. This is perhaps due to an unusually high degree of sensitivity on issues of the eye; iris-scan biometrics, where the patterns of the iris are read, which requires less effort on the part of the user, is also frequently met with similar expressions of hesitation.

Retina-scan devices read through the pupil; this requires the user to situate their eye within 1/2 inch of the capture device, and to hold still while the reader ascertains the patterns. The user looks at a rotating green light as the patterns of the retina are measured at over 400 points. By comparison, a fingerprint may only provide 30-40 distinctive points (minutiae) to be used in the enrollment, template creation, and verification process. Retina-scanning has a very high level of accuracy compared to most other biometrics.

Retina-scanning can be quite accurate but requires the user to look into a receptacle and focus on a given point. This is not particularly convenient if you wear glasses or are concerned about having close contact with the reading device. For these reasons, retina-scanning is not warmly accepted by all users, even though the technology itself works well.

4.1.4 Iris-Scan Technology

Iris recognition uses the unique features of the human iris to provide an unmatched identification technology. So accurate are the algorithms used in iris recognition that the entire planet could be enrolled in an iris database with only a small chance of false acceptance or false rejection [4.2, 4.4-4.5].

Iris identification technology is a tremendously accurate biometric. Only retina-scan can offer nearly the security that iris-scan offers, and the interface for retina-scan is thought by many to be more challenging and intrusive. More common biometrics provide reasonably accurate results in verification schematics, whereby the biometric verifies a claimed identity, but they cannot be used in large-scale identification implementations like iris recognition.

An iris-based biometric, on the other hand, involves analyzing features found in the colored ring of tissue that surrounds the pupil. Iris-scan, undoubtedly the less intrusive of the eye-related biometrics, uses a fairly conventional camera element and requires no close contact between the user and the reader. In addition, it has the potential for a higher than average template-matching performance. Iris biometrics work with glasses in place and it is one of the few technologies that can work well in identification mode. Ease of use and system integration have not traditionally been strong points with iris-scanning devices, but you can expect improvements in these areas as new products emerge.

In some banks, new ATMs with iris-recognition technology have been used to control access to bank accounts. After enrolling once (a "30 second" process), the customer needs only to approach the ATM, follow the instruction to look at the camera, and be recognized within 2-4 seconds [4.44].

Again, the benefits of such a system are clear, that is, the customer who chooses to use an ATM with iris recognition will have a quicker, more secure transaction. Although one may question whether the risk of fraud at ATM's is very large, this type of integration makes long-term sense. First, ATMs are large, omnipresent, secured devices which, the public knows, visually record every transaction. It is a small cognitive leap to envision them moving from their current configuration to being biometrically enabled. Second, iris technology is being put before the public in a non-coercive, unobtrusive, fairly low-risk setting. As the accuracy and reliability of the technology are proven through time, the public should be accepting of less traditional implementations. Like the vast majority of biometric companies, iris recognition vendors are very eager to participate in securing Internet commerce. The potential market for the vendors whose technology is most widely embraced is unimaginably large.

4.1.5 Facial-Scan Technology

Similar to finger-scan and voice-scan biometrics, there are various methods by which facial-scan technology recognizes people. All share certain commonalities, such as emphasizing those sections of the face that are less susceptible to alteration, including the upper outlines of the eye sockets, the areas surrounding the cheekbones, and the sides of the mouth. Most technologies are resistant to moderate changes in hairstyle, as they do not utilize areas of the face located near the hairline. All of the primary technologies are designed to be robust enough to conduct one-to-many searches, that is, to locate a single face out of a database of thousands, and even hundreds of thousands, of faces [4.2, 4.4-4.5, 4.27].

Facial-scans can be used to control entry to buildings or computer networks by comparing the image of a person seeking access against the scan taken of that person at an earlier date, that is, a one-to-one check [4.47].

Facial-recognition solutions employ the same four-step process that all biometric technologies do, namely, sample capture, feature extraction, template comparison, and matching. The sample capture takes place in the enrollment process, during which the system takes multiple pictures of the face, usually from slightly different angles, to increase the system's ability to recognize the face. After enrollment, certain facial features are extracted and used to create a template. The specific features extracted vary depending on the type of facial-recognition technology used. No images of faces are stored. Instead, the templates consist of numeric codes that are usually encrypted. Many templates can be stored on one system because each is less than 1K in size, compared to between 150K and 300K for a facial image. When someone logs in using a facial-scan system, the template created upon attempted login is compared to a stored template for that person (one-to-one matching) or to a database of stored templates (one-to-many matching).

Face recognition involves the analysis of facial characteristics. This technique has attracted considerable interest, although many people do not completely understand its capabilities. Some vendors have made extravagant claims, which are very difficult, if not impossible, to substantiate in practice for facial-recognition devices. Because facial-scanning needs an extra peripheral not customarily included with basic PCs, it is more of a niche market for network authentication. However, the casino industry has capitalized on this technology to create a facial database of scam artists for quick detection by security personnel.

4.1.6 Handwriting and Signature Verification

Signature verification involves analysis of the way a user signs their name. Signing features, such as speed, velocity, and pressure, are as important as the finished signature's static shape. Signature verification enjoys a synergy with existing processes that other biometrics do not. People are used to signatures as a means of transaction-related identity verification, and most would see nothing unusual in extending this to encompass biometrics. Signature-verification devices are reasonably accurate in operation and obviously lend themselves to applications where a signature is an accepted identifier.

Electronic-signature verification is also gaining ground for retail and e-commerce applications. The implementation includes installation of electronic-signature software and the solution utilizes electronic signatures to automate processing of some lease-end documents. The solution is part of a transition from paper lease-end documents to electronic documents, which will reduce operation costs and provide an easy-to-use, legally binding electronic signature. E-Pad [4.45] captures a handwritten signature and converts it to a biometric e-signature, offering enhanced workflow and faster processing times. Electronic signatures may be bound into Microsoft Word and Outlook documents, Adobe Acrobat files, and many other forms and transactions. They also feature a handwriting profile that can be used to authenticate the identity of the signer. Surprisingly, relatively few significant signature applications have emerged compared with other biometrics methodologies. But if your application fits, it is a technology worth considering [4.2, 4.4-4.5].

4.1.7 Voice-Scan Technology

Of all the above-mentioned human traits used in biometrics, the one that humans learn to recognize first is the voice characteristic. Infants can identify the voice of their mothers and telephone users can identify a caller on a noisy telephone line. Furthermore, the bandwidth associated with speech is much smaller than the other image-based human traits. This implies quicker processing and smaller storage space [4.2, 4.4-4.5, 4.26, 4.29].

A speaker-recognition system can be divided into two categories, namely, text-dependent and text-independent systems. In text-dependent systems, the user is expected to use the same text (keyword or sentence) during training and recognition sessions. A text-independent system does not use the training text during recognition session. Both systems perform the following tasks: feature extraction, similarity analysis, and selection. Texture extraction uses the spectral envelope to adjust a set of coefficients in a predictive system. One voice sample can then be compared for similarity with another sample by computing the regression between the coefficients. This is a similarity analysis. A number of normalization techniques have been developed to account for variation of the speech signals.

A voice security system is responsible for an innovative method of security that dramatically reduces fraud and can prevent one's property from being use, if stolen or obtained fraudulently. This new breakthrough allows speaker-verification to be burned onto an existing microprocessor within a device. Examples of use of this technology are cell phones (to eliminate cell phone fraud), ATMs (to eliminate PIN fraud), and automobiles (to dramatically reduce theft and carjacking). This method is the only standalone technology that does not require management of a large user database, thus protecting the privacy of the user's biometric data. The software, algorithms and templates can be stored on the microprocessor that a device already employs to operate the functions of the electronic hardware inside [4.42].

Voice authentication is not based on voice recognition but on voice-to-print authentication, where complex technology transforms voice into text. Voice biometrics has the most potential for growth, because it does not require new hardware, that is, most PCs nowadays already come with a microphone. However, poor voice quality and ambient noise can affect verification. In addition, the enrollment procedure has often been more complicated than with other biometrics, leading to the perception that voice verification is not user friendly. Therefore, voice authentication software needs improvement. One day, voice may be integrated with finger-scan technology. Because many people see finger-scanning as a higher form of authentication, voice biometrics will most likely be relegated to replace or enhance PINs, passwords, or account names.

4.2 Potential Application Areas

Biometrics applications are not limited to the areas mentioned in the last section. In fact, as long as a system needs to recognize people, it can incorporate biometrics.   In the law enforcement community, matching finger images or part of palm images is the most common method to process criminal suspects and bring guilty criminals to justice. Also we have seen many times in movies the police ask the witness to describe the criminal's physical features such as hair color, the length, width, and shape of the face, etc.; and they then reconstruct a picture of the criminal. In some movies, we see the criminal call the victim over the phone and the police can record the voice of the criminal and search for the criminal according to the voice. All these scenes are examples of finding people using their unique physical features (finger, palm, face, etc.) or behavioral trait (voice), and automatic biometrics can help in all these examples. It is not difficult to understand that the law enforcement community is the largest biometrics user group. Police forces throughout the world are using the Automatic Fingerprint Identification System to assist in crime detection. There are many biometrics vendors earning significant revenues in this area [4.9, 4.11-4.12, 4.14-4.15].

Businessmen always play an important role in spreading a new technology. As automatic biometrics technologies become more and more mature in the law enforcement area, they are also introduced in civilian applications by biometrics product vendors. Usually most civilian biometrics applications are some kind of access control. We may simply classify all the civilian biometrics applications as either physical access control or data access control. Physical access control ensures only authorized individuals can physically access secure areas while data access control secures access to sensitive data. Securing benefit systems against fraud, preventing illegal immigrants from entering a country, or prisoners from leaving a prison all belong to physical access control, while Internet banking, telephone banking, ATM, and Web Store belong to data access control. Automatic biometrics is a rapidly expanding market. Fraud is an ever-increasing problem and security is becoming a necessity in many walks of life. Civilian access control, therefore, will not be restricted to the application areas mentioned below and will branch out to other market opportunities as soon as a need is identified.

4.2.1 Benefit Systems

When applying biometrics in benefit systems, it plays a different role from that in banking or in physical access control. In banking or physical access control or other methods of access control, all unique physical features or behavioral traits are registered in a system before the system is used. When somebody needs to access the system, their unique feature is captured at that point and the system checks the newly captured feature against the template in the database to decide whether it is from the same person. This will prevent unauthorized people from accessing the system. In benefit systems, however, people do not need to register their features first. Only when they need to get the benefit is their unique feature extracted and stored in the system. The system checks whether this person has already registered and received the benefit before, by checking the database templates. Biometrics is well placed to capitalize on this phenomenal market opportunity, and vendors are building on the strong relationship currently enjoyed with the benefits community.

4.2.2 E-Commerce Applications

E-commerce developers are exploring the use of biometrics and smart cards to more accurately verify a trading party's identity. For example, many banks are interested in this combination to better authenticate customers and ensure non-repudiation of online banking, trading, and purchasing transactions [4.5, 4.9, 4.13].

Banks may embrace biometrics technologies from various aspects. Automated teller machines (ATMs) and transactions at the point of sale, telephone banking, Internet banking, and many other banking applications are vulnerable to fraud and can be secured by biometrics. Fig. 4.3 shows various biometrics and banking services and where they can be applied.

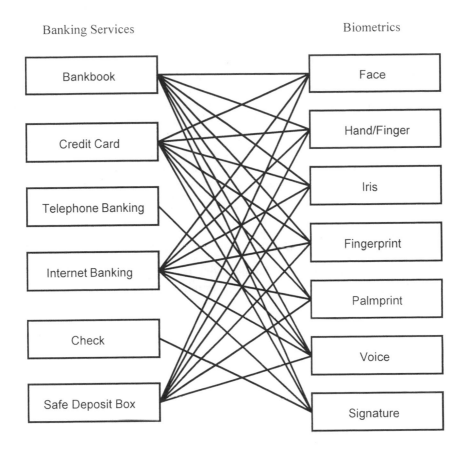

Fig. 4.3   Biometrics applications in banking

Point-of-sale (POS) system vendors are working on the cardholder verification method, which would enlist smart cards and biometrics to replace signature verification. MasterCard estimates that adding smart-card-based biometric authentication to a POS credit card payment will decrease fraud by 80%.

Merchants use biometrics to obtain secure services over the telephone through voice authentication. Voice authentication systems developed by Nuance Communications are currently deployed nationwide, by both the Home Shopping Network and Charles Schwab. The latter's marketing catch phrase is: "No PIN to remember, no PIN to forget."

4.2.3 Computer Systems

Currently, computer systems use passwords as their secure guards. On one hand, remembering tens of passwords and changing passwords very often becomes a headache for almost everyone who uses a computer; on the other hand, a password itself does not have direct connection to the end-user. If somebody gets the password, they will be considered as a legal user by the computer system even though he is a criminal and meanwhile, if a legal user forgets their password, they will be refused access to their own computer. Biometrics technology binds the authority directly to the end-user and removes the need for various passwords. Voice and fingerprint recognition are now the most promising techniques in this area.

4.2.4 Immigration

Terrorism, drug-running, illegal immigration, and an increasing throughput of legitimate travelers are putting a strain on immigration authorities throughout the world. It is essential that these authorities can quickly and automatically process law-abiding travelers and identify the lawbreakers. Biometrics is being employed in a number of diverse applications to make this possible. The US Immigration and Naturalization Service is a major user and evaluator of a number of biometrics. Systems are currently in place throughout the US to automate the flow of legitimate travelers and deter illegal immigrants. Elsewhere biometrics is capturing the imagination of countries such as Australia, Bermuda, Germany, Malaysia, and Taiwan.

4.2.5 National Identity

Biometrics is beginning to assist governments as they record population growth, identify citizens, and prevent fraud occurring during local and national elections. Often this involves storing a biometrics template on a card that in turn acts as a national identity document. Finger scanning is particularly strong in this area and schemes are already under way in Jamaica, Lebanon, The Philippines, and South Africa.

4.2.6 Telephone Systems

Global communication has truly opened up over the past decade, while telephone companies are under attack from fraud. Once again, biometrics is being called upon to defend this onslaught. Speaker ID is a technique for recognizing people by their voices. It is obviously well suited to the telephone environment and is catching these new markets quickly.

4.2.7 Monitoring Time and Attendance

Currently, some factories and companies use cards to monitor the movement of their employees. When they come to work, they need to punch a hole on their cards and another hole when they leave. Such things can be assisted by biometrics. With a biometrics system, employees may press their fingers on a small platform when they come or leave. This may prevent some forms of cheating. But using such a system to monitor employees' movement is still in question because some people think it may violate an employee's privacy.

4.2. 8 Covert Surveillance

One of the more challenging research areas involves using biometrics for covert surveillance. Using facial and body recognition technologies, researchers hope to use biometrics to automatically identify known suspects entering buildings or traversing crowded security areas such as airports. The use of biometrics for covert identification as opposed to authentication must overcome technical challenges such as simultaneously identifying multiple subjects in a crowd and working with uncooperative subjects. In these situations, devices cannot count on consistency in pose, viewing angle, or distance from the detector.

4.3 Multiple Authentication Technologies

From an application standpoint, widespread deployment of a user authentication solution requires support for an enterprise's heterogeneous environment. Support for legacy applications, client-server applications, and Web-based applications is extremely important. However, the complexity of this process is exacerbated by the number of application-specific identities one has to manage. This is compounded by the fact that individual authentication devices or methods may be required to maintain additional identities [4.2, 4.5, 4.11, 4.16].

When it comes to selecting and deploying specific verification methods for enterprise-wide use, one size does not fit all. Any solution should enable the selection of different methods, depending on the users, and be flexible enough to enable dynamic, multifactor authentication, allowing you to dial up the appropriate level of security without sacrificing convenience.

The distributed environment of an enterprise – organizationally, geographically, and technologically – means that employees access information from various access channels. For example, an employee who may access data from their desktop one day may use their laptop remotely the next day. The increasing use of PDA and other wireless devices makes it obvious that users must be authenticated regardless of the channel of access in the digital environment.

Finally, user authentication as a security infrastructure cannot be considered in isolation, often it is through a multifaceted security approach in which combinations of security solutions are deployed. An authentication solution should seamlessly extend the organization's existing security infrastructure.

Consolidating and streamlining user authentication enables the creation of an "Authentication Hub," as shown in Fig. 4.4, providing a single point of control to deploy and manage a combination of authentication methods such as passwords, smart cards, tokens, and biometrics (fingerprint, voice, face, iris, and signature recognition).

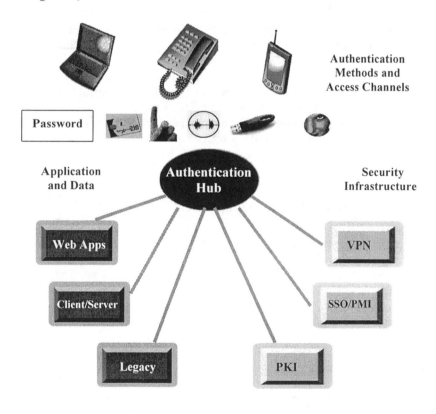

Fig. 4.4   Unified authentication management

An infrastructure that provides unified authentication management allows organizations to manage user authentication through context-based security policies and integrate authentication with existing security solutions such as virtual private networks (VPNs), access management, and public-key infrastructure (PKI). It mitigates interoperability problems between multiple applications, authentication methods, access channels, and platforms, thus driving cost savings, convenience, and security.

When implemented as a strategic component of the security infrastructure within the enterprise, the unified authentication management solution:

- Implements centralized authentication policies for a large number of users.
- Integrates the administration of many forms of authentication.
- Tailors authentication methods to specific information assets, sizes of transactions, roles of individuals and groups, and access channels and entry points.
- Provides a single point for managing user authentication for heterogeneous applications – legacy, client-server, and Web-based.
- Enables convenient but secure access to applications and data in a heterogeneous environment, allowing you to dial up the appropriate level of security without sacrificing user convenience.
- Streamlines the administration tasks necessary to enable convenient and cost effective implementation of strong authentication security policies such as enrollment, verification, policies, and unenrollment of users when multiple authentication methods (smart cards, tokens, fingerprint devices) are deployed.
- Extends existing security infrastructures – VPNs, privilege management (or SSO: single sign-on), policy making and implementation (PMI), and PKI – and seamlessly supports the adoption and migration to advanced authentication methods.

A major problem with biometrics is how and where to store the user's template. Because the template represents the user's personal character, its storage introduces privacy concerns. Furthermore, storing the template in a centralized database leaves that template subject to attack and compromise. On the other hand, storing the template on a smart card enhances individual privacy and increases protection from attack, because individual users control their own templates.

Vendors can enhance security by placing more biometric functions directly on the smart card. Some vendors have built a fingerprint sensor directly into the smart card reader, which in turn passes the biometric to the smart card for verification. At least one vendor, Biometric Associates, has designed a smart card that contains a fingerprint sensor directly on the card. This is a stronger secure architecture because cardholders must authenticate themselves directly to the card.

PKI uses public- and private-key cryptography for user identification and authentication. There are some advantages over biometrics: PKI is mathematically more secure, and it can be used across the Internet. The main drawback of PKI is the management of the user's private key. To be secure, the private key must be protected from compromise; to be useful, the private key must be portable. The solution to these problems is to store the private key on a smart card and protect it with a biometric.

In the Smart Access common government ID card program, the US General Services Administration is exploring this union of biometrics, smart cards, and PKI technology. The government of Finland is also considering using these technologies in the Finnish National Electronic ID card.

4.4 How to Select a Biometrics System

4.4.1 Difficulty in Selecting a Biometrics System

The performance of a biometrics system is greatly impacted by many factors, such as humidity, light, noise, and the end user's attitude to and familiarity with the system. Therefore, for accuracy, testing should be performed in real working circumstances. High levels of accuracy in one application do not qualify a system for an entirely different application. The quoted performance figures of a biometric system only can be applied to the specific application for which they are quoted. Each application is widely different in terms of system workload and throughput, environmental factors, and other variables [4.2, 4.5, 4.17-4.18, 4.28, 4.33, 4.36].

For example, the same fingerprint-verification system may have very high accuracy in a university restaurant while it may work badly in a village where most people have their fingerprints worn heavily.

This is not to say that the performance rulers, the fault accept rate (FAR) and the fault reject rate (FRR) are meaningless, just that the two rates may vary in diverse environments. The FAR and FRR provided by the developer can be used as a guide to understand a system's general ability.

In one sentence, a biometrics system's performance is application sensitive, and making a biometrics system adaptive to a particular application needs significant consideration.

University of Glamorgan
Learning Resources Centre -
Treforest
Self Issue Receipt (TR4)

Customer name: MR DAVID
COURT
Customer ID: ******4216403

Title: Payment technologies for e-commerce
ID: 7312505390
Due: **15/03/2012 23:59**

Total items: 1
08/03/2012 13:49

Thank you for using the Self-Service
system
Diolch yn fawr

4.4.2 Various Factors: Whether a Biometrics System Is Needed

Before applying biometrics, we must make clear what the business driver is. What is the main goal of the whole project? What are the constraints of the project, like deadlines, budgets, etc.? What security level is needed? What is the current system? What is the weakness of the current system? Is it necessary to apply biometrics? Can biometrics solve the existing problems? Are there any other choices for securing the system? Will biometrics cause any trouble for the system? Can biometrics integrate well with the current system? Will users of the system accept this new work style? Simply put, making sure biometrics is needed is the first step when applying this new technology.

4.4.3 Comparison of Different Biometrics Techniques

Tables 4.1 and 4.2 are two tables of comparison for existing biometrics systems. Factors considered in biometrics system evaluation are discussed below.

Vulnerability to Fraud

Biometrics systems aim at providing high-level security, so whether a biometrics trait is hard to mimic is an essential consideration in the construction of such applications. Extreme measures, such as gouging out eyes or truncating fingers to defraud a biometrics system, have appeared in some movies.

Ease of Use

One springboard for biometrics system popularity is to allow the public to get rid of the bother of remembering tens of passwords and keeping strings of keys. Such systems could be really user friendly, preventing headaches greater than a lost room key. Some biometric devices are not user friendly. For example, users without proper training may experience difficulty aligning their head with a device for enrolling and matching facial templates, while face, fingerprint, voice, and palm technologies are easy to use.

Intrusive for Human Beings

Certain biometrics systems are seen to be more intrusive than others. For example, retina capture involves exposing eyes to a bright beam, while voice-scan seems non-intrusive. However, sometimes, a higher accuracy may be gained using a more intrusive approach. Places where high levels of security are needed have to choose such intrusive methods. For example, workers at a nuclear power plant would probably acknowledge the need for a degree of intrusiveness, as security is a very important issue in that environment.

Applicability

Physical characteristics vary and some individuals will not be able to use a bio-metrics system. No single biometrics system can capture and match biometrics data for the global population in all circumstances. Human beings are as diverse and unpredictable as environments. Some individuals have damaged fingers, limbs, voice boxes, or eyes. This may make verification and identification with a single biometrics system impossible; but it may be possible to use a multiple-biometrics system. Also, this does not mean that a single biometrics system is un-able to perform a task in an application where a minority of people cannot have a biometrics sample captured. It is simply that the minority cannot use the system automatically and must be dealt with in an appropriate manner.

Speed of Verification

Response time is a key issue for any computer system and for biometrics systems.

Size of Storage for One Biometrics Template

For an identification system, this factor directly affects the overall database size and searching speed. For a verification system, where the registered template is stored in some special media such as barcodes, magnetic cards, or smart cards, this factor could determine the cost of a card.

Long-Term Stability

The biometrics feature chosen to identify a person in a system should be stable for at least as long as the system is to be used, so that the system can work correctly during its lifetime.

Maturity of Technology

Some biometrics features, such as fingerprints and signatures, have been used for a long time and their accuracies have been proven widely. Meanwhile, other bio-metric systems, such as face-scanning and voice-scanning, are newcomers to this area and need to be proven in real-time applications.

From Tables 4.1 and 4.2, retina-scan appears to have the highest crossover accuracy. Even though iris-scan has a high cross over accuracy, its user acceptability is low. Fingerprints and hand geometries are equally "unique."

Signature dynamics and voice dynamics have the lowest accuracy rates. In addition, these two techniques rely on behavioral measurements as opposed to physical measurements. In general, behavioral biometrics is less reliable than physical biometrics.

Retina-scan has a high accuracy but also has a high data-collection-error rate and a low user-acceptability. For this reason, retina-scan broadly exists only in science fiction movies and not in real-life applications!

The fingerprint biometric has a low data-collection-error rate and a high user-acceptability. Further, fingerprint technology has been heavily invested in, and applied to both the identification and the authentication problem. Finally, fingerprint biometrics has the highest acceptance in the identification community and virtually every large biometrics system in operation today uses fingerprint biometrics. Notwithstanding its association with "criminal" applications, fingerprint biometrics is generally accepted by clients.

Table 4.1   Comparison of various biometrics techniques

Technical factor	Hand geometry	Retina	Fingerprint
False rejection rate	0.2 percent, one try	12.4 percent (one try), 0.4 percent (three tries)	1% - 5%, three tries
False acceptance rate	0.2 percent, one try	0 no false acceptances	0.01 - 0.0001 percent (three tries)
Vulnerability to fraud	Almost impossible to secretly obtain hand-geometry data. However, when the person cooperates, this seems not at all impossible	No counterfeits seem possible. False eyes, contact lenses, or eye transplants cannot breach the security of this device	Dummy fingers and dead fingers will be detected when high-security platen is installed
Ease of use	The first time one needs to get used to it. After some experience it is not difficult	Difficult to use. Socially difficult to accept because people do not like to have their eyes scanned	Easy to use, but it is associated with criminal investigations
Universality	Not suitable for people who have rheumatic hands or related physical impairments	Suitable for everyone with eyes	Not for people with damaged fingerprints due to daily handling of rough material
Speed of identification	Less than 3 seconds	1.5 seconds	Average verification time 2 seconds. Maximum is 20 seconds
Size for storage of template	Only 9 bytes	40 bytes	1203 bytes. After compression it is smaller than 800 bytes
Long-term stability	Sizes of hands will change for children and can change when someone gains or loses a lot of weight	The retinal vascular pattern is very stable. Only a few diseases or injuries will change this pattern	Sizes of fingerprints change for children. Apart from that they always remain the same
Maturity of technology	Worldwide used in many systems	Used in a fair number of systems	Worldwide used in many systems

Table 4.2   Comparison of various biometrics techniques

Technical factor	Iris	Retina	Face	Finger-scanning	Voice	Hand geometry	Finger geometry	Palm	Signature
Level of Accuracy	Very high	Very high	High	High	High	High	High	High	High
Ease of use	Medium	Low	Medium	High	High	High	High	High	High
Vulnerability to fraud	Very high	Very high	Medium	High	Medium	High	High	High	Medium
Intrusive for human beings	Medium	Medium	High	Medium	High	High	Medium	Medium	Very high
Long-term stability	High	High	Medium	High	Medium	Medium	Medium	High	Medium
Industry standards	-	-	-	ANSI/NIST Data Interchange & FBI Image Compression Standards	Speaker Verification API (SVAPI)	-	-	See finger scanning	-
Factors that may affect performance	Glasses worn by end user	-	Poor lighting, aging of face, glasses, facial hair	Dry, dirty or damaged finger images; age, gender, and race of end-user	Background and network noise, colds, and other factors can change the voice	Diseases such as arthritis and rheumatism in end-users	See Hand Geometry	Dry, dirty, or damaged palm images, age, gender, and race of end-user	Illiteracy; signatures that constantly change or are easily imitated

Deciding When to Apply Biometrics, and What Should Be Considered?

Of course, investigating various existing biometrics systems and products is mandatory. Besides this, there are still many questions that should be answered. What
kind of biometrics system is required? Is it an identification system or a verification system? What are the characteristics of the end-user population? What are the
ages, genders, ethnic origins, and occupations of the end-user group? In case
something is wrong with the biometrics system, what will be the substitute
method? What is the accuracy of the biometrics system? Will the population of the
system grow? What does the environment look like? At last, a detailed testing plan
must be prepared.

4.5 Summary

Biometric devices will continue to improve, becoming even more accurate and reliable as technology evolves. As biometric technologies are more widely accepted,
the proliferation of applications should multiply into many phases of our daily activities. The growing interest in the combined use of biometrics and smart cards
should also cause an increased growth path for both technologies in the future.
Hopefully, in the near future, standards will be available which allow multiple
reader technologies from various manufacturers to be utilized within the same system.

4.6 References

[4.1]   International Biometrics Industry Association (IBIA). http://www.ibia.org
[4.2]   International Biometrics Group (IBG). http://www.biometricgroup.com/
[4.3]   The Biometrics Consortium. http://www.biometrics.org
[4.4]   Biometrics Research. http://biometrics.cse.msu.edu
[4.5]   S. Liu, M. Silverman: A practical guide to biometric security technology.
         IEEE Computer Society, IT Pro – Security.
         http://www.computer.org/itpro/homepage/Jan_Feb/security3.htm
[4.6]   East Shore Technologies. http://www.east-shore.com/
[4.7]   Fingerprint Technologies. http://www.fingerprint.com/
[4.8]   FingerPrint USA. http://www.fpusa.com/
[4.9]   Biometrics Reports. http://www.biometrics.org/REPORTS/CTSTG96/
[4.10]   The Biometrics Consulting Group, LLC. http://biometric-consulting.com
[4.11]   Association for Biometrics (AfB), UK. http://www.afb.org.uk/
[4.12]   Australian Biotechnology Association. http://www.aba.asn.au/

[4.13]   Financial Services Technology Consortium. Biometrics fraud prevention.
         http://www.fstc.org/
[4.14]   Security Industry Association (SIA). http://www.siaonline.org/
[4.15]   The Human Identification Project. http://www.asti.dost.gov.ph/
[4.16]   GSA's SmartGov. http://policyworks.gov/smartgov/
[4.17]   Biometrics in Human Services User Group. http://www.bioapi.org
[4.18]   Biometrics and Security.
         http://www.infosyssec.org/infosyssec/biomet1.htm
[4.19]   A. K. Jain, et al. (eds.) (1998) Biometrics: personal identification in net-
         worked society. Kluwer, Boston.
[4.20]   B. Miller (1994): Vital signs of identity. IEEE Spectrum 32 (2): 22–30.
[4.21]   D. Zhang (2000) Automated biometrics: technologies & systems. Kluwer,
         Boston.
[4.22]   D. Zhang (ed.) (2002) Biometrics solutions for authentication in an e-
         world. Kluwer, Boston.
[4.23]   M. Eleccion (1973) Automatic fingerprint identification. IEEE Spectrum
         10(9): 36–45.
[4.24]   G. Lawton (1998) Biometrics: a new era in security. Computer 16–18.
[4.25]   A. Jain, et al. (1997) On-line fingerprint verification. IEEE Trans PAMI
         19(4): 302–313.
[4.26]   J.P. Campbell (1997) Speaker recognition: a tutorial. Proc IEEE 85(9):
         1437–1462.
[4.27]   L. Hong, et al. (1998) Integrating faces and fingerprints for personal iden-
         tification. IEEE Trans PAMI 20(12): 1295–1307.
[4.28]   J. Daugman (1993) High confidence visual recognition of persons by a
         test of statistical independence. IEEE Trans PAMI 15: 1148–1161.
[4.29]   Y. Zhang, D. Zhang (2000) A novel text-independent speaker verification
         method based on the global speaker model. IEEE Trans SMC (Part
         A) 30(5): 598–602.
[4.30]   D. Sims (1994) Biometrics recognition: our hands, eyes and faces give us
         away. IEEE Comput Graphics & Apps.
[4.31]   J. D. Woodward (1997) Biometrics: privacy's foe or privacy's friend?
         Proc IEEE 85(9): 1480–1492.
[4.32]   A. Davis (1997) The body as password. Wired, July Issue.
[4.33]   D. R. Richards (1995) Rules of thumb for biometrics systems. Security
         Manage, October Issue.
[4.34]   G. Lawton (1998) Biometrics: a new era in security. IEEE Computer,
         August Issue.
[4.35]   R. Mandelbaum (1994) Vital signs of identity. IEEE Spectrum, February
         Issue.
[4.36]   M. Golfarelli, D. Maio, D. Maltoni (1997) On the error-reject trade-off in
         biometrics verification systems. IEEE Trans PAMI 19(7): 786–796.
[4.37]   R. P. Wildes (1997) Iris recognition: an emerging biometrics technology.
         Proc IEEE 85(9): 1348–1363.

[4.38]   C. Seal, D. McCartney, M. Gifford (1997) Iris recognition for user validation. British Telecommunications Engineering 16.
[4.39]   A. K. Jain, H. Lin, P. Harath, R. Bolle (1997) An identity-authentication
system using fingerprints. Proc IEEE 85(9): 1365–1388.
[4.40]   A. Jain, H. Lin, R. Bolle (1997) On-line fingerprint verification. IEEE
Trans PAMI 19(4): 302–313.
[4.41]   A. R. Roddy, J. D. Stosz (1997) Fingerprint features: statistical analysis
and system performance estimates. Proc IEEE 85(9): 1390–1421.
[4.42]   http://www.nwfusion.com/research/biometrics.html
[4.43]   http://www.veridicom.com/technology/Biometric%20Applications.pdf
[4.44]   http://www.iris-scan.com/iris_recognition_applications.htm
[4.45]   http://www.biometritech.com/features/deploywp4.htm
[4.46]   http://www.vanguard-fire-security.com/security.htm
[4.47]   http://www.fcw.com/geb/articles/2002/0311/web-face-03-04-02.asp
[4.48]   http://hydria.u-strasbg.fr/~norman/BAS/intro_to_biometrics.htm
[4.49]   http://www.computer.org/itpro/homepage/jan_feb01/security3b.htm

5 Smart Cards and Applications

Weidong Kou[1], Simpson Poon[2], and Edwin M. Knorr[3]

[1] University of Hong Kong
    Pokfulam Road, Hong Kong

[2] School of Information Studies
    Charles Sturt University, Australia

[3] Department of Computer Science
    University of British Columbia, Canada

5.1 Introduction

A smart card is a plastic card with an embedded integrated circuit (IC). A smart card resembles a credit card, with the difference being a chip and (for most smart cards) its metal contacts. A host computer or smart card terminal runs the off-card application and communicates with the card's embedded chip to exchange data and commands. The plastic card usually conforms to physical standards for bank/credit cards, and is a convenient and acceptable way of carrying the chip. Smart cards may contain a microprocessor, random access memory (RAM), read only memory (ROM), and electrically erasable programmable read-only memory (EEPROM). The first patent for a smart card was issued in 1974 to Roland Moreno of France.

Depending on how communication takes place, the smart card can be either contact-based or contactless. For contact-based smart cards, communication takes place through the contacts. The visible contacts cover an area approximately 1cm×1cm (i.e., 100 mm^2); however, the chip itself is usually no more than 25 mm^2. For contactless smart cards, communication takes place through wireless transmission.

Smart cards have some type of non-volatile storage, and can be classified according to whether or not they have a microprocessor. Over half of the smart cards in circulation today do not contain a microprocessor. Such cards are referred to as memory (smart) cards, and are used primarily for storing information or value. These cards have been successfully used for years (primarily in Europe

and Asia) for electronic payment in pay phone, vending, and transportation applications, among others.

Smart cards with an embedded microprocessor are sometimes thought of as
truly "smart" cards - at least in terms of processing functionality. These cards can
perform very reliable security functions, such as authentication, digital signatures,
and encryption. A microprocessor allows a smart card to operate independently of
a host computer or smart card terminal, thereby enabling essential security operations, such as the creation of a digital signature without the signing key ever leaving the card. These smart cards play a crucial role in information and network security, digital identification, order authorization, and payment processing in
electronic commerce applications.

Smart cards have a huge market potential. Currently, billions of smart cards are
in use. According to a 1998 report by Gemplus and the Smart Card Industry Association, approximately 805 million smart cards were issued in 1996, and 2.8 billion cards were forecast for 2000. A more recent report from SchlumbergerSema,
however, reports that only 1.8 billion cards were issued worldwide in 2001, and
furthermore, this figure represents only a 1% increase from 2000. This mild increase stands in contrast to the annual 20% growth rate in recent years, but
SchlumbergerSema predicts increases of 7% and 10%, respectively, in 2002 and
2003. Much of this growth is expected to be driven by smart-card-enabled PKI
applications, including wireless applications, national ID programs, and network
access for enterprise applications.

In terms of applications, prepaid phone cards are still the most popular, followed by mobile communications, and banking. Table 5.1 shows the usage of
smart cards. Multi-application cards include applications such as healthcare, loy-
alty points, secure remote access, and "electronic purse" applications for electronic payment. On electronic-purse cards, real money is represented as a string of
bits, and is exchanged among parties.

Table 5.1 Smart card breakdown[1]

By Application	2000 actual	2003 estimate
Pay Phones	1,040,000,000	990,000,000
Mobile Communications	450,000,000	550,000,000
Banking	120,000,000	220,000,000
Others	180,000,000	357,000,000
Total	1,790,000,000	2,117,000,000

---

[1] Source: SchlumbergerSema, March 2002

By Region	2000 actual	2003 estimate
Europe, Middle East, Africa	895,000,000	974,000,000
Asia Pacific	519,000,000	656,000,000
Latin America	340,000,000	402,000,000
North America	36,000,000	85,000,000
Total	1,790,000,000	2,117,000,000

By Technology	2000 actual	2003 estimate
Memory Cards	1,126,000,000	1,155,000,000
Microprocessor	664,000,000	962,000,000
Multiapplication	115,000,000	530,000,000
(of which are Java Cards...)	(53,000,000)	(336,000,000)

5.2 Fundamentals of Smart Card Systems

A smart card *system* is a distributed computing system consisting of smart cards, smart card readers, smart card operating systems, file systems, and communication interfaces. In this section, we describe the components of a typical smart card system.

5.2.1 Smart Cards

Depending on chip type and method of communication with the reader, smart cards can be classified into different categories. First, the chip can either be a memory chip or a microprocessor. Second, smart cards can communicate with readers either using the contacts on the cards, or wirelessly (in the case of contactless cards). In the latter case, radio waves are used to energize and communicate with the chip. Third, smart cards come in at least two sizes: the size of a standard bank/credit card, and a smaller size for a subscriber identification module (SIM) for global system for mobile communications (GSM) cellular phones.

Memory Chips

Smart card memory chips are designed in accordance with their intended applications. The types of memory used for smart cards include:

- Random access memory (RAM):
  This type of memory is used as a short-term work area. Memory contents are lost when the power is switched off.

- Read-only memory (ROM):
  This type of memory is used for storing software.

- Erasable programmable read-only memory (EPROM):
  This type of memory can only be changed once, and is often used in pre-paid service cards, such as telephone calling cards that count off minutes of use. (For telephone applications, the cards can be discarded when there are no units of value left because the cards cannot be reloaded with value.)

- Electrically erasable programmable read-only memory (EEPROM):
  This type of memory can store programs or data. The contents of the memory are preserved when power is switched off, and the memory can be modified up to about 100,000 times.

The architecture of a memory chip varies, depending on the intended application. An example is shown in Fig. 5.1. In particular, a smart card memory chip may contain the following data for communication with the reader:

- Smart card issuer
- Smart card serial number
- Counter logic
- Secret codes or keys

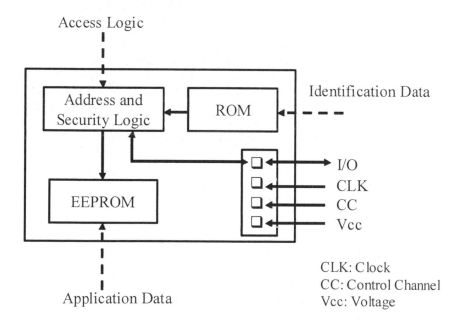

Fig. 5.1 Architecture of a memory smart card

Microprocessor Chips

As shown in Fig. 5.2, microprocessor chips for smart cards contain a CPU, RAM, ROM, EEPROM, I/O control port, and operating system. The CPU is usually an 8-bit processor, which is a smaller and slower version of the CPU used in a typical PC; however, the smart card's CPU could be a 16-bit, 32-bit, or 64-bit version instead. Besides the processor, there are memory components: ROM, which contains the chip's operating system; RAM, which serves as the processor's working memory; and EEPROM, which stores data and program code. Typically, with respect to memory size, RAM is in the range of 256 bytes to 1 KB, ROM is in the range of 16~32 KB, and EEPROM is in the range of 1~16 KB. The connection to outside the chip is via the I/O control port.

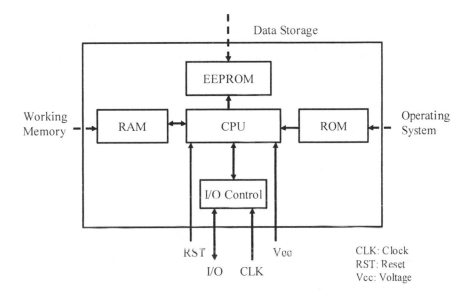

Fig. 5.2 Architecture of a microprocessor smart card

A smart card chip may have an arithmetic co-processor for cryptographic functions. Some chips also have a random-number generator that can facilitate mutual authentication and secure electronic payment.

Contact Smart Cards

Contact smart cards make their physical interface with a smart card reader through an eight-pin contact, as defined in Part 1 of the ISO 7816 standard. These pins are defined as I/O, reset, clock, ground, Vpp (programming voltage), etc. Note that the contacts may become dirty, worn (through use), or damaged (intentionally or unintentionally). Also, hackers use the contacts to launch security attacks. Contactless smart cards are a workaround to most of these problems.

Contactless Smart Cards

Contactless smart cards communicate with a card reader through an antenna embedded in the card. Many such cards have approximately a 10-cm range, but there are systems that work up to a distance of 1 m. The antenna on a smart card can be quite small (e.g., less than 1 cm in diameter). Through an antenna, a contactless smart card can collect its power from a radio frequency (RF) field generated by the card reader. The RF field also transfers information to and from the card.

Since there is no need to insert a contactless smart card into a card reader, such cards can be more convenient. A successful contactless smart card application for public transportation is the Octopus card in Hong Kong, which we describe in detail later in this chapter. Another successful contactless application is access control (via employee badges).

5.2.2 Smart Card Readers

A smart card reader is a device that sets up a communication link or interface between a smart card and a host, such as a PC. Smart card readers are also known as *card acceptance devices* (CADs). They interface with a host through RS232 serial ports, parallel ports, USB ports, PCMCIA slots, infrared IRDA ports, or floppy disk slots. They can also be integrated with a computer keyboard, or embedded into various devices or terminals, such as bank ATMs, kiosks, vending machines, TV set-top boxes, cellular phones, personal digital assistants (PDAs), or handheld computers.

Since a smart card contains no independent power source or clock signal to drive its processor, one of the functions that a reader needs to perform is to provide the card with both power and a clock. In the case of a contact smart card, this is done via the contact pins. In the case of a contactless smart card, the task is accomplished via the embedded antenna.

Depending on whether the smart card is a memory or a microprocessor card, the reader either acts as a translator between the host and the card, or it directly passes commands from the host to the card. For a memory smart card, the reader views the physical card structure to get the exact data address and perform the translation. For a microprocessor smart card, the operating system and logic stored on the smart card directly interpret the commands that have been passed by the reader from the host to the card.

Smart card readers can be classified into two categories: stationary readers and mobile readers. Stationary readers have a permanent connection to the host and are usually powered by the host through the data interface. The host drives the reader and the card, and is responsible for all signaling functions, including initialization and communication. Mobile readers, on the other hand, are stand-alone devices that are battery-powered. A mobile reader initializes communication with the smart card. The host is only concerned with communication with the reader (and not with the smart card).

5.2.3 Smart Card Operating Systems

A smart card operating system typically contains a few thousand bytes of code, and it loads, operates, and manages one or more applications on the card. Unlike DOS, Windows, Unix, or Linux, smart card operating systems are tiny and do not support the rich functionality that these other operating systems provide, such as providing user interfaces or controlling external resources other than the I/O port.

A smart card operating system allows a card reader to send a command to a smart card. The card executes the command, returns a result (if appropriate), and waits for the next command.

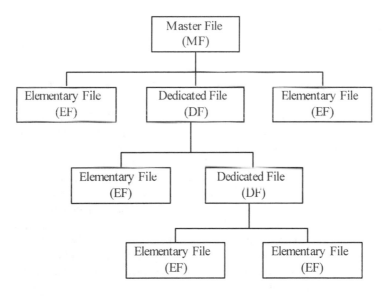

Fig. 5.3 A hierarchical file system for a smart card

Different smart card manufacturers offer different operating systems. Through-out the 1980s and 1990s, various smart card operating systems have been developed for specific applications, such as a data repository. These operating systems are written into ROM. They are proprietary and specific to a smart card chip. A hierarchical file structure, such as that shown in Fig. 5.3, has been used in these systems. Here, the master file serves as the root of the hierarchical file structure, a dedicated file is a directory, and an Elementary File is a leaf node.

As a smart card evolves from a data-storage device to a transaction device, a hierarchical file structure may not be the best choice. New data structures have been created using the industry standard "Create Table" and "Create View" SQL statements (i.e., from the database community). The key advantage is to allow different applications to share a common data structure.

In addition to sharing, it is important for an application not to read or overwrite another application's data, without that other application's consent. This means that the smart card operating system must control memory allocation for each application (e.g., for loading or retrieving data from RAM and EEPROM storage areas).

Given that a smart card application may need to be updated after a smart card is issued, and that various smart card readers may need to access information on the card, new extensions are required for smart card operating systems. Such extensions include an application programming interface (API) and an object-oriented programming language (e.g., Java) that can be used on many different platforms ranging from PCs to hand-held devices.

5.2.4 Communication Interface

Communication between a smart card and a reader typically goes through a half-duplex physical channel on which the reader and the card can only transmit in turn (i.e., the other party has to be in reception mode). In this section, we examine how communication protocols on top of this half-duplex physical channel are established, and how data is transferred.

When establishing communication between a smart card and a reader, it is always the reader that takes the initiative. The card never transmits data without an external request from the reader. To illustrate, consider a contact smart card. When the card is inserted into the reader, five contacts on the card are electrically activated, and the card automatically executes a power-on-reset. Then, the answer to reset (ATR) is sent to the reader. The reader may optionally send a PTS (protocol type select) request command to the card after it successfully evaluates the ATR, and the card responds to the reader with a PTS-response. Both ATR and PTS are independent of the transmission protocol, and they are used for initialization and for setting various transmission parameters. After initialization, the reader sends the card the first command. The card processes the command and sends a response. This kind of command-response protocol is how the reader and the card communicate.

Communication between the card and the reader takes place serially through a bit-serial data stream. The bit order for converting a byte into the bit-serial data stream must be considered. In the direct convention, the first data bit after the start bit is the lowest in the byte, where the start bit is used for indicating the beginning of each serially transmitted byte. A parity bit is at the end of each byte. One or two stop bits may also be added after the parity bit.

In terms of transmission, a basic question is whether data should be transferred in byte mode or in block mode. In answer to this question, there are two transmission protocols at the data link layer, namely T=0 and T=1 protocols. The T=0 protocol is the asynchronous, half-duplex, byte-oriented protocol, which is covered by the ISO/IEC 7816-3 standard, dominating in Europe and widely used in various smart card systems (e.g., GSM applications). The T=1 protocol is the asynchronous, half-duplex, block-oriented protocol, which is covered by the ISO/IEC 7816-3 Amendment 1 standard. The data structures used in the exchange between the reader and the card in the command-response protocol are called transmission protocol data units (TPDUs).

On top of the data link layer protocols (T=0 and T=1), application-layer protocols can be defined for smart card applications to exchange control and information between the card and the reader. There are two application protocols that have been defined in the ISO/IEC 7816-4 standard. One protocol is for providing a file system for storing and retrieving information on a smart card, and the other is for accessing security services on the card. The former is defined in the form of a collection of functions for selecting, reading, writing, and erasing files, while the latter is defined in the form of a series of security functions. To support these two protocols, the ISO/IEC 7816-4 standard defines data units in the application layer, called application protocol data units (APDUs), which are used for data exchange between the card and the reader.

Fig. 5.4 is a high-level summary of our discussion about the communication model between a smart card and a smart card reader.

Application Layer	ISO/IEC 7816-4 ISO/IEC 7816-7
Data Link Layer	ISO/IEC 7816-3 (T=0) ISO/IEC 7816-3 Amd. 1(T=1)
Physical Layer	ISO/IEC 7816-3 (Contact cards) ISO/IEC 10536-3 (Contactless cards)

Fig. 5.4 Communication model between a smart card and a reader

Before discussing the communication protocols in further detail, let us examine the TPDU and APDU data structures. Fig. 5.5 shows the TPDU data structure for a command with the transmission protocol T=0, which consists of a header and optionally a data section. The header has five fields: a class byte (CLA), an instruction byte (INS), and three parameter bytes (P1-P3), where parameter P3 is a length datum to indicate the length of the data byte transferred to or from the card. The data structure for a response with T=0 consists of an acknowledge byte (ACK), a flow control byte (NULL) to let the reader know that the card is still processing the command and is not yet ready to receive another command, a status return code (SW1), and optionally a return code (SW2) to indicate the amount of data (if the response contains data).

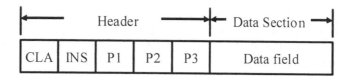

Fig. 5.5 TPDU command data structure with T=0

The transmission protocol T=1 is block-oriented. There are three types of blocks in the T=1 protocol: information block (I-block), receive ready block (R-block), and supervisory block (S-block). Each block contains two mandatory fields (prolog and epilog), and one optional field (information), as shown in Fig. 5.6. The prolog field consists of three bytes: node address byte (NAD), protocol control byte (PCB), and length byte (LEN). The information field contains the application layer's data (APDU) and it may be up to 254 bytes in length. The epilog field contains an error detection code with a length of either 1 or 2 bytes.

	Prolog field		Information field	Epilog field
Node address (NAD)	Protocol control byte (PCB)	Length (LEN)	APDU	EDC
1 byte	1 byte	1 byte	0 to 254 bytes	1 to 2 bytes

Fig. 5.6 T=1 transmission block structure

There are two APDU data structures: the command APDU structure and the response APDU structure. The command APDU structure consists of a header and a body, as shown in Fig. 5.7. The header includes CLA, INS, P1, and P2 fields. The body may be of variable length or it may be absent (when the data field is empty). The Lc field specifies the length of data sent to the card. The Le field indicates the length of data to be sent back from the card. There are four cases for the command APDU structure:

Case 1: No data is to be exchanged, and the command APDU structure only contains the header.

Case 2: No data is transferred *to* the card, but data is transferred *from* the card. The command APDU structure contains the header and the length (Le) of data returned from the card.

Case 3: Data is transferred *to* the card, but not *from* the card. The command APDU structure contains the header, the length (Lc) of data transferred to the card, and the data field.

Case 4: Data is transferred both to and from the card. The command APDU structure contains the header, the length (Lc) of data transferred to the card, the data field, and the length (Le) of data returned from the card.

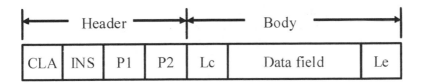

Fig. 5.7 Data structure of an APDU command

The response APDU structure consists of an optional body and a mandatory trailer, shown as in Fig. 5.8. The body contains the data field. The data length is determined in the Le field of the previous command APDU structure. The trailer contains two bytes, SW1 and SW2, which are the designated return codes for the response to the command.

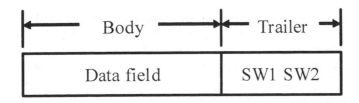

Fig. 5.8 Data structure of an APDU response

5.3 Java Card

A Java Card implementation of a smart card application runs programs written in a subset of the Java programming language, in byte-code form. (Java Card technology can also be applied to other resource-constrained devices.) Java Card defines a runtime environment supporting the smart card's memory, communication protocols, security, and application execution. It changes the landscape of the smart card world for the following reasons:

- **Platform independence**
  Applications written for one smart card platform can run on other platforms (from different vendors), provided that those platforms support Java Card technology.

- **Ability to run multiple applications**
  Downloadable Java byte-code enables multiple applications from multiple vendors to be run securely on a single smart card. For example, a single Java Card can be used as an electronic purse, an employee badge (for accessing buildings), a healthcare card, and a telephone card.

- **Ease of upgrades**
  Java Card technology allows the card issuer to: (a) upgrade existing applications on a card, and (b) download new, additional applications to a card.

- **Compatibility with existing standards**
  Java Card technology is compatible with existing smart card standards, such as ISO 7816 and EMV (Europay, MasterCard, Visa).

- **Security**
  The Java virtual machine implements Java-language security policies even though the Java Security Manager class is not supported by Java Card. This means that the level of access to all methods and instances of variables is strictly controlled. Java's "no pointers" feature prevents malicious programs from accessing data in memory.

- **Availability of sophisticated Java application development tools**
  There are a number of integrated Java development tools from leading software vendors such as Borland, IBM, Microsoft, Sun, and Symantec. Java Card developers can choose a tool to create and debug Java Card applications. This is in contrast to traditional smart card application development where a smart card application is coded in assembly language, compiled into machine code, and then burned into ROM. The traditional development method needs a relatively long time to develop and deploy a smart card application, and once the application is deployed it is hard to

make changes. With Java development tools, a Java Card application can be developed and deployed easily and quickly. Furthermore, the deployed Java Card applications can be easily upgraded.

- **Large and growing pool of experienced Java programmers**
  Due to Java's popularity, there is a large and growing pool of experienced Java programmers. Java programmers can easily become Java Card programmers; consequently, the cost of acquiring and training Java Card programmers is minimized.

Due to the resource constraints of smart cards, Java Card only supports some of the features of the Java language (e.g., small primitive data types, 1-D arrays, Java object-oriented features, Java packages, classes, interfaces, and exceptions), but preserves many benefits of the Java language, including productivity, security, robustness, tools, and portability. The Java Card virtual machine is split into two parts: one part running off-card, and the other part running on-card. The assumption is that many processing tasks that require significant resources or that do not have to be executed at runtime can be run on the off-card part of the Java Card virtual machine.

Java Card separates the smart card system and its applications, and uses a well-defined high-level API for application requests for system services and resources. Java Card technology defines a platform consisting of three parts:

- **Java Card virtual machine (JCVM)**
  The JCVM consists of two separate pieces: the Java Card interpreter and the Java Card converter.

  o **Interpreter**
    This is the on-card part of the Java Card virtual machine, providing runtime support for the Java language model. The interpreter executes Java byte-code instructions and Java applets, controls memory allocation and object creation, and enforces runtime security.

  o **Converter**
    This is the off-card part of the Java Card virtual machine. The converter loads and preprocesses all the Java class files that make up a Java package and converts the package to a converted applet (CAP) file. It also verifies the Java-class load images, checks for violations, initializes static variables, optimizes the byte-code, and allocates storage.

- **Java Card runtime environment (JCRE)**
  The JCRE consists of the Java Card system components that run inside a smart card, and serves as the operating system of the smart card. It manages card resources, executes Java applets, and ensures on-card system

and applet security. It is also responsible for network communication.
JCRE has three layers, as shown in Fig. 5.9. The bottom layer contains
the JCVM and the native methods that support the low-level communication protocols, memory management, and implementation of cryptographic functions. The middle layer contains system classes that manage
transactions and communication, and control applet creation, selection,
and deselection. The upper layer contains framework classes, industry-
specific extensions, and the installer. The framework classes define the
APIs that make the creation of an applet relatively easy. The industry-
specific extensions are the add-on libraries supplied by specific industries
or businesses to provide additional services. The installer is used for easily upgrading existing applications and for downloading new applications
after the smart card has been issued.

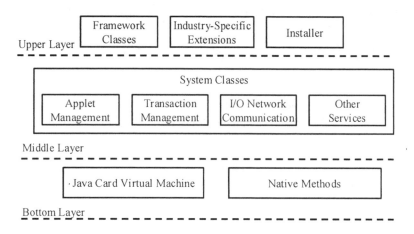

Fig. 5.9 Three-layered Java Card runtime environment

- **Java Card API**
  The Java Card API defines the calling conventions for programming
  smart card applications, by which the applications can access the JCRE
  and native methods. It specifies a subset of Java that is tailored for use in
  smart cards and other devices with limited memory. The Java Card API
  consists of four packages: three are core packages, and one is an extension package. They are java.lang, java.framework, javacard.security, and
  javacardx.crypto. These packages contain a set of customized compact
  classes supporting smart card standards, such as ISO 7816, and providing
  cryptographic services. The significance of the Java Card API is that it
  frees smart card developers from the development limitations (e.g., a
  proprietary assembly language) imposed by specific smart card manufacturers.

5.4 Smart Card Standards

In order for smart cards to be used en masse in the marketplace, interoperability between smart card systems from different vendors must be supported. Thus, there must be a standard upon which every vendor agrees. A standard is an open specification that lays down the rules, guidelines, or requirements that (a) have been proposed and agreed to, with the consensus of many interested parties, and (b) have been adopted by a recognized standards organization, such as the international organization for standardization (ISO) or the international electrotechnical commission (IEC).

Many standards organizations, such as ISO, IEC, European Telecommunications Standards Institute (ETSI), and American National Standards Institute (ANSI), have been actively involved in smart card standardization efforts. As a result, a set of standards on smart cards has been produced. Some of these standards are listed in Table 5.2. These standards play a key role in promoting the interoperability of smart card systems from different manufacturers and vendors.

Table 5.2 Selected smart card standards

Standard	Subject
ISO/IEC 7810	Physical characteristics
ISO/IEC 7811	Recording techniques: magnetic stripe & embossing
ISO/IEC 7812	Numbering system
ISO/IEC 7813	Financial transaction cards
ISO/IEC 7816	Contact cards
ISO 10373	Test methods
ISO 10536	Contactless cards
ISO 14443	Remote coupling communication cards

ISO/IEC 7810 defines the physical characteristics of smart cards, including visual and physical durability, embossing, and the location of a magnetic stripe. The information that identifies the cardholder and supports the transaction via the card may be conveyed via either a magnetic stripe, or a chip. ISO/IEC 7811 defines how to encode the information. ISO/IEC 7812 specifies how to construct the card identification number, which is up to 19 characters long and has three components: issuer ID number, individual account ID number, and check digit. ISO/IEC 7813 defines the location of embossed characters on the card. ISO/IEC 7816 is for contact smart cards, and specifies the following distinct parts:

- Physical characteristics (Part 1)
- Dimensions and locations of contacts (Part 2)

- Electronic signals and transmission protocols (Part 3)
    - o Protocol type T=1, asynchronous half-duplex block transmission protocol (Part 3, Amendment 1)
    - o Revision of protocol type selection (Part 3, Amendment 2)
- Inter-industry commands (Part 4)
- Numbering system and registration procedure for application identifiers (Part 5)
- Data elements for interchange (Part 6)
- Query language commands (Part 7)
- Security architecture (Part 8)
- Inter-industry enhanced commands (Part 9)
- Synchronous cards (Part 10)

ISO 10373 defines the test methods for smart cards. ISO 10536 covers contactless smart cards and defines a close-coupled card having a range up to 10 cm. It comprises the following parts:

- Physical characteristics (Part 1)
- Dimension and locations of the coupling elements (Part 2)
- Electronic signals and reset procedures (Part 3)
- Answer to reset and transmission protocols (Part 4)

ISO 14443 is a specification for contactless cards that changes the contact description to an antenna, and defines the protocol for communication over the air. It consists of the following four parts:

- Physical characteristics (Part 1)
- Radio frequency interface (Part 2)
- Transmission protocols (Part 3)
- Transmission security features (Part 4)

In addition to these ISO/IEC standards, there are smart card industry de facto standards and other regional standards. For example, the following standards define the operation of a smart card for various applications.

- EMV: This specification for payment systems based on ISO 7816 defines the content, structure, and programming of chip-based payment cards. It defines how smart cards exchange information with a payment terminal (e.g., PIN checking), and how security is enhanced by preventing the reading of certain low-level information.
- PC/SC: The PC/Smart Card architecture is an open architecture defined by various smart card and PC operating-system vendors including CP8 Transac, Schlumberger, Siemens Nixdorf, HP, and Microsoft. It defines a general-purpose architecture for multiple applications to share smart

card devices attached to a system through low-level device interfaces, device-independent APIs, and resource management.

- OpenCard: The Open Card Framework (OCF) specifications are open specifications allowing applications to be independent of the specific design of smart cards from different manufacturers. The difference between Open Card and Java Card is that Open Card runs Java on the host or terminal side, whereas Java Card runs (a subset of) Java on the smart card itself.
- ETS 300 608: This is a specification from the European Telecommunications Standards Institute defining a smaller-sized smart card (SIM card) to fit into GSM phones (GSM 11.11).

5.5 Smart Cards and Security

Smart cards are excellent vehicles for implementing security. They are a crucial part of security infrastructures. In the following sections, we examine the role of smart cards in key management, digital signatures, identification, authentication, and authorization.

5.5.1 Smart Cards in Key Management

Key management is essential for security, and is the hardest part of security. Secure electronic commerce applications rely on secure algorithms or protocols involving keys, and the key information must be kept secret. It is not easy to invent a new security algorithm/protocol that will be adopted widely for electronic commerce applications; it is even harder to keep key information secret.

There are millions of users of electronic commerce applications. It can be quite challenging to create, distribute, store, retrieve, and destroy keys for millions of users. Although an asymmetric cryptographic system, as discussed in previous chapters, can be used to solve the key management problem, a problem remains about how to keep one's private key confidential. Smart cards offer a solution to this problem. An individual's private key can be stored on a smart card with the aid of a PIN. The PIN can be used to generate a key to encrypt the private key. Then, if the smart card is lost or stolen, no one will be able to access the private key without knowing the PIN.

5.5.2 Smart Cards in Digital Signatures

A digital signature is a piece of data that is created with a signer's private signature key and is a function of the message being digitally signed. To generate a digital signature, a private signature key is required. As we discussed in the last section, smart card can be used for storing this private key.

A digital certificate is an electronic set of credentials for a signer, issued by a trusted authority called a certificate authority (CA). This confirms both the signer's identity and their public key. In some digital-signature implementations, a digital certificate of the signer is required as an appendix to the signed message. This makes the verification process simpler, since the certificate accompanies the message. In this case, it is no longer necessary to obtain the signer's digital certificate from an X.500 directory in a public key infrastructure. Smart cards can be used to store one's digital certificate in addition to one's private signature key.

5.5.3 Smart Cards in Identification

Identification is essential to secure electronic commerce. Smart cards can be used as a means of identification, in place of other forms of ID, such as passports. Various governments have expressed interest in national ID cards, including Malaysia, Hong Kong, and Singapore. Such cards can be used to securely store personal ID, healthcare information, and other data (including financial data), on a single smart card. For example, the Hong Kong Special Administration Region government plans to issue citizen identification cards, that is, smart cards containing personal identification information.

As mentioned in Section 5.5.1, if an individual's smart card containing encrypted or protected information is lost or stolen, no one else will be able to use it. In this regard, smart cards can be a better form of identification than passports. The use of a smart card for identification can provide more efficient processing of individuals at international border checkpoints.

The use of smart cards can also reduce fraud in healthcare and welfare systems. These two systems are well known for abuse and high costs (e.g., due to claims by ineligible recipients, or due to multiple claims in one or more jurisdictions). Banks and credit card companies can save millions of dollars in losses due to fraud, again by using smart cards as a form of cardholder identification.

5.5.4 Smart Cards in Authentication

As discussed in Chapters 2-3, authentication is the process by which an entity's identity is verified. Authentication is typically based one of the following three criteria:

- Something a person knows, such as a PIN or password
- Something a person possesses, such as a smart card

- Something a person uniquely has and cannot easily change, such as a fingerprint, iris image, facial image/structure, voice pattern, etc.

Smart cards can utilize all three of these criteria for authentication. First, a smart card can have a PIN that is only known to the owner of the card. Second, like a bank (ATM) card, each smart card has a unique serial number. Third, unlike a typical bank card, a smart card can store much more information, including information about fingerprints, iris images, etc., that serve to uniquely identify the cardholder (see Chapter 4). Such biometric information can be used to achieve a very high level of security.

Besides authentication via a PIN and the presence of the card, third-party authentication can be performed (either locally or remotely) using a private signature key stored on a smart card. To authenticate the cardholder, the cardholder's digital signature may be verified using a signature-verification process via a third party (i.e., a certificate authority). This third-party authentication is extremely useful for electronic commerce conducted over the Internet.

5.5.5 Smart Cards in Authorization

In electronic commerce, the authorization of a purchase or of a payment for the purchase is required, which can be carried out using smart cards. In the business-to-consumer (B2C) e-commerce applications, the *secure electronic transaction* (SET) protocol (see Chapter 10 for the detailed information about SET) can be used for authorization. In the business-to-business (B2B) e-commerce applications, if the dollar amount of the order is high, multiple levels of authorization may be required. For example, the order may have to be accompanied by the digital signature of the chief financial officer (CFO). To enable secure authorization, a smart card is an ideal tool because a given smart card is unique to the CFO, and no other individual will be able to create the CFO's digital signature. Hence, the likelihood of someone creating a bogus purchase order is minimized.

Smart cards can also be used to implement a hierarchical security scheme for access control, whereby certain individuals within a company are permitted to modify (i.e., add, update, or delete items from) a purchase requisition before it is sent for authorization. This gives authorized individuals the ability to override details on a purchase requisition. Digital certificates can be used to authenticate these individuals.

5.5.6 Summary of Smart Cards and Security

A smart card can be issued to an authorized person and be carried around by that person. The significance of smart cards is that they can be used to securely store the private keys, the digital certificates containing the public keys, and the cryptographic algorithms. Given that a private key never leaves the smart card, and the cryptographic algorithms on the card are used for security purposes, no third party can intercept the private key by listening to the communication between the card and the reader. In addition, the private key on the card can be protected using a PIN. This enables only the authorized person to make use of the private key for security purposes. The smart card system can even prevent further use of the card by locking out the card after a few unsuccessful PIN attempts.

5.6 Smart Card Applications

Smart cards have been widely adopted for many applications throughout the world, but especially in Europe and Asia Pacific. Typical smart card applications include:

- Electronic payment
- Access control
- Telecommunications
- Healthcare
- Transportation
- Identification

5.6.1 Electronic Payment

Smart cards play an important role in payment processing in electronic commerce. They can be used to store and process "value" or digital money, and they can be used to add an additional level of security to a credit card or debit card.

A *stored value* smart card cannot be reloaded, and is issued with some fixed amount of value or money (e.g., $20). As a user purchases goods or services with the card, the monetary value on the card is gradually decremented. Stored value cards have limited hardware functionality and do not contain a microprocessor. The card is decremented by a host application that interfaces with the smart card through a card reader.

An *electronic purse*, on the other hand, is a reloadable smart card. It contains a microprocessor, not only to perform monetary calculations but also to securely store the digital money, to authenticate the host application, and to perform secure communication with the host. A PIN can be used to "lock" the funds on a card to prevent other people from using the card. A Mondex card is an example of an electronic purse. Mondex digital money can even be exchanged between two smart cards belonging to family or friends, using a device called an electronic wallet.

To prevent a hacker from counterfeiting digital money, it is essential that the smart card guard against unauthorized access. Increases and decreases in monetary value must only take place with accepted host applications, using accepted protocols. Digital certificates are required used to authenticate the host and the smart card.

Not only can smart cards be used in credit card or debit card payment processing, they can be used to write digital signatures for electronic cheques. Electronic cheques are based upon a bank account debit system, and are paperless cheques that can be sent electronically from one entity to another. The receiving entity can endorse the cheque via another digital signature, and e-mail it to a bank.

Finally, we note that privacy is an integral part of payment processing. Smart cards can facilitate privacy through digital signatures or the use of anonymous digital money.

5.6.2 Access Control

Smart cards can be used to facilitate authorization to physical or logical sites and resources. For example, smart cards can be used in corporate, government, and military environments for physical access control to buildings, rooms, and parking lots. In addition, smart cards can be used for controlling access to, and operation of, designated physical assets, such as:

- Machines
- Vehicles
- Computer equipment
- Telecommunication equipment
- Laboratory research equipment
- Dangerous arms
- Other equipment

There is great potential in employing biometrics in ID cards for strict physical access control of military, government, and financial facilities and assets. Such applications became even more important following the September 11, 2001 terrorist attacks against the United States.

With respect to logical access, smart cards can serve as a form of identification for remote, online access to workstations, files, databases, and networks. Smart cards can be used to implement security using biometrics, without the need for a central, online database. In particular, they can replace many USERID/password scenarios with automated equivalents, and can provide a very high level of security. For situations where individuals are often working from different terminals, smart card solutions for network access are particularly attractive. Network security will become increasingly important for the Internet.

5.6.3 Telecommunications

Smart cards have been used in telecommunications for years. Typical applications include payment cards for public telephony, and subscriber identity modules (SIM) cards for GSM mobile communications.

Advantages of using smart cards for public telephony include reduced costs of operation since there is no need to collect cash, and theft deterrence (i.e., there is no money available to be stolen).

The use of SIM cards in mobile telephony has enhanced security of GSM because with SIM cards, user authentication, integrity, and confidentiality of voice and data can be provided.

5.6.4 Healthcare

Smart cards are used in healthcare in various ways, including facilitating registration/information in emergency-care situations. For example, in an emergency, a doctor other than the patient's regular physician can access the patient's health information (e.g., blood type, allergies, medicines, special needs, contact information).

Medical insurance companies like smart cards because smart cards can provide information about a patient's insurance eligibility and coverage. They can also be used in an electronic claim submission procedure since both insurance data and patient information can be read and verified from the smart card.

Smart cards are good vehicles for controlling healthcare costs by preventing fraud, especially in public healthcare systems where there may be no good way of verifying eligibility for medical services. Some states or provinces (e.g., British Columbia, Canada) have far more healthcare-benefit cards (not smart cards) in circulation than there are people in the population.

Electronic prescriptions with the physician's digital signature can be stored on smart cards, thereby reducing errors or misunderstandings, minimizing potential drug interactions, and reducing fraud (e.g., some patients visit many physicians, or forge prescriptions, in order to obtain drugs for resale). Healthcare professionals can also use smart cards to control access to unattended workstations in hospital wards.

5.6.5 Transportation

Smart cards have been successfully deployed in transportation applications in many cities, including Hong Kong and Shanghai in China. These applications include:

- Drivers' licenses
- Parking permits
- Taxi payments
- Local public transportation
- Train and air travel
- Electronic toll collection

Transportation is a smart card application that can reach a critical mass of people. In Section 5.7, we will take a close look at Octopus cards in the Hong Kong local transportation fare-collection system.

5.6.6 Identification

Smart cards are emerging as an excellent tool for personal identification in corporate, government, and university applications. Many organizations are using, or plan to use, smart cards as employee badges for multiple purposes. As mentioned previously, some nations are in the process of deploying smart cards as national identification cards.

In many university campuses, all-purpose student ID cards have been used for various purposes, including electronic payments for applications such as:

- Vending machines
- Laundry machines
- Photocopiers
- Meal payments in cafeterias

These student cards can also be used for identification or access in the following applications:

- Course registration
- Student union or club activities
- Libraries
- Athletic facilities
- Medical care

5.7 A Case Study in Smart Cards: Hong Kong's Octopus Card

5.7.1 The Rise of the Octopus Card

The history of the Octopus card started in June 1994 when Hong Kong's five major public transportation operators, namely, Mass Transit Railway Corp. (MTRC)[2], Kowloon-Canton Railway Corp. (KCRC)[3], Kowloon Motor Bus Company (KMB), Citybus Ltd., and the Hong Kong and Yaumatei Ferry systems (HKF), formed a joint venture company, Creative Star Limited (CSL), to develop an automated fare collection system based on contactless smart cards. The fare collection contract, valued at US$55 million, was awarded to ERG Australia Limited and its subsidiary AES Prodata, which subsequently awarded the contactless card portion of the contract to Sony and Mitsubishi Corporation. These contactless, reloadable smart cards, known as Octopus cards, were introduced to the general public in September 1997.

An estimated 10 million passenger journeys are made each day on Hong Kong's wide variety of public transportation services. According to a 1998 report by Industry Canada, the Creative Star Octopus System, when launched, was the largest, integrated, contactless, smart card, fare collection system in the world, and accounted for approximately US$13 million[4] in daily transactions.

Here is how the system works. Each of the operators' computer networks is linked to the Creative Star Clearing House system, which in turn apportions revenue to the operators and deposits funds into the appropriate bank accounts. In mid-2000, there were 6.5 million cards in use, with millions more to follow. Users have the ability to reload their cards with cash (HK$100 is a typical amount). Cardholders can reload their cards in any MTRC and KCRC station, as well as in any of the 368 7-Eleven convenience stores within Hong Kong. Octopus cards can also be used for other kinds of applications, such as purchasing food or merchandise, and even serving as an employee badge (Leong, 2000).

In 1998, Creative Star negotiated with Mondex and VisaCash to incorporate an electronic-purse function into its originally closed system, with the MTRC still owning a 67.8% stake in Creative Star.

---

[2] MTRC is the metropolitan underground railway system in Hong Kong.

[3] KCRC is an electric railway system that connects the Kowloon peninsula to the New Territories.

[4] At the time of writing, US$1 equals approximately HK$7.8.

5.7.2 Debit Cards in the Passenger Transportation Industry

Although various payment-processing applications already exist for smart cards, transit fare collection requires special considerations to ensure its success (Goldfinger, 1988). We itemize these criteria, modeling them as network goods, as follows.

Deployment and Apprehension

When smart cards were initially introduced for fare collection, there was some apprehension due to technology "hiccups", and the fact that passengers had to adjust to a new system. In those cases where an existing system was already in place (e.g., magnetic stripe cards), a smooth and short cutover was required to ensure the success of the smart card deployment. Some technical hiccups and customer apprehension had been experienced in previous smart card pilot studies (e.g., Mondex in Manhattan, New York City, in 1998, although that pilot did not involve the transportation sector). The bottom-line is that customers and vendors demand smooth rollouts; otherwise, they will lose confidence in the new technology and be more resistant to embracing it.

Co-operation Among Linked Fare Systems

In the case of passenger transportation applications, smart card systems often suffer from incompatibility with other fare systems at either the technology or the business level. At the technology level, vendors using incompatible technologies may develop different kinds of smart card systems that are adopted by different transportation providers. Sometimes, many smart card fare systems are used in one mode of transportation (e.g., buses), but not in another. Sometimes, due to different governing and policy-making bodies, the smart card systems are not integrated, even though there is a logical flow of passengers between two transportation systems (e.g., from trains to buses). And of course, customers are inconvenienced if they need to deal with multiple cards for similar applications.

Contactless Requirements

As mentioned earlier, the term "contactless" means that a transaction performed using a smart card does not require physical contact between the card and the card reader. In fact, many successful transportation-ticketing systems are contactless, and this is important for a number of reasons (Goldfinger, 1998). The user flow rate in some of these systems can be as high as one million or more per day (averaging 19 users per second). During peak hours, the flow rate can be two to three times the average hourly flow rate for the day. In order to handle such a volume, it is important to make sure that the processing time per user is as short as possible.

The critical delay for processing is often not due to transaction processing time, but due to human activity (i.e., locating or fetching the card, and then placing it into the reader). Slot-based cards require the user to physically place the card into a slot and this is the major source of delay for such systems, especially when customers are carrying bags or packages, and there is a queue of passengers boarding.

5.7.3 Analyzing the Success of the Octopus Card

When the Octopus card was introduced in 1997, there were already smart card systems in use, mainly in the form of debit systems introduced by major credit card companies, namely, VisaCash by Visa International, and Mondex by MasterCard. Both VisaCash and Mondex had two key competitive advantages: a large international customer base, and backing by two of the world's largest credit card companies. Both VisaCash and Mondex were in trials around the world. In Hong Kong, Mondex had just launched a trial of its smart card technology, and the results were positive. Given that the Octopus system was still in its infancy, traditional wisdom would have pointed to the demise of an unproven smart card system targeting a local application (i.e., passenger transportation), especially since a magnetic, debit card system was already in place. However, there were a number of factors that made the Octopus card a success, which we outline as follows.

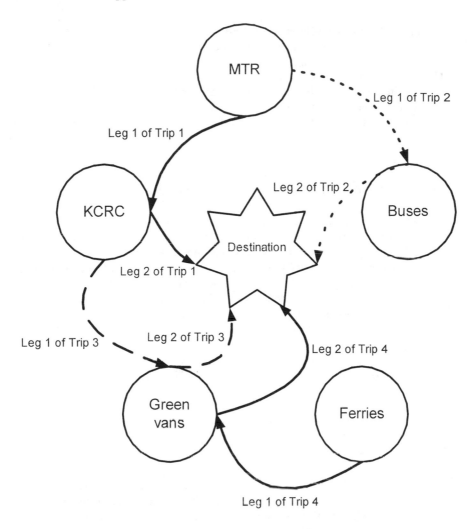

Fig. 5.10 Examples of types of multi-leg trips made in Hong Kong
(Source: Poon & Chau, 2001)

A High-Density City with a Heavy Reliance on Public Transportation

Hong Kong is special in the sense that it has one of the highest population densities in the world, combined with a relatively low rate of private vehicle ownership. The highly congested road system and the high cost of car ownership mean that many Hong Kong people use public transportation for their day-to-day activities. The passenger-transportation sector in Hong Kong includes the MTRC, KCRC, bus companies, ferries, and other auxiliary transit systems, such as the "green vans" (a public, light bus system having designated routes). On average, an individual needs to make at least one return trip using the public transport system to go to work, attend school, etc. Given a population of 7.5 million people, if 70% of the population were doing one such trip per day, and spending on average HK$16.00 (approx. US$2.00) per return trip, then the daily transactions of the Octopus system would total approximately US$11 million. Due to the way the Hong Kong passenger transportation system is set up, passengers often need more than one mode of transportation; consequently, the daily transaction volume can be even higher.

Sector Wide Adoption with a Common Technological Standard

Although the use of a stored-value card for local transportation payments has been in place for over two decades in Hong Kong, the diffusion of such an application beyond the Mass Transit Railway Corporation (MTRC) and the Kowloon-Canton Railway Corporation (KCRC) was a recent development. The early stored-value card system used by the railway systems was based on magnetic stripes, and required insertion of the card into 'a reader slot at a turnstile. For all other modes of public transportation in Hong Kong (e.g., ferries, buses and mini-buses), payments were made by tendering the exact fare using coins into an on-board coin box.

Creative Star Limited was created and backed by the biggest passenger transportation companies in Hong Kong. These companies together operated more than 70% of the passenger transportation business in Hong Kong. Their unanimous adoption of the Octopus card generated an instant critical mass. A critical mass is an essential property for the flow of network goods. This also reflects a spirit of cooperation because the member companies jointly owning Creative Star were direct competitors in some cases.

It has been pointed out that if both the current and new systems coexisted, chances are that the old system would jeopardize the adoption of the new one because of the existing infrastructure and habitual usage (Goldfinger, 1998). In the case of the Octopus card system, the deployment was a quick conversion over a period of a few months, and users had no choice but to use the new system.

As this chapter was written, a sector-wide adoption situation had been achieved with about 40 passenger transportation companies accepting the Octopus card. Almost 7 million cards had been issued by early 2001, of which 1.4 million were sold to children under 18 years of age (Rader and Maghiros, 2001).

Captured Market with Reasons for Adoption

Although coin payment has been well accepted in Hong Kong's passenger transportation system, it has nevertheless been a hassle because of the "exact fare" rule that requires passengers to have the exact amount ready, usually in the form of coins. Getting change is difficult because there is often no money-change facility near the terminals or bus stops. Sometimes, the only way to get change is from nearby shops or other passengers, neither of which is a welcoming move.

The Octopus card, on the other hand, offers a number of conveniences, especially when considering the contactless property. For those people who have their Octopus cards buried under their belongings in a handbag, for example, there is no need to physically place the card into a reader because the card can be read where it is, providing the card is sufficiently close to the reader. The contactless nature of the card allows for fast scanning. In fact, transaction processing takes less than 300 milliseconds. The fact that there is a captured market of about 7 million cards, with constant use, means that there is a critical mass for this payment infrastructure. More importantly, the clearing and settlement of payments (via HSBC bank, at the time of writing) taking place between Creative Star and the transportation operators, take less time (i.e., less than 24 hours), compared to the considerably longer process involving coin boxes (Leong, 2000).

Fending Off Competition from VisaCash and MasterCard

When the Octopus card was launched, Visa International and MasterCard were both involved in debit-card trials in Hong Kong. Although both Visa and Master-Card had a much larger customer base and a long track record in the credit card industry, the captured market, contactless nature, and focused application have proven to be important criteria for success. Both VisaCash and Mondex were using contact-based cards, whose transaction times would have been at least as long as it takes for the card holder to place the card into the reader. In the Hong Kong passenger transportation industry, this process was too time-consuming, especially during rush hour. More than 3 million transactions take place per day, during an 18-hour period of operation. During rush hour, however, there might be up to 1.8 million transactions occurring, averaging about 600,000 per hour. Clearly, the contactless nature of the Octopus card and its short transaction time are key reasons for its success.

Expanding to be a Micro-Payment Provider

The original intent of the Octopus card was to provide a means of payment within the passenger transportation industry. In fact, under the original governance of the Hong Kong Monetary Authority (HKMA) Banking Ordinance, Octopus transactions were to be confined to the transportation and related sectors. However, Octopus can derive up to 15% of the equivalent core transactions from non-transportation sectors. In April 2000, Creative Star Limited was granted a deposit-taking licence by the HKMA, which broadened the card's scope of use (Leong,

2000). Octopus cards can be used for payments at shops in the fast-food sector, kiosks, phone booths, and soft-drink vending machines (Rader and Maghiros, 2001). They can be reloaded not just at MTRC and KCRC train stations, but also at 7-Eleven convenience stores using dedicated devices, and even at the point of transaction if one has an account with the Dah Sing Bank or Standard Chartered Bank. For example, if there are insufficient funds on the card at the time of usage, and the holder has an appropriate credit card from the bank, then the bank will automatically transfer/upload HK$250 to the Octopus card, without any special handling charge (Dah Sing Bank, 2002). This means that passengers can bypass sales counters and add-value machines. The above reasons make the Octopus card the most mobile-friendly micropayment system in Hong Kong.

5.7.4 Future Developments in the Octopus System

The Octopus card is in a strategic position to expand its market share, including non-transportation applications. Fig. 5.11 illustrates some of the potential paths for expansion.

All-Purpose Micropayment System

One potential development path is to have the Octopus card be an organizational charge card. In some organizations, there is a need to have an internal charge card to allow employees to use company resources on a pay-per-use basis. For example, in a university, students have to pay for different services such as photocopying and recreational facilities. The Octopus card is well positioned to take on the role of a university-wide charge card, thereby enabling students to use various resources and pay via an internal Octopus system.

Transaction Services Outsourcing

The strength of the Octopus system, besides its application in the passenger-transportation industry, is its transaction-clearing system. The high daily transaction volume means Octopus's clearing system rivals that of mid-size banks in Hong Kong (Rader and Maghiros, 2001). The Octopus system, in conjunction with HSBC's Hexagon system, can settle this volume of payments within 24 hours. This very efficient clearing system can be positioned as an outsourcer for other high-volume transaction environments, enabling the Octopus clearing system to become the universal backend for major transaction establishments.

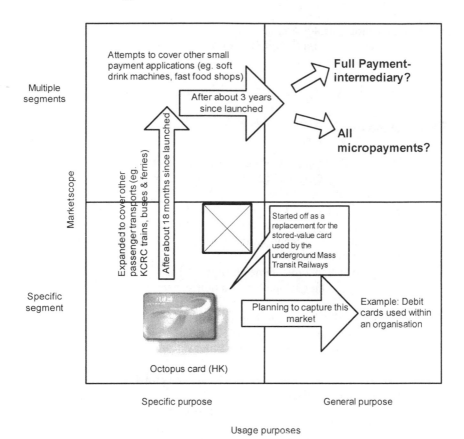

Fig. 5.11 Strategic orientation of the Octopus card and its future
(Source: Poon & Chau, 2001)

5.8 Summary

In this chapter, fundamentals of smart cards have been introduced, including smart card chips, readers, operating systems, and communication interface. Then, the information of Java Card has been provided. In addition, a set of smart card standards have been presented. The utilization of smart cards in implementing security and possible smart card applications have been discussed. Finally, a case study of Hong Kong's Octopus cards has been presented.

Smart cards, plastic cards with an embedded IC chip, are excellent vehicles for electronic payment and other applications, such as identification, access control, telecommunications, healthcare, and transportation. They are also crucial for implementing security. Currently, billions of smart cards are in use, and the market potential of smart cards is huge.

5.9 References

[5.1]   Dah Sing Bank: http://www.dahsing.com.hk/etopup.htm
[5.2]   W. Ford, M. S. Baum (2001) Secure electronic commerce (2nd ed.). Prentice-Hall, New York.
[5.3]   C. Goldfinger (1998) Economics of financial applications of the smart card: a summary overview. http://www.fininter.net/Archives/fasc.htm
[5.4]   M. Hendry (2001) Smart card security and applications (2nd ed.). Artech House, Boston London.
[5.5]   Hong Kong Economic Times (2000) The largest eCommerce network in Hong Kong – the Octopus transaction system. September 27, 2000, IT2–IT3.
[5.6]   W. Kou (1997) Networking security and standards. Kluwer, Boston Dordrecht London.
[5.7]   E. Leong (2000) Octopus extends its reach. FinanceAsia.com, July 19, 2000.
[5.8]   S. Poon, P. Y. K. Chau (2001) Octopus: the growing e-payment system in Hong Kong. Electronic Markets 11(2): 1–10.
[5.9]   M. Rader, I. Maghiros (2001) Electronic Payment Systems Observatory Newsletter, No. 5. http://epso.jrc.es/newsletter.
[5.10]   B. Schneier (2000) Secrets and lies: digital security in a networked world. Wiley, New York.
[5.11]   Sun Microsystems (2002) Java Card platform security: technical white paper. http://java.sun.com/products/javacard
[5.12]   The World Bank Group (2002) The Octopus system (presentation by the Hong Kong MTR Corporation). http://lnweb18.worldbank.org/External/lac.nsf/Sectors/Transport/0D8952
[5.13]   U. Hansmann, M. S. Nicklous, et al. (2002) Smart card programming. Springer, Berlin Heidelberg New York.

6 Wireless Infrastructure

Weidong Kou

University of Hong Kong
Pokfulam Road, Hong Kong

6.1 Introduction

Wireless e-commerce (or mobile commerce) is projected to become a US$12.4 billion market by 2005 in Asia-Pacific, excluding Japan, according to International Data Corp (IDC). Mobile commerce applications such as mobile banking, email, wireless gaming, and stock trading already are available in the marketplace. For example, NTT DoCoMo's i-mode service in Japan, which provides email, web access, wireless banking, stock information service, flight information, online reservations, news and weather, yellow page service, fortune telling, online games, and digital content retrieval from its partners, in addition to regular cellular-phone functions. DoCoMo was formed in July 1992. It had sales of 4.6 trillion yens in fiscal 2000 year ended by March 31, 2001. It was reported that the subscriber number of the i-mode service exceeded 28 million as of October 2001. We see some countries, for example, Korea, where wireless subscription numbers exceed wired customers. A recent statistical report (October 2001) shows that China now has the largest hand-phone user base in the world, with a total of over 120 million users, or 10% penetration rate. In Hong Kong, over 5 million people out of a total of 7 million have a cellular phone. The penetration rates in European countries are also high. All this evidence shows that the growth of mobile commerce is phenomenal and its potential is huge.

Payment is essential for commerce transactions. Mobile commerce transactions also need to have payment in place. To enable the payment process in mobile commerce, we need to have a wireless infrastructure. In this chapter, we will examine various components of such a wireless infrastructure for e-payment and for mobile commerce in general, including wireless communication infrastructure, wireless and pervasive computing infrastructure including wireless and pervasive devices, wireless application protocol (WAP), and wireless security.

6.2 Wireless Communications Infrastructure

The Internet is the basis of the World Wide Web, and is the infrastructure that has taken the current form of e-commerce to center stage in the past few years. The Internet has been an interconnected computer network through cables since it was born more than thirty years ago. The rapid development of wireless technologies means the Internet going through a revolution. The Wireless Internet is emerging. Accessing information anytime and anywhere is becoming a reality. This change sets mobile commerce rolling. The essential part of the advances in wireless technologies is wireless communication infrastructure.

There are three main areas of the wireless communication infrastructure: the transmission and media access, the mobile network, and the mobile services. The transmission and medium access area covers wireless transmission technologies (such as multiplexing and modulation) and medium access technologies (such as TDMA and CDMA). The mobile network area addresses the network system architecture and protocols. The mobile services deal with voice and data services such as mobile-prepared services, mobile voice IP, and international roaming.

In wireless communication, radio transmission takes place via different frequency bands. It starts at several kilo-Hz. It can go as high as over one hundred mega Hz. As there exists interference in the radio transmission, and as radio frequencies are scare resources, the frequencies used for transmission are all regulated.

In order to ensure low interference between different senders, multiplexing schemes have been introduced in four dimensions: space, time, frequency, and code. The space-division multiplexing is a scheme to ensure that there is wide enough distance between senders to avoid interference due to radio transmissions from the different senders. The time-division multiplexing scheme allows senders to use the same frequency but at different times. The frequency division multiplexing scheme is to subdivide the frequency dimension into several non-overlapping frequency bands. Different senders are assigned to different frequency bands. The code-division multiplexing scheme is relatively new, and it resolves the interference problem by assigning senders to different codes, and the distances between these codes are wide enough to avoid the interference. As the many codes can be designed, the code-division multiplexing scheme offers much more flexibility than the space, time, and frequency division multiplexing schemes do.

In wireless networks there is a need to translate the binary bit stream into an analog signal first. This translation is referred to as digital modulation. There are three basic techniques for digital modulations: amplitude shift keying (ASK), frequency shift keying (FSK), and phase shift keying (PSK). In the ASK technique, the binary values, 1 and 0, are assigned to two different amplitudes. The FSK technique assigns the two binary values, 1 and 0, to two different frequencies. The PSK technique makes use of shifts in the phase of a signal to present the two binary values, 1 and 0, for example, shifting the phase by 180 degrees when the value of data changes. After digital modulation, wireless transmission requires an analog modulation, which is a technique to shift the center frequency of the baseband signal generated by the digital modulation up to the radio carrier frequency. There are three different analog modulation schemes: amplitude modulation (AM), frequency modulation (FM), and phase modulation (PM). These modulation schemes have been widely used, for example, AM and FM radios.

In wireless communication networks, how to allow a mobile-phone user to access the wireless networks is the problem that the medium-access control technology is meant to resolve. The typical algorithms for the medium-access control include space division multiple access (SDMA), frequency division multiple access (FDMA), time division multiple access (TDMA), and code division multiple access (CDMA). SDMA is a technology for allocating a separate space to mobile users in the wireless network. FDMA deals with allocating frequencies to transmission channels according to the frequency division multiplexing scheme. TDMA is to allocate certain time slots for wireless communications. CDMA is to separate different users through the codes used in the code division multiplexing.

The wireless communication systems are cellular, that is, they are designed as a network of cells. In the center of each cell, there is a base transceiver station (or, simply, a base station) that comprises radio equipment for transmitting and receiving radio signals, including antennas, signal processing, and amplifiers. Each cell has a coverage area. A mobile-phone user may move from one cell to another. This movement is called roaming. The process of switching such a user from one cell to another while the user is engaging a call is referred to as a handoff or handover.

The popular wireless communication systems include global system for mobile communications (GSM), general packet radio service (GPRS), and code division multiple access (CDMA) systems. Among them, the most popular one is the GSM system that has been used in more than 130 countries worldwide, including most countries in Europe and Asia, excluding Japan. GSM has initially been developed and deployed in Europe to provide a mobile phone system that offers the roaming service to users throughout Europe. Now, GSM supports the integration of different voice and data services and permits an easy system upgrade to higher data rates. GPRS was designed for data services by providing packet-mode transfer for applications, such as web requests and responses, and it promises to provide users with a high-capacity connection to the Internet. CDMA is a digital spread-spectrum system initially developed by a US-based company called Qualcomm, and it has been standardized by the Telecommunications Industry Association (TIA). The CDMA standard is known as Cellular IS-95.

An example of the wireless communication systems is shown in Fig. 6.1. A mobile station (MS) can be held by either a pedestrian or a motion vehicle. The MS communicates with a base transceiver station (BTS). The BTS is managed by a base station controller (BSC) which is connected to either a mobile service switching center (MSC) or a gateway mobile service switching center (GMSC). The MS information is usually stored in a home location register. The MS information can be static and dynamic. The static information includes the mobile subscriber ISDN number, subscribed services, and the authentication key information. The dynamic information includes the current location area of the MS. When an MS leaves the current location area, to localize a user in the worldwide network, this information needs to be stored and updated in a very dynamic database, which is called visitor location register (VLR). The VLR is associated with a MSC, storing the information of the MS who is currently visiting the location area associated to the MSC. The GMSC connects to the public switched telephone network (PSTN). The operation and maintenance center (OMC) monitors traffic and provides management functions such as subscriber and security management, and accounting and billing. The authentication center (AUC) is to protect mobile user identity and data transmission.

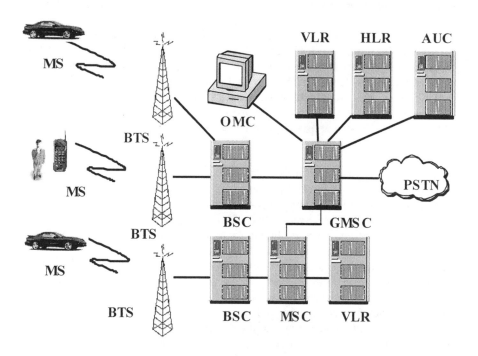

Fig. 6.1 An example of the wireless communication systems

By having the wireless communication systems in place, various mobile services have been provided to the mobile users, such as mobile voice and data services. The mobile data services include messaging services and wireless web services. The examples of the mobile messaging services are messaging through
short message service (SMS), cell broadcast service (CBS), and unstructured sup-
plementary services data (USSD). The examples of wireless web services include
mobile commerce and mobile payment services.

6.3 Wireless Computing Infrastructure

The evolution of computing infrastructure has gone from the client-server infrastructure model, to the network computing infrastructure model. It is now moving
toward the wireless computing infrastructure model. In the client-server computing infrastructure model shown in Fig. 6.2, many clients connect to a server. The
server is a center of computing, to provide a variety of services that clients request. The client machines were equipped with dedicated client software. This
model was very effective before the Internet was adopted.

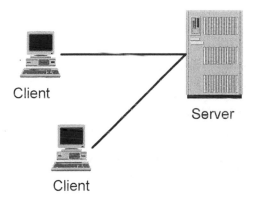

Fig. 6.2 Client-server computing infrastructure model

The Internet has changed the computing infrastructure. In the 1990s, many
leading players in the computing industry looked into network computing. In the
network computing infrastructure model shown in Fig. 6.3, the clients connect to
the Internet, and the Internet connects a variety of servers. The client machines do
not need special client software. Only standard Internet browser such as Netscape
or Microsoft Internet Explorer is needed. This saves a huge effort for companies to

develop different client software. Through the Internet, clients can access much wider applications than they used to. The network computing infrastructure model coupled with the revolutionized Internet, has indeed changed the computing industry, corporate IT infrastructure, and people's daily lives.

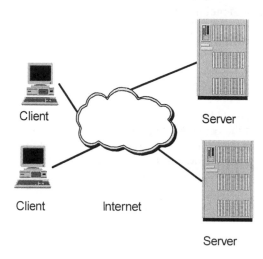

Fig. 6.3 Network computing infrastructure model

In the late 1990s, wireless communication was rapidly developed. Cellular phones and a variety of other wireless devices have become popular. The wireless communication infrastructure together with Internet technology makes another evolution step possible, resulting in the wireless computing infrastructure model shown in Fig. 6.4.

In addition to wireless communication infrastructure, the wireless computing-infrastructure model includes flexible and mobile devices, such as personal digital assistants (PDAs), mobile phones, pagers, hand-held organizers, and home-entertainment systems. These wireless devices connect to the Internet and provide quick access to many wireless applications. With enhanced security, electronic commerce transactions can also be conducted through these wireless devices. The differences between the network computing infrastructure model and the wireless computing infrastructure model are:

- In the wireless-computing-infrastructure model, client machines are no longer only the desktop PCs or laptop computers as those in the network computing infrastructure model. They can be any hand-held device with wireless communication capability.

- In the wireless-computing-infrastructure model, communication between clients and servers are no longer through wired lines as the case of the network computing infrastructure model. The communication is carried out through a wireless network and the Internet.
- In the wireless-computing-infrastructure model, there are two sets of communication protocols, one set is wireless protocols and the other set is the wired Internet protocols. This is different from the network computing infrastructure model in which, there is only wired Internet protocols.

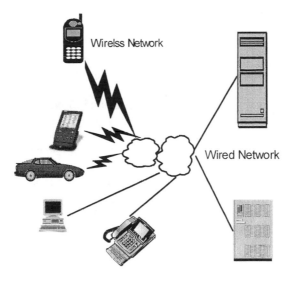

Fig. 6.4 Wireless computing infrastructure model

The challenges for the wireless-computing-infrastructure model include powerful wireless e-commerce applications for massive wireless users that are still to be developed and deployed, wireless-device capability-management systems, and personalization for different users, and the associated user management by the wireless service providers. Given the limitations that wireless devices have, the server software must be highly scalable and flexible. Mobility will also make the wireless applications be more interesting and challenging.

In the wireless-computing-infrastructure model, to make mobile commerce transactions successful, there are three very important principles: security, connectivity, and simplicity. The importance of the security model is obvious, as without the proper security protection of the consumer's financial account information and other private information, mobile commerce is not going to succeed. The connectivity loss during the mobile-commerce transaction will create the trustworthiness problem on mobile commerce for consumers. People will not accept that their mobile-commerce transactions (such as mobile payments) are aborted due to a broken connection. Given a limited capacity of a mobile device and the reliability of the wireless connection compared to that of the wired connection, it is easy to see that simplicity and reliability are important for completing a mobile-commerce transaction instantly.

6.4 Wireless Application Protocol

6.4.1 WAP Overview

The wireless application protocol (WAP) is a suite of emerging standards to enable mobile Internet applications. The WAP standards have been created as a result of the WAP Forum that was formed in June 1997 by Ericsson, Motorola, and Nokia. The WAP Forum is designed to assist the convergence of two fast-growing network technologies, namely, wireless communications and the Internet. The convergence is based on rapidly increasing numbers of mobile-phone users and the dramatic affect of e-business over the Internet. The combination of these two technologies will have a big impact on current e-business practice, and it will create huge market potential.

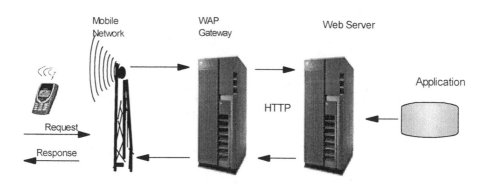

Fig. 6.5 The WAP architecture

The WAP standards consist of a variety of architecture components, including an application environment, scripting and markup languages, network protocols, and security features. These components and features together define how wireless data handsets communicate over the wireless network and how content and services are delivered. With the WAP standards, a wireless data handset can establish a connection to a WAP compliant wireless infrastructure, request and receive the content and services, and present the content and services to the end user. This WAP-compliant wireless infrastructure may include the handset, the server side infrastructure, such as the proxy server (WAP gateway), the web server, the application server, and the network operator (telecommunication company). The WAP architecture is shown in Fig. 6.5.

The WAP architecture can also be presented through the WAP protocol stack shown in Fig. 6.6. The WAP protocol stack covers the complete picture from bearers to applications. The bearers are the various wireless networks that WAP currently supports. The transport layer is an interface common to the underlying wireless network, and it provides a constant service to the upper layers in the WAP stack, such that the bearer services are transparent to the upper layers. In other words, with the transport layer, the specific network characteristics can be masked. The security layer provides security for the transport layer, based on the industry standard protocol, the transport layer security (TLS) protocol. The transaction layer provides a lightweight transaction-oriented protocol for mobile thin clients. The session layer provides the application layer with the capability to select connection-oriented or connectionless services. The application layer deals with a general-purpose environment for applications.

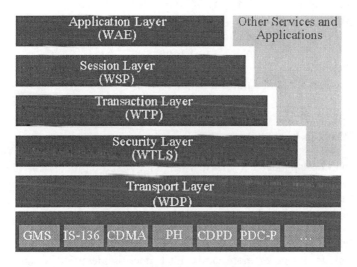

Fig. 6.6 The WAP protocol stack

The WAP protocols in Fig. 6.6 include wireless application environment (WAE), wireless session protocol (WSP), wireless transaction protocol (WTP), wireless transport layer security (WTLS), and wireless datagram protocol (WDP).

.. the following sections, we discuss these protocols with a focus on WAE by providing more detailed information.

6.4.2 Wireless Application Environment

The wireless application environment (WAE) consists of a set of standards that collectively define a group of formats for wireless applications and downloadable content. WAE specifies an application framework for wireless devices, such as cellular phones, pagers, and PDAs. WAE has two logical layers, namely, user-agent layer and format-and-service layer. The components of the user-agent layer include browsers, phone books, message editors, and other items on the user device side, such as wireless telephony application (WTA) agent. The components of the format-and-service layer include common elements and formats accessible to the user agents, such as WML, WMLScript, and WAP binary XML content format (WBXML).

A WAP microbrowser has the following capabilities:

- Submission requests to the server
- Reception of responses from the server
- Converting and parsing the data
- Interpreters from WML and WMLScript files
- Ability to interact with the appropriate WAP layer
- Local cache and variable management
- Wireless session protocol processing
- Effective management of local hardware resources, such as RAM, ROM, small screen, and input and output

Wireless Markup Language

Wireless markup language (WML) is a language based on the extensible markup language (XML). WML is optimized for small screens and limited memory capacity, and it is for content intended for lightweight, wireless devices such as mobile phones and personal digital assistants (PDAs).

A WML document is called deck. A page of a WML document is called card. A deck consists of one or more cards. Each deck is identified by an individual URL address, similar to an HTML page. A WML deck requires a browser that will format the deck for the benefit of the user. The browser determines the final shape of the deck. Sometimes, people use the analogy of HTML to explain WML. In the analogy, a WML deck corresponds to an HTML page. However, there are differences between a WML deck and an HTML page. While each HTML file is a single viewable page, a WML deck may contain multiple cards, each of which is a separate viewable entity. WML files are stored as static text files on a server. During the transmission from the server to the browser, the WML files are encoded in binary format by the wireless connection gateway, and then sent to the browser. This is also different from HTML, where there is no need for such an encoding process.

WML contains commands for navigating in decks. Each WML command has two core attributes, namely, id and class. The id is the attribute for an individual name to the elements inside a deck, while the class is the attribute that links the element to one or several groups. A WML deck, at its most basic level, is constructed from a set of elements. Elements are identified by tags, which are enclosed in angle brackets. Each element must include a start tag (<el_tag>) and an end tag (</el_tag>). The content is included between the start and end tags. An empty element that has no content can be abbreviated by a single tag (<el_tag/>).

Because WML is based on the XML language, a WML document must follow the XML rule to contain the XML specified document type definition (DTD) at the beginning of the WML code, which is referred to as deck header or document prolog, as follows:

```
<?xml version="1.0"?>
<!DOCTYPE wml PUBLIC "-//WAPFORUM//DTD WML 1.1//EN"
http://www.wapforum.org/DTD/wml_1.1.xml>
```

A deck is defined by the <wml> and </wml> tags that are required in every WML document. Within a deck, each card is defined by the <card> and </card> tags. Both <wml>...</wml> and <card>...</card> are formatting commands. The <wml>...</wml> commands summarize the deck. The <card>...</card> commands summarize the text, images, input fields, and any other objects of a card in the deck.

Cards are the basic units of WML, defining an interaction between mobile device and the user. Each card may contain three different groups of elements: content elements (such as text, tables, and images), tasks and events (such as <onevent>, <timer>, and <do>), and data entry (such as <input> and <select>).

WMLScript

WMLScript is a simple scripting language based on ECMAScript (ECMA-262 standard) with modifications to better support low-bandwidth communication and thin clients. WMLScript is part of the WAP application layer.

WMLScript complements the WML by adding simple formatting capabilities to make the user interfaces more readable, for example, the capabilities of checking the validity of user input and generating messages and dialog locally to reduce the need for expensive round-trip to show alerts. These capabilities are not supported by WML as the content of WML is static. WMLScript provides programmable functionality that can be used over narrowband communication links in clients with limited capabilities. With WMLScript, more advanced user interface functions can be supported and intelligence can be added to the client. WMLScript also provides access to the device and its peripheral functionality and reduces the amount of bandwidth that is needed for sending data back forth between the server and the client.

WMLScript is similar to JavaScript. For example, WMLScript includes a number of operators such as assignment and arithmetic operators, which are similar to those in JavaScript. However, there are major differences between WMLScript and JavaScript. First, WML contains references to the URL address of a WMLScript function, whereas JavaScript functions are normally embedded in the HTML code. Second, WMLScript must be compiled into binary WMLScript code prior to its execution in a WAP device, while there is no such requirement for JavaScript.

Although WMLScript is based on ECMAScript as we mentioned before, there are differences between WMLScript and ECMAScript. First, like JavaScript, ECMAScript is not encoded in a binary form while WMLScript has to be. Second, to form WMLScript, many advanced features of the ECMAScript language have been dropped to make WMLScript smaller, and easier to compile into binary WMLScript code.

WMLScript syntactically resembles C language. It has basic types, variables, expressions, and statements. Unlike C, WMLScript cannot be used to write stand-alone applications. There is no built-in support for reading and writing files. Because it is an interpreted language, scripts or functions can run only in the presence of an interpreter, which is supplied as part of the WAP user agent. WMLScript is a weakly typed and object-based language, in which variables must be declared before they can be used in expression. In WMLScript, there is no main program or routine. Functions are created to perform specific tasks and they are invoked through a WML call. When a WMLScript function is invoked, the WAP gateway accesses the source code, compiles it into binary WMLScript code, and then sends the execution function to the WAP user agent. WMLScript code is written in normal text files with the file extension "wmls."

Each WMLScript file contains at least one function. Each function is composed of statements that perform the appropriate processing. The structure of a WMLScript function is as follows:

```
extern function function_xyz (parameter list)
{ // start of the statements
      statement_1;
      statement_2;
```

```
        statement_n;
    }// end of the statements
```

With this structure and the file extension "xmls," a simple WMLScript example to set a first day of the week, which is included in the file named "setday.xmls," is listed as follows:

```
extern function SetDay(givenDay)
{
    if (givenDay > 0 && givenDay <= 7) {
        var newDay = givenDay;
    }
    else {
        newDay = 1;
    }
    return newDay;
}
```

To invoke a WMLScript function, a reference to the WMLScript function must be included in a WML document. The call will be routed from the WAP browser through the WAP gateway to the server. The server then sends the binary WMLScript code to the WAP browser. The WAP browser has an interpreter that is able to execute WMLScript programs in their binary format. Using our example, the reference to the WMLScript can be as simple as follows:

```
<do type="ACCEPT" label="Set Day">
<!--Calling the WMLScript function: -->
    <go href="setday.xmls#SetDay($(givenDay))"/>
</do>
```

Wireless Telephony Application Interface and Wireless Telephony Applications

One of the major mobile services is voice. How can we set up a call or receive an incoming call using a WAP enabled mobile device? This is the problem that Wireless Telephony Application Interface (WTAI) addresses. WTAI is designed to allow wireless network operators access the telephony features of WAP device. Through either a WML deck/card or WMLScript, using the WTAI function libraries, a mobile phone call can be set up and an incoming call can be received. In addition, text messages can be sent or received, and phonebook entries can be manipulated on the WAP device.

Wireless telephony applications (WTA) is a collection of telephony-specific extensions for call and feature control mechanisms that make advanced mobile network services available to the mobile users. It provides a bridge between wireless telephony and data. The WTA applications can use the privileged WTAI.

From the architecture point of view, a WTA server communicates with the WAP gateway to deliver and manage telephony services; on the client side, there is a WTA framework which has three components as follows:

1. User agent: This agent supports the WTAI libraries, renders WML, and executes WMLScripts.
2. Repository: It provides persistent client-side storage for wireless telephony applications.
3. Event Handling: This deals with incoming-call and call-connected events to be delivered to a wireless telephony application for processing, which may also invoke WMLScript library interfaces to initiate and control telephony operations.

Wireless telephony supports in WAP make WAP suitable for creating mobile applications through voice services. The compact form, encryption, and error handling capabilities of WAP enable critical wireless payment transactions.

WBXML

WAP Binary XML Content Format (WBXML) is defined in the Binary XML Content Format Specification in the WAP standard set. This format is a compact binary representation of the XML. The main purpose is to reduce the transmission size of XML documents on narrowband communication channels.

A binary XML document is composed of a sequence of elements and each element may have zero or more attributes. The element structure of XML is preserved while the format encodes the parsed physical form of an XML document. This allows user agents to skip elements and data that are not understood. In terms of encoding, a tokenized structure is used to encode an XML document. The network byte order is big-endian, that is, the most significant byte is transmitted first. Within a byte, bit-order is also big-endian, namely, the most significant bit first.

6.4.3 Wireless Session Protocol

The Wireless session protocol (WSP) is a protocol family in the WAP architecture, which provides the WAP Application Layer with a consistent interface for session services. WSP establishes a session between the client and the WAP gateway to provide content transfer: the client makes a request, and then the server answers with a reply through the WAP gateway. WSP supports the efficient operation of a WAP micro-browser running on the client device with limited capacity and communicating over a low-bandwidth wireless network. The WSP browsing applications are based on the HTTP 1.1 standard, and incorporated with additional features that are not included in the HTTP protocol, for example, the connection to the server shall not be lost when a mobile user is moving, resulting in a change from one base station to another. The other additional features that WSP supports include:

- **Binary encoding**:
  Given the low bandwidth of the wireless network, the efficient binary encoding of the content to be transferred is necessary for mobile Internet applications.

- **Data push functionality**:
  Data push functionality is not supported in the HTTP protocol. A push is what is performed when a WSP server transfers the data to a mobile client without a preceding request from the client. WSP supports three push mechanisms for data transfer, namely, a confirmed data push within an existing session context, a non-confirmed data push within an existing session context, and a non-confirmed data push without an existing session context.

- **Capability negotiation**:
  Mobile clients and servers can negotiate various parameters for the session establishments, for example, maximum outstanding requests and protocol options.

- **Session suspend/resume**:
  It allows a mobile user to switch off and on the mobile device and to continue operation at the exact point where the device was switched off.

WSP offers two different services, namely, the connection-oriented service and the connectionless service. The connection-oriented service has the full capabilities of WSP. It operates on top of the wireless transaction protocol (WTP), supports session establishment, method invocation, push messages, suspend, resume and session termination. The connectionless service is suitable for these situations where high reliability is not required or the overhead of session establishment and release can be avoided. It supports only basic request-reply and push, and does not rely on WTP.

6.4.4 Wireless Transaction Protocol

The wireless transaction protocol operates on top of a secure or insecure datagram service. WTP introduces the notion of a transaction that is defined as a request with its response. This transaction model is well suited for web content requests and responses. It does not handle stream-based applications (such as telnet) well.

WTP is responsible for delivering the improved reliability over datagram service between the mobile device and the server by transmitting acknowledge messages to confirm the receipt of data and by retransmitting data that has not been acknowledged within a suitable timeout period.

WTP supports an abort function through a primitive error handling. If an error occurs, such as the connection being broken down, the transaction is aborted.

WTP is message-oriented and it provides three different types of transaction services, namely, unreliable one-way, reliable one-way, and reliable two-way transactions. The transaction type is set by the initiator and it is contained in the service request message sent to the responder. The unreliable one-way transactions are stateless and cannot be aborted. The responder does not acknowledge the message from the initiator. The reliable one-way transactions provide a reliable datagram service that enables the applications to provide reliable push service. The reliable two-way transactions provide the reliable request/response transaction services.

6.4.5 Wireless Transport Layer Security

The wireless transport layer security (WTLS) protocol is a security protocol based on the *transport layer security protocol* (TLS) [6.10] (see Section 6.7). TLS is a derivative of the *secure sockets layer* (SSL), a widely used security protocol for Internet applications and payment over the Internet (for more information about SSL, see Section 11.6 of Chapter 11). WTLS has been optimized for the wireless communication environment. It operates above the transport protocol layer.

WTLS is flexible due to its modular design. Depending on the required security level, it can be decided whether WTLS is used or not. WTLS provides data integrity, data confidentiality, authentication, and denial-of-service protection. The data integrity is to ensure that data sent between a mobile station and a wireless application server is unchanged and uncorrupted. The data confidentiality is to ensure that data transmitted between the mobile station and the wireless application server is private to the sender and the receiver, and it is not going to be understood by any hackers. The authentication is to check the identity of the mobile station and the wireless application server. The denial-of-service protection is to prevent the upper protocol layers from the denial-of-service attacks by detecting and rejecting data that is replayed or not successfully verified.

6.4.6 Wireless Datagram Protocol

The wireless datagram protocol (WDP) in the WAP architecture specifies how different existing bearer services should be used to provide a consistent service to the upper layers. WDP is used to hide the differences between the underlying bearer networks. WDP layer operates above the bearer services and provides a consistent interface to the WTLS layer.

Different bearers have different characteristics. The bearer services include short message, circuit-switched data and packet data services. Since WAP is designed to operate over the bearer services, and since the bearers offer different types of quality of service with respect to throughput, error rate, and delays, the WDP is designed to adapt the transport layer to specific features of the underlying bearers. The adaptation results in a family of protocols in the WDP layer, dealing with each supported bearer network protocol. When a message is transmitted through WAP stack, depending on the underlying bearer network, a different WDP protocol may be used. For example, for an IP bearer, the user datagram protocol (UDP) must be adopted as the WDP protocol, and for a short message service (SMS) bearer, the use of the source and destination port numbers becomes mandatory.

6.4.7 WAP Gateway

A WAP gateway as shown in Fig. 6.7 is a proxy server that sits between the mobile network and the Internet. The purpose of this proxy server is to translate between HTTP and WSP. The reason for the translation is that the web server connected to the Internet only understands the HTTP protocol while the WAP-enabled mobile client only understands the WSP. The WAP gateway also converts a HTML file into a WML document that is designed for small-screen devices. In addition, the WAP gateway compiles the WML page into binary WML which is more suitable for the mobile client. The WAP gateway is transparent to both the mobile client and the web server.

Fig. 6.7 WAP gateway

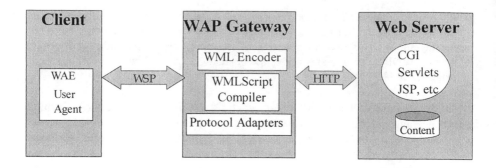

Fig. 6.8 WAP model

Fig. 6.8 shows the WAP model using the WAP gateway. How the WAP gateway processes of a typical request for a document can be illustrated as follows:

1. The mobile user makes a request for a specific document using the WAP phone.
2. The WAE user agent on the WAP phone encodes the request and sends it to the WAP gateway.
3. The WAP gateway decodes and parses the encoded request.
4. The WAP gateway sends a HTTP request for the document.
5. The web server answers with a response to the WAP gateway.
6. The WAP gateway parses and encodes the response.
7. If the content-type is WML then the gateway compiles it into binary WML.
8. The WAP gateway sends the encoded response to the WAP phone.
9. The WAE user agent on the WAP phone interprets and presents the document to the mobile user.

6.5 Wireless Security

Wireless security is becoming more and more important as transaction-based mobile commerce applications (such as mobile payment, banking, and buying stock via cellular phones or handheld devices) take off.

The basic security needs for mobile commerce are similar to that for electronic commerce over the wired Internet, such as authentication, confidentiality, non-repudiation, and data integrity. However, implementing them in the wireless world is more difficult than it is to implement them in the wired world. This is simply because the limitations that wireless have, including limited bandwidth, high latency, and unstable connections. In addition, limited battery power and limited processing power that the wireless devices have also make the sophisticated security algorithms difficult to run on these devices.

As we discussed in the previous section, WAP does specify an SSL like security protocol, namely, wireless transport layer security (WTLS). However, there are some drawbacks in WTLS. First, WTLS only provides security protection from the mobile client to the WAP gateway where the wireless communication ends. In the wired Internet environment, when a web client (web browser) starts an SSL session with web server, the web client and web server are communicated directly, and the end-to-end security protection is provided through the SSL session. This means when one sends a credit card number over SSL, only the receiving web server will be able to receive it. The situation is different in the WTLS. The credit card number will be securely protected between the mobile device and the WAP gateway. It will be in the clear form at the WAP gateway. Then, an SSL session will be established between the WAP gateway and the Web server for securely transmitting the credit card number over the Internet. This means that there is no end-to-end security protection for the wireless transactions since there is a potential security hole in the WAP gateway. Second, the CCITT X509 certificate is too large for the mobile phones, and the limitations of the processing power and battery for the wireless devices make it difficult to perform the sophisticated computation of the public-key encryption. In summary, WAP security has two issues: (1) there is no end-to-end security protection, and (2) there is a lack of certificates for mobile devices.

People are currently addressing these two security issues. As a result, simplified certificates have been defined for mobile devices. The research on how to use currently available mobile devices to perform the computation of public-key encryption is ongoing. For example, elliptic curve cryptography (ECC) requires far fewer resources and it looks very promising for wide deployment to CPU-starved wireless devices.

6.6 Summary

The convergence of wireless technologies and the e-commerce over the Internet lead to emerging and fast growth of mobile commerce. As the result, mobile commerce and mobile payment have attracted more and more attention of the academic researchers and business leaders. Being able to conduct e-commerce and make payment anywhere and anytime is becoming reality. However, because of the limitations that wireless have, conducting e-commerce and making payment in the wireless world is more difficult than in the wired world. Understanding the wireless infrastructure that the wireless applications rely on is important for developing and deploying such applications.

In this chapter, we discussed the wireless infrastructure for mobile payment and fore mobile commerce in general, including wireless communication infrastructure, wireless computing infrastructure, wireless application protocol, and wireless security.

6.7 Appendix

Overview of the Transport Layer Security

The transport layer security (TLS) [6.10] is a protocol that provides privacy and data integrity between two communicating applications. The TLS is application protocol independent, that is, higher-level protocols can layer on top of the TLS protocol transparently. The TLS protocol is composed of two layers:

- **TLS record protocol**: This protocol provides connection security and is used for encapsulation of various higher-level protocols, such as the TLS handshake protocol to be discussed below. It has the following two basic properties.

   o   The connection is private. Data encryption is used for ensuring the communication privacy, and is based on symmetric cryptographic algorithms, such as DES or RC4. The keys for symmetric encryption are generated uniquely for each connection and are based on a secret negotiated by another protocol (e.g., the TLS handshake protocol). The record protocol can also be used without encryption.

   o   The connection is reliable. A message integrity check based on a keyed MAC is used for protecting message transport. Secure hash functions, such as SHA and MD5, are used for MAC computations. In the case of that another protocol uses the record protocol and negotiates security parameters, the record protocol can operate without a MAC.

- **TLS handshake protocol**: This protocol allows the server and client to authenticate each other, and negotiate an encryption algorithm and cryptographic keys. It has the following three basic properties.

   o   The authentication between the server and client can be based on a public-key cryptographic algorithm, such as RSA or DSS. Although the authentication can be mutual, the mutual authentication is optional. Generally speaking, one-way authentication is required.

o   It is secure for the negotiation of a shared secret between the server and client.

o   The negotiation is reliable.

Because the TSL is a derivative of SSL, the actual handshake exchanges are similar to that of SSL. The descriptions of the main SSL exchanges can be found in Section 11.6 of Chapter 11.

6.8 References

[6.1]   WAP. http://www.ini.cmu.edu/netbil.
[6.2]   Wireless Application Protocol Forum Ltd. (1999) Official wireless application protocol. Wiley, New York.
[6.3]   S. Mann, S. Sbihli (2000) The wireless application protocol. Wiley, New York.
[6.4]   S. Singhal, et al. (2001) The wireless application protocol. Addison-Wesley, New York.
[6.5]   J. Schiller (2000) Mobile communications. Addison-Wesley, New York.
[6.6]   U. Hansmann, et al. (2001) Pervasive computing handbook. Springer, Berlin Heidelberg New York.
[6.7]   C. Sharma (2001) Wireless Internet enterprise applications. Wiley, New York.
[6.8]   Y. B. Lin, I. Chlamtac (2001) Wireless and mobile network architectures. Wiley, New York.
[6.9]   A. Dornan (2001) The essential guide to wireless communications applications. Prentice-Hall, New York.
[6.10] T. Dierks, C. Allen (1999) The TLS protocol version 1.0. http://www.ietf.org/rfc/rfc2246.txt.

7 Payment Agents

Amitabha Das

School of Computer Engineering
Nanyang Technological University, Singapore

7.1 Introduction

In a broad sense, a software agent is a computer program that acts autonomously on behalf of a person or organization. Software-agent technology seems able to provide attractive solutions in the field of electronic commerce. An agent-based architecture for electronic commerce allows the creation of a virtual marketplace in which a number of autonomous or semi-autonomous agents trade goods and services. The introduction of software agents acting on behalf of end-consumers could reduce the effort required from users when conducting electronic commerce transactions, by automating a variety of activities. The personalized, continuously running autonomous nature of agents makes them well suited for mediating consumer behavior with respect to information filtering and retrieval, personalized evaluations, complex coordination, and time-based interactions. Agents are able to examine a large number of products before making a decision to buy or sell. This not only eliminates the need to manually collect information about products but also allows the negotiation of an optimal deal with the various sellers of a good.

7.1.1 Agent-Based Electronic Commerce Systems

During the hay day of the dotcoms, several agent-based e-commerce systems came into existence, e.g., PersonaLogic, Firefly, BargainFinder, and Jango. All of them disappeared within a short while. PersonaLogic allowed users to specify product features and used a constraint satisfaction algorithm to filter through the product space to retrieve an ordered set of products. Firefly used an automated collaborative filtering method to rate and recommend products to shoppers. BargainFinder and Jango were systems that could take a product name as the input, obtain price information from other websites, and perform a price comparison.

More advanced systems in which buyer and seller agents cooperate to constitute a virtual market have also been developed in academic institutions (e.g., [7.1-7.6]). Among them Kasbah [7.1] is a multi-agent system where agents filter through ads on behalf of their owners and find those that their users might be interested in. The agents then proceed to negotiate to buy and sell items. MAGMA [7.6] is a prototype of a virtual marketplace system, which consists of multiple trader agents, an advertising server, and a bank. Trader agents are responsible for buying and selling goods. They also handle the price negotiations. Advertising server provides a classified advertisement service that includes search and retrieval of ads by category. Bank provides a set of basic banking services that includes checking accounts, lines of credit, and electronic cash.

7.1.2 Use of Agents for Payment

In none of the agent-based e-commerce systems discussed above are the agents used for executing the actual transaction involving transfer of money. Besides, in all the above systems, the agents are immobile. They do not support mobile users, and for activities that require a large number of interactions between remote agents they leave much to be optimized.

However, when the system is based only on static agents that reside in sites controlled entirely by their owners, there is no real reason for not allowing the agents to execute the payment operations. The security concerns in this case are not different from those when the payment involves manual intervention by the transacting parties. In spite of that, so far, the introduction of a system in which the agents carry out autonomously the entire process of e-commerce transaction starting from information gathering to the completion of the transaction has not materialized. The real reason for this is perhaps the lack of confidence in the competence of the agents to take decisions that are intelligent enough.

The security concerns, however, change drastically when it comes to the introduction of *mobile agents*. A mobile agent is a program that represents a user and can migrate autonomously from node to node in a computer network to perform some computation on behalf of the user. It is not bound to the system where it begins execution. It can suspend its execution at an arbitrary point, transport itself to another node, and resume execution there.

The mobile-agent paradigm offers several advantages compared to traditional approaches, such as a reduction in communication costs, better support of asynchronous interactions, enhanced flexibility in the process of software distribution, and the offer of increased performance and robustness. The use of mobile agents has been particularly promising in the fields of information retrieval, network management, electronic commerce, and mobile computing.

Information-retrieval applications often download and process large amounts of information from the server over the network while generating a comparatively small amount of result data. This can be supported much more efficiently if a mobile agent representing a query moves to the server where the data are actually stored, rather than having to move all of the data across the network for filtering. Then vendors can set up online shops with products or services for sale. Mobile agents can help customers locate the best offerings, can negotiate deals, and can even conclude transactions on behalf of their owners.

Finally, an important application of mobile agents concerns mobile computing. A portable computer's network connectivity is often achieved through low-bandwidth wireless links, hence it is likely to be slow. Besides, to minimize power consumption and transmission costs, users will not want to remain online while some complicated query is handled on their behalf by the fixed computing resources. Mobile agents offer a promising way of achieving this: users simply submit mobile agents that embody their queries and log off, waiting for the agents to deposit their results, ready to be picked up at a later time.

7.2 Security Implications of Mobile-Agent-Based Systems

The fact that mobile agents can and do execute in hosts other than the ones controlled by their owners gives rise to a number of security concerns that do not exist in the case of static agents. The most important and the most difficult-to-handle security threat arises from the fact that the third-party host has complete access and observability of the code of the mobile agents. As a result, it is extremely easy for a malicious host to either spy on confidential information, or tamper with the execution of the mobile agents.

This appears to be a severe limitation on the applicability of mobile agents in tasks involving confidentiality or security, such as electronic payment operation. However, a number of possible remedies have been suggested to overcome this problem. We will briefly examine these before we embark on the task of designing a secure payment protocol for mobile agents in untrusted host environments.

7.3 Security Techniques Protecting Mobile Agents

Methods that protect an agent against attacks can be categorized into those that prevent attacks and those which detect attacks. The detection methods use cryptographic and other techniques to detect tampering with the code and/or data carried by the mobile agent. The detection techniques are useless in preventing an attack, such as the theft of confidential information, and only serve to help in post mortem analysis. In the context of payment protocols, such methods can come in handy in detecting whether the payment has been redirected maliciously to an unintended recipient.

On the other hand, the prevention techniques are more relevant in thwarting attacks. Some of the prevention techniques proposed in the literature are *sliding encryption* [7.7], trail obscuring, code obfuscation [7.8], and computing with an encrypted function [7.9-7.10]. These are briefly discussed below.

7.3.1 Methods for Protecting Mobile Agents

Sliding Encryption

A mobile agent uses this technique [7.7] to encrypt acquired data by using a public key. The key is public, so theft is not an issue. Decryption can only be performed with the corresponding private key. The mobile agent uses sliding encryption to hide what it is carrying, so potentially malicious hosts that the mobile agent visits cannot steal any data.

This technique is applicable when mobile agents gather information in small chunks from multiple sources and it is necessary to prevent any host other than the source of a given piece of information from seeing it. As an example, consider a scenario where a mobile agent is collecting product information from multiple vendor sites and accumulating the information in its buffer. When it visits a host, the host can potentially see all the information the mobile agent is carrying and can possibly tamper with it for its own commercial gain or to affect the operations of the predecessor nodes.

A straightforward use of public key cryptography can result in substantial storage overhead for an agent. As an example, suppose that the agent is required to collect 4 bytes of data from each of 1024 different sites. If it uses a 128-byte public key, then it must encrypt the 4 bytes of data collected from a node into at least a 128-byte ciphertext before it moves on to a subsequent node. Consequently, in the end, the agent must have the capacity to carry 128 Kbytes of ciphertext which contains only 4 Kbytes worth of plaintext.

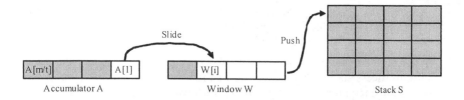

Fig. 7.1 Data structures used for sliding encryption

The technique of sliding encryption [7.7] helps to reduce the size of the cipher-text substantially by using the method of chain ciphering (see Fig. 7.1). The scheme described is based on the RSA [7.11] public-key encryption algorithm, but it is general enough to accommodate any other public-key encryption algorithm. The essentials of the scheme are described below.

Assume that the granule of plaintext that is collected from each site is of a small fixed length u. This is concatenated with randomly generated v bytes to construct a word of size $v+u$ in which the random word occupies the upper-order bytes. Let us call this composite word X which is of length $t = u+v$. The length of the RSA public key used is m. Both m and t are powers of 2, and $m \gg t$.

The data structures used by the agent for sliding encryption include an accumulator A of m bytes, an m-byte window W, and a stack S, each stack element $S[i]$ being m bytes long. The accumulator is divided into m/t entities, each t bytes long. $A[1]$ contains the least-significant bytes of A, and $A[m/t]$ contains the most-significant bytes. We will denote the public-key encryption function by E() and the corresponding private-key decryption by D(). The functions E() and D() include an uneven Feistel-like preprocessing and postprocessing as in [7.12].

The mechanism works as follows. Initially the stack is empty, and the accumulator is initialized to a random non-zero positive integer K. After the piece of information is collected at the first site, the composite word X1 is formed by concatenating it with the randomly generated v bytes. Then A[1] is replaced by X1, and the resultant content of the whole accumulator is encrypted using E(). A[1] now contains the lowest-order bytes of the ciphertext. Then we set $W[m/t] = A[1]$. The remaining part of the ciphertext in the accumulator is carried unchanged and serves as a link in the chain ciphering process.

In the next node, the composite word X2 is similarly formed from the information picked up at that node, then A[1] is replaced by X2. The modified content of the accumulator is now encrypted using E(), and again the lowest bytes of the ciphertext, which now occupy A[1], slide into $W[(m/t)-1]$.

After all the m/t slots in the window W are full, it is pushed onto the stack S, and the sliding restarts from slot $W[m/t]$.

After all the nodes are visited and the mobile agent returns to its owner, the decryption process starts. This makes use of the private key and the process simply reverses the encryption steps sequentially, retrieving the hidden pieces of information in reverse order.

Trail Obscuring

This method depends on changing a mobile agent binary image to make it hard to identify by pattern matching. A mobile agent attempts to obscure its path through the network by constantly modifying its own binary image so that it cannot be identified as the same mobile agent by different hosts which are colluding in an attempt to track the mobile agent. This works in a situation where anonymity is required, such as an anonymous monetary donation or auction bid. It may also aid in surviving malicious hosts trying to stop specific behavior that can be identified by analyzing the mobile agent's path.

One important component of traceability of a mobile agent is its state information. If a group of adversary nodes compare the state information of a mobile agent captured in the snapshots taken by them, it can be possible to determine the order in which the nodes were traversed. Therefore, to thwart such attacks, the state information associated with an agent must be concealed. As an example, if sliding encryption is used as described above, then the state information will consist of the accumulator values, the window values, the stack, the stack pointer, and the index to the next location in the window where the next value of A[1] will slide into. In this case, one has to devise ways to conceal the real state using various techniques. For details the reader is referred to [7.7].

However, trail obscuring is not a foolproof method. A major problem of this approach is that mobile agents cannot encrypt and decrypt themselves, because, if they could, then any host could also do the same as it too will have access to the decryption key. Suppose that a subset of all the nodes visited by the mobile agent colludes to trace the agent's itinerary by taking snapshots of the agent while it was visiting each node of this subset. Under such circumstances, it is impossible to make an agent completely untraceable if all the adversaries are connected directly, and the agent cannot modify itself without being caught just before moving out of an adversary node.

Code Obfuscation

This method was discussed in [7.8]. Most of the above security problems can be solved if the host is not able to determine the relation between single lines of code and their semantics and the relation between memory bits and the semantics of data elements, respectively. A host can of course modify code, data and control flow anyway, but not with a computed effect. For a host this results in three choices:

- Host can execute the agent undisturbed.
- Host can execute the agent by switching some bits, not knowing about the effect on the execution.
- Host can take the agent without executing it.

An attacker needs a certain amount of time to read the data, understand the code and, thereafter, manipulate both in a meaningful way. The basic idea of the approach described now is simply not to give them enough time to do this. According to [7.8] this can be achieved by a combination of code mess-up and a limited lifetime of code and data.

With the employment of code mess-up techniques, Hohl has developed a non-cryptographic agent protection scheme that is built up like any cryptographic mechanism: readable input (i.e., code and data) is transformed to an unreadable form by a mechanism that cannot be inverted easily with the current knowledge.

Code mess-up does cost something, both in terms of speed and of space, and the processing model is more complex due to expiration aspects. Therefore, this scheme should be mainly used for agents that need to be protected, e.g., because they carry money or other sensitive data. The global usage of this mechanism even for nonsensitive applications may be too expensive, but because a code mess-up infrastructure is needed only for protected agents, agents of both protection levels can exist and interact in parallel. Hohl claims that it is possible to practically protect agents from malicious hosts by using code mess-up techniques. However, future work has to prove this claim.

Computing with Encrypted Function (CEF)

This method of concealing the computations of an agent from its host is proposed in [7.9] and [7.10]. Instead of using the more general term *program*, the authors differentiate between a function and the program that implements it. Thus, the goal is to encrypt functions such that their transformation can again be implemented as programs. The resulting program will consist of cleartext instructions that a processor or interpreter understands. What the processor will not be able to understand is the "program's function." With the requirements of mobile agents in mind, we can state the problem that we want to solve, as follows.

Alice has an algorithm to compute a function f. Bob has an input x and is willing to compute $f(x)$ for her, but Alice wants Bob to learn nothing substantial about $f(\cdot)$. Moreover, Bob should not need to interact with Alice during the computation of $f(x)$. To let Alice and Bob work together in the way described above, we assume that a function f can be transformed (encrypted) to some other function $E(f)$. The encryption hides the function f and may or may not also contain the encryption of the output data. We let the notation $P(f)$ stand for the program that implements the function f. In this protocol Alice does not send to Bob the program $P(f)$ for the plain function f but the program $P(E(f))$ for the encrypted function $E(f)$. Bob only learns about the program $P(E(f))$ that he has to apply to his input x and the result of this computation that he has to return to Alice. The simple protocol for noninteractive computing with encrypted functions looks like this:

(1) Alice encrypts $f(x)$.
(2) Alice creates a program $P(E(f))$ which implements $E(f)$.
(3) Alice sends $P(E(f))$ to Bob.
(4) Bob executes $P(E(f))$ on x.
(5) Bob sends $P(E(f))(x)$ to Alice.
(6) Alice decrypts $P(E(f))(x)$ and obtains $f(x)$.

Noninteractive computing with encrypted functions is a challenge for cryptography. The challenge is to find encryption schemes for arbitrary functions. The authors of [7.9] identified some specific function classes (i.e., polynomials and rational functions) for which they could find encrypting transformations.

Their approach of studying algebraic homomorphic encryption schemes (HES) yields a first and simple scheme for CEF. However, they leave it open whether the CEF approach is applicable to arbitrary functions, that is, they don't even claim to have achieved a complete solution for the case of all polynomials. However, within the restricted setting of polynomials and rational functions they can prove first positive results that falsify the "general belief on mobile code vulnerability" for nontrivial cases.

7.4 Secure Payment Protocols Using Mobile Agents in an Untrusted Host Environment

With the above background we are now in a position to explore ways to design payment protocols for mobile agents that offer security against malicious hosts. In order to do that we need to define precisely the context in which the mobile agents operate and the specific threats of attacks they face. The following two sections define these parameters.

7.4.1 Model for the Mobile-Agent-Based E-Commerce Environment

There are mainly four parties in the payment system [7.13-7.14]: a bank B, a customer U, a merchant M, and a *trusted third party* (TTP). A TTP is an impartial entity that is trusted by both the customer and the merchant and whose testimony is accepted in a court of law as valid evidence. In addition, we assume the existence of a trusted certification authority that can certify the validity of the public keys of the different parties. Both customer U and Merchant M have accounts with the bank B. An electronic payment system consists of protocols that allow customer U to make a payment to the merchant M. The customer's site can create some buyer agents to do the information gathering, negotiation, and payment for him. The merchant's site can create some seller agents to interact with the customer or buyer agent. The bank can create one or more bank agents that can interact with the buyer agent and seller agent, providing some services, such as creating accounts, withdrawing and depositing money, transfering money, etc. TTP is used to provide a non-repudiation service in case any party should deny sending or receiving information in the protocol.

The buyer agents for the customer are hosted by a network of mobile agent hosts (MA hosts). These hosts provide a resident and executive environment for all these buyer agents.

In order to make the payment, the mobile agents have to communicate and transfer messages to one another. So the system must provide a mechanism for finding the current location of an agent and the MA host. All the entities, such as the customer U, Merchant M, Bank B, TTP, and all the MA hosts are assigned unique names. So that an agent can specify its desired destination when it migrates, a name server is provided which maps a symbolic name to the current location of the named entity. The locations of the customer, merchant, Bank, TTP, and MA hosts do not change often, whereas the location of a mobile agent is more likely to change. Whenever a mobile agent arrives or migrates to a new host, it should contact and inform the name server regarding its change of address, so that it can be located afterwards.

Threat Model

In this model, one or more agents representing a customer need to transfer sensitive payment information to the merchant site. The customer agents are hosted by a network of MA hosts. Both the MA hosts and the merchant site can be malicious. The following is a list of assumptions regarding the nature of the potential attacks in the scenario described above:

A1. At the most *m-1* malicious hosts may collude to steal sensitive information from the customer agent.

A2. The mobile agents travel through secure channels, i.e., no one other than the intended recipient can gain any information by eavesdropping on the communication channels.

A3. The merchant may deny that he has received the electronic money, and spend the money as his own later.

A4. The merchant site host works independently and does not collude with malicious MA hosts to cheat the customer.

A5. There is a "trusted third party" which is honest, and both the customer and the merchant trust that the TTP will execute its role correctly. The TTP has no role to play in the protection of the customer agents against malicious MA hosts.

7.4.2 A Secure Payment Protocol

Since electronic payment necessarily involves processing and transfer of confidential information, mobile payment agents are extremely vulnerable to attacks by malicious hosts. The CEF technique described above can be an effective tool to protect mobile agents from malicious hosts, but its applicability is quite restricted because of the limited current knowledge of the functions. An alternative is to ensure that at no point in time is the confidential information completely accessible to the untrusted hosts. This approach is adopted in the following protocol by making use of secret sharing schemes. The basic protocol described below [7.13-7.14] is based on Shamir's secret sharing scheme [7.15] and can use any digital cash scheme such as Chaum's digital cash [7.16] or the more efficient e-cash scheme of Stefan Brands [7.17-7.18]. But it can be adapted to many other payment methods and can be based on other secret sharing techniques as well.

7.4.3 Main Phases of the Protocol

There are four phases in the payment protocol:

1. **Withdrawal phase:** In this phase the customer withdraws electronic cash from their bank. The specifics of this phase will depend on the e-cash

scheme being adopted, and the subsequent phases are largely independent of this phase. At a conceptual level, it suffices to view this phase as generating some tokens which we call e-cash.

2. **Distribution phase:** In this phase, the customer encrypts the e-cash using a secret key and divides the secret key into several small shares using an (m, n) threshold scheme.

3. **Payment phase:** In this phase, m mobile agents work together and each passes its share of the secret key to the merchant's site. The merchant then reconstructs the secret key and deciphers the e-cash. Payment by e-cash typically involves a token transfer phase followed by an authentication phase in which the payee poses a challenge and the payer responds with appropriate values. The authentication phase can be handled by a single agent. For the sake of simplicity, we will confine our attention to the phase involving the transfer of the token only.

4. **Verification and transfer phase:** The merchant signs the e-cash deciphered in the payment phase and forwards it to bank B. The bank verifies that the e-cash submitted is not fake or duplicated and credits the amount to the merchant's account.

The core Secure Payment protocol consists of the Distribution Phase and the Payment Phase. In what follows we describe these phases in detail. But before we do so, the notation used is explained.

Notation:

- M: The merchant (or payee).
- s: Secret key for encrypting e-cash.
- C: The e-cash to be transferred as payment.
- $e_s(m)$: Message m symmetrically encrypted using secret key s.
- $d_s(g)$: Encrypted message g decrypted using secret key s.
- $(m)^k$: Message m asymmetrically encrypted with a public/private key k.
- $S_X(m)$: Message m digitally signed by X.
- Share$_i$: The share of the secret carried by the ith agent.
- $H(\cdot)$: One-way collision-free hash function. We will denote $H(\text{Share}_i)$ as $H(i)$.
- $Lagent$: A leader agent used to organize the transfer of the shares, any of the mobile agents carrying a share of the secret can be a leader agent
- P_x and V_x : The public/private key pair of party x.

- F_{REC}, F_{SUB}, F_{CON}: Flags used to identify the steps of transferring the shares in the protocol. They indicate the intended purpose of a (signed) message. F_{REC}, F_{SUB}, and F_{CON} indicate that the objective of the step is transferring a receipt, submitting a document, and confirming the receipt of a document, respectively.
- TTP: On-line trusted third party providing security services accessible to the public.

The steps of the two core phases are described below.

7.4.4 Distribution Phase

The steps of this phase are as follows:

1. Distribute the secret keys using a secret sharing scheme

The customer distributes s using the secret sharing scheme, an (m, n) threshold scheme. For this purpose an arbitrary polynomial of degree $m - 1$ is generated:

$$f(x) = a_0 + a_1x + a_2x^2 + \cdots + a_{m-1}x^{m-1}, \text{ where } a_0 = s .$$

The coefficients $a_1, a_2, \ldots a_{m-1}$ are chosen randomly from the set $Z_p = \{0, 1, \ldots, p - 1\}$ and are kept secret and discarded after the shadows are handed out. p is a prime larger than the number of possible shadows (shares), and the largest possible secret. All arithmetic is done modulo p.

The n shadows are obtained by evaluating the polynomial at n random different points, $y_i = f(x_i)$. The values of $x_i (i = 1, \ldots, n)$ are made public whereas $y_i (i = 1, \ldots, n)$ are kept secret and act as the n shares $share_i (i = 1, \ldots, n)$.

It is easy to see that when any m shadows come together, linear algebra can be used to solve for the coefficients of the polynomial, including the constant term, $a_0 = s$.

2. Compute n message digests for n shares

A hash function is used to compute $H(i) = H(share_i)$, $i = 1, \ldots, n$.

3. Prepare *n* mobile agents

The customer creates n agents, each agent assigned a unique name Agent$_i$ $(i = 1,...,n)$, and will carry the encrypted e-cash $e_s(C)$, a share of the secret s, and a set of n ordered pairs $\{x_j, H(j)\}, j = 1,...,n$.

4. Dispatch *n* mobile agents to *n* hosts

The n agents are dispatched to n distinct hosts. Each agent will carry the following information:

$$\text{Agent}_i, e_s(C), \text{share}_i, \{\text{Agent}_j, x_j, H(j), j = 1,...,n\}.$$

5. Register the location of these *n* mobile agents

After dispatching a mobile agent, the customer's site should register at the name server for the new location of the dispatched mobile agent. The name server maintains a hash map, each record of which is a pair, the agent name and the location. The location consists of a hostname and a port number. It can be resolved using the domain name server (DNS). The agent name is unique, so that the customer and other mobile agents can communicate with it or control it while it travels on its itinerary. So the content of the hash map is:

$$\{\text{Agent}_i, \text{Location (Hostname : PortNumber)}\}.$$

7.4.5 Payment Phase

The payment phase begins when one of the mobile agents of the customer initiates the payment process after receiving the payment order from the merchant. This agent will be designated as the leader agent or *Lagent*. The payment order (PO) consists of a number of components, as given below:

$$PO = S_M(Tid, Lagent, M, Goods\_desc, Amount, Time)$$

where
     Tid = unique identifier for the transaction being carried out,
     $Goods\_desc$ = description of the goods being purchased,
     $Amount$ = the amount to be paid to the merchant,
     $Time$ = the time when the payment order is made,
     $S_M(message)$ = indicates that the message is signed by M.

The *Lagent* will randomly select the other $m-1$ mobile agents and send the payment order signed by the merchant. After the other $m-1$ mobile agents have verified the payment order, they will send their shares to the merchant. The merchant sends a signed acknowledgment to *Lagent* after the merchant has received $m-1$ shares. The *Lagent* then sends the last share to a TTP from which the merchant collects it.

The steps of this phase are explained below.

1. Initialization

The *Lagent* randomly selects $m-1$ Agents from the information it carries, finds the locations of these $m-1$ mobile agents from the *name server*, and sends the following information to the selected mobile agents: the message digest of its share $\{x_j, H(j)\}$, the merchant identity M, and the payment order signed by M.

Other mobile agents can authenticate *Lagent* using the message digest. They verify the payment order using the merchant's public key. If anything inconsistent is found, the payment is stopped and the problem is reported to the owner.

2. Other *m-1* mobile agents send shares to the merchant

All the selected mobile agents send their shares of the secret key to the merchant:

$$Agent_i \rightarrow M : (Tid, Share_i, x_i)^{P_M} .$$

3. Merchant sends the acknowledgement to *Lagent*

After $m-1$ shares have been received by the merchant, the merchant computes the message digests of the $m-1$ shares using the same hash function $H(\cdot)$. Then the merchant sends the following message as a receipt to *Lagent*:

$$M \rightarrow Lagent : S_M \{F_{REC}, Tid, M, Lagent, m-1 \text{ pairs } (x_i, H(i))\} .$$

4. *Lagent* sends its share as the last share to the TTP

Lagent verifies that each share received by the merchant is valid by comparing each message digest in the receipt with the one carried by itself. After that *Lagent* sends the m th (or last) share to the TTP.

$$Lagent \rightarrow TTP : (F_{SUB}, Tid, Lagent, M, e_s(C), Share_m, x_m)^{P_{TTP}} .$$

5. *M* and *Lagent* retrieve the confirmed message from the TTP

Both *Lagent* and M have to retrieve the confirmed message from the TTP as part of the non-repudiation evidence required in a dispute. It is assumed that even in the case of network failures, both parties will eventually be able to retrieve the message from the TTP.

$$M \leftrightarrow TTP : (F_{CON}, Tid, Lagent, M, e_s(C), Share_m, x_m)^{V_{TTP}},$$

$$Lagent \leftrightarrow TTP : (F_{CON}, Tid, Lagent, M, Share_m, x_m)^{V_{TTP}}.$$

The two-sided arrow ($\leftrightarrow$) indicates that the transfer is initiated by the recipient through an ftp call.

6. Reconstruction of the secret key

Once the merchant gets all m shares, they reconstruct the secret key s using the Lagrange interpolation formula:

$$s = a_0 = \sum_{j=1}^{m} Share_j \prod_{1 \leq k \leq m, k \neq j} \frac{x_k}{x_k - x_j}. \tag{1}$$

7. Payment

The merchant decrypts the e-cash using $C = d_s(e_s(C))$, signs the e-cash with the merchant's private key V_M, and forwards it to the bank.

7.4.6 Correctness of the Protocol

We show that the secure payment protocol (SPP) presented above provides adequate protection under the threat model presented in the previous section. We do so through a couple of simple claims.

Claim 1. The protocol SPP ensures that the e-cash is protected against spying/stealing by $m - 1$ or fewer malicious MA hosts.

Proof. The e-cash is protected by encryption and it requires at least m agents to reconstruct the encryption key. Since all the transfers take place through secure channels, and at no point of the protocol has any one agent access to more than one share, this property is trivially guaranteed provided that the agent itinerary ensures that no MA host is ever visited by more than $m-1$ agents.

Note that the protocol will fail if there is collusion between the merchant and the host of *Lagent*.

Since the merchant receives $m-1$ shares from the other $m-1$ agents, the merchant simply needs to pass them to the host of the *Lagent*, who then uses that information to extract the e-cash.

Claim 2. The protocol produces evidence to support non-repudiation for both the customer and the merchant.

Proof. The nonrepudiable evidence is generated at steps 3, 4, and 5 of the payment phase. At step 3, the merchant signs and sends message digests of the $m-1$ shares already received by them. If these digests are not all valid, the *Lagent* will not complete the payment. If they are valid, they serve as evidence of M's receipt of the $m-1$ shares.

In step 4, the *Lagent* passes the last share as well as the encrypted e-cash to the TTP. This message is protected by encryption using the public key of the TTP. This ensures that the merchant cannot spy on the last share from this message.

This message need not be signed by *Lagent* as the TTP is trusted. (Otherwise it could have passed the message clandestinely to the merchant, later corrupting the data and producing untenable non-repudiation evidence.)

In step 5, both M and *Lagent* retrieve the message using ftp, which serves as the non-repudiable evidence of transfer of the last share as well as the e-cash.

In summary, at the end of this protocol, if *Lagent* wants to prove that the shares have been received, it presents

$$S_M(F_{REC}, Tid, M, Lagent, m-1 \text{ pairs } \{x_i, H(i)\})$$

and $$(F_{CON}, Tid, Lagent, M, e_s(C))$$

to the judge. The first piece of evidence confirms that M received the $m-1$ shares, and the second piece confirms that the last share was deposited with the TTP, which means that the merchant has access to it.

7.4.7 Efficiency of the Protocol

The message complexity of the protocol can be computed as follows. In the initialization phase, the *Lagent* sends $m-1$ messages of $O(1)$ length to $m-1$ participating agents. Each of the agents transfers its share to the merchant, using altogether $m-1$ messages of $O(1)$ length.

The merchant sends the single acknowledgement message of length $O(m-1)$ in step 3. In steps 4 and 5, three messages are transmitted, each of length $O(1)$. Thus altogether, the complexity of the messages communicated is $3O(m-1)+ 3O(1)$, whereas the total number of messages transferred is $3(m-1)+3 = 3m$.

The parameter m can be viewed as a measure of untrustworthiness of the host network. Therefore, it can be said that the cost of protection increases linearly with the number of untrustworthy hosts in the network. The secret key is distributed to n shares, m of them is enough to reconstruct the secret, $n \geq m$.

The larger m and n are, the more secure and reliable the protocol is. But at the same time, the cost increases. To select m and n one needs to find a good balance among the safety, reliability, cost, and efficiency of the protocol.

It is worth noting here that the protocol involves the TTP only for the transfer of the last share. So the TTP remains unaffected by the choice of m.

7.4.8 Limitations of the Protocol

The protocol discussed above is a very basic one and has several drawbacks that must be addressed effectively before it can be put to practical use. First of all, since the secret key is revealed at the end of each payment operation, the protocol requires a different key to be used for each payment transaction.

Second, since the value of the e-cash token is fixed at creation, this protocol cannot be used in cases where the amount to be paid is not known before the creation of the mobile agents.

Third, there are important additional security issues that need to be addressed. For example, if m or more of the mobile agents pass through any given untrusted host in the course of their nomadic lifetime, that host can gather all the information necessary to reconstruct the secret. To avoid this possibility, one can either preplan the itineraries of all the mobile agents or the mobile agents need to consult a central controlling agent for clearance to move to an intended site.

Another possible attack can be mounted in which a malicious host that hosts any one agent creates a fake merchant identity and makes up a payment order in which it makes itself the recipient site. However, any payment protocol is vulnerable to such an attack, and the only effective way to address this is by making the certification process more reliable.

7.4.9 An Electronic-Check-Based Payment Protocol

The constraints imposed by the SSP protocol presented above, namely the single use of secret keys and the predetermined amount of the payment can be removed with some modifications if the requirement for anonymity is given up. In what follows, we describe a modified version of the SSP protocol that uses electronic checks rather than e-cash and thus no longer provides anonymity to the customer.

The exposure of the secret key at the end of each transaction can be avoided by using a homomorphic secret sharing scheme [7.19]. We can partition the private key in a way that each mobile agent can partially encrypt or sign the message without revealing their share to the combiner. After the last partial signature, the document is completely signed with the shared private key, and none of the shareholders learns about any other shares. The combiner can get the whole signature after each mobile agent has signed without knowing the private key. This concept is explored further in [7.20].

Let g be an encryption function, if g is homomorphic it satisfies the following equation:

$$g(k_1 + k_2) = g(k_1) \times g(k_2) . \tag{2}$$

If $k_1 + k_2$ is the encryption key, then a threshold cryptographic system may be constructed [7.21]. As an example, in computing an RSA signature one computes $g_h(s) = h^s \bmod n$, where $h = H(message)$ is the message digest, s is the secret key, $n = p \times q$ is the public modulus, and p and q are two distinct large primes. From (1), and with careful choice of p and q, Shamir's scheme satisfies the property

$$s = \sum_{i \in Q} (\text{constant}_{i,Q} \times s_i) , \tag{3}$$

where Q is a quorum subset of the set of all participants, called A, and $|Q| = m$ is the threshold value. From (1), the terms $\text{constant}_{i,Q}$ can be obtained from the known values of x_i as follows:

$$\text{constant}_{i,Q} = \prod_{i,k \in Q, k \neq i} \frac{x_k}{x_k - x_i}.$$ (4)

Hence, when combined with a homomorphic g, one obtains:

$$g_h(s) = g_h \sum_{i \in Q} \text{constant}_{i,Q} \times s_i$$ (5)

$$= \prod_{i \in Q} g_h(\text{constant}_{i,Q} \times s_i)$$

$$= \prod_{i \in Q} g_h(s_i)^{\text{constant}_{i,Q}}$$

Thus, an RSA signature can be computed using partial signatures, yet both the private key s and the various shadows remain secret even after combining the shares.

The payment protocol based on e-check is described briefly in the following steps:

Step 1. The customer first distributes her private key s using a polynomial of degree $m-1$, and gets n shadows s_i by evaluating the polynomial at n different points x_i. The customer creates n mobile agents with $\{x_i, s_i\}$ and dispatches them to n different hosts through secure channels.

Step 2. Whenever any of the customer agents, say $agent_j$, wishes to make a payment against a properly authenticated payment order sent by the relevant merchant, it creates an e-check C of an appropriate amount, computes $h = H(C)$ and then a partial signature $g_h(s_j)$. The agent sends $\{C, g_h(s_j), x_j\}$ along with proper identifiers to the merchant through a secure channel. At the same time it sends the payment order and a copy of the check C to randomly selected $m-1$ other customer agents.

Step 3. All the *m-1* customer agents that receive the above message generate their own partial signature $g_h(s_i)$ and send $\{g_h(s_i), x_i\}$ along with proper identifiers to the merchant through a secure channel.

Step 4. After collecting m partial signatures, the merchant combines them to obtain the fully signed e-check $g_h(s)$ using the formula given in (5).

Note that a TTP can be involved if a non-repudiation service is needed. In this case, the leader agent will send its partially signed check through the TTP instead of sending it directly to the merchant and a protocol similar to the one described using e-cash can be used to ensure proper documentation.

It may be noted that since this protocol involves the signature of the customer, it does not support the anonymity of the customer.

7.4.10 Possibility of Combining Anonymity with Reuse of Secret Key by Payment Agent

To protect a payment agent from malicious usurpation, one must ensure that no agent ever has complete knowledge of a validated instrument of payment, such as cash or a signed check. As we have seen in the preceding section, using a threshold encryption scheme, a set of mobile agents can generate an e-check of arbitrary amount independently of any intervention by the owner and can complete payment in a secure manner. However, this process requires the customer agents to give up anonymity. The question is whether it is possible to combine the flexibility of making payments in arbitrary denominations a multiple number of times using a single secret key while retaining anonymity. With the available cryptographic techniques that seems to be impossible at the time being. Whether it is possible at all is debatable, and it is best to withhold any conclusion until it is proven formally either way.

7.5 Summary

In this chapter, we have addressed the problem of protecting sensitive information carried by mobile agents from malicious hosts, and proposed two payment protocols using Shamir's secret sharing scheme. One of the protocols is based on electronic cash that allows the customer to carry out transactions anonymously. But it imposes two constraints, namely, the amount to be paid must be predetermined, and secondly for each payment transaction a new secret key needs to be used. The second protocol, which is based on electronic check payment, removes these constraints at the cost of anonymity. The protocols guarantee protection of confidential data, such as electronic cash, against concerted attack by a known maximum number of malicious hosts. In addition, by making optional use of a TTP in a minimal way, it produces non-repudiable evidence of transfer of funds from the customer to the merchant.

7.6 References

[7.1]   A. Chavez, P. Maes (1996) Kasbah: an agent marketplace for buying and selling goods. In: Proceedings of the First International Conference on the Practical Application of Intelligent Agents and Multi-agent Technology.

[7.2]   J. G. Lee, J. Y. Kang, E. S. Lee (1997) ICOMA: an open infrastructure for agent-based intelligent electronic commerce on the Internet. In: Proceedings of the International Conference on Parallel and Distributed Systems.

[7.3]   P. Maes, R. H. Guttman, A. G. Moukas (1999) Agents that buy and sell: transforming commerce as we know it. Comm ACM (March Issue).

[7.4]   A. Moukas, R. Guttman, P. Maes (1998) Agent-mediated electronic commerce: an {MIT} media laboratory perspective. In: Proceedings of ICEC Conference, 1998.

[7.5]   M. Tsvetovatyy, M. Gini (1996) Toward a virtual marketplace: architectures and strategies. In: Proceedings of the First International Conference on the Practical Application of Intelligent Agent and Multi-agent Technology (PAAM'96), Blackpool, 1996.

[7.6]   M. Tsvetovatyy, M. Gini, B. Mobasher, Z. Wieckowski (1997) MAGMA: an agent-based virtual market for electronic commerce. J Appl Artificial Intelligence.

[7.7]   A. Young, M. Yung (1997) Encryption tools for mobile agents: sliding encryption. In E. Biham (ed.) Fast software encryption – FSE'97, LNCS 1267. Springer, Berlin Heidelberg New York.

[7.8]   F. Hohl (1997) An approach to solve the problem of a malicious host. Report No. 1997, Universität Stuttgart, Fakultät Informatik.

[7.9]   T. Sander, C. Tschudin (1997) Towards mobile cryptography. Technical Report, International Computer Science Institute, Berkeley.

[7.10] T. Sander, C. Tschudin (1997) Protecting mobile agents against malicious hosts. In: Mobile agent security, Springer, Berlin Heidelberg New York.

[7.11] M. Bellare, P. Rogaway (1994) Optimal asymmetric encryption. In: Eurocrypt 94, LNCS 950. Springer, Berlin Heidelberg New York.

[7.12] R. Rivest, A. Shamir, L. Adleman (1978) A method for obtaining digital signatures and public key cryptosystems. Commun ACM 21(2): 120–126.

[7.13]   A. Das, G. Yao (2001) A secure payment protocol using mobile agents in an untrusted host environment. In: W. Kou, et al. (eds.) Electronic commerce technologies – ISEC 2001, LNCS 2040. Springer, Berlin Heidelberg New York.

[7.14]   G. Yao (2001) Security mechanisms for mobile agent-based e-commerce systems. Master's Thesis, Nanyang Technological University.

[7.15]   A. Shamir (1979) How to share a secret. Commun ACM 22:612–613.

[7.16]   D. Chaum (1989) Online cash checks. In: Proceedings of Advances in Cryptography–Eurocrypt'89, LNCS 434. Springer, Berlin Heidelberg New York.

[7.17]   S. A. Brands (1993) An efficient off-line electronic cash system based on the representation problem. Technical Report CSR9323, Computer Science Department, CWI, US.

[7.18]   S. Brands (1994) Untraceable off-line cash in wallet with observers. In: Advances in Cryptology–CRYPTO'93. Springer, Berlin Heidelberg New York.

[7.19]   J. C. Benaloh (1997) Secret sharing homomorphisms: keeping shares of a secret secret. In: A. Odlyzko (ed.), Advances in Cryptology, Proc. of Crypto'86, Santa Barbara, CA, US, Aug. 1987.

[7.20]   Y. Desmedt (1997) Some recent research aspects of threshold cryptography. In: E. Okamoto, et al. (eds.), Information security, LNCS 1396. Springer, Berlin Heidelberg New York.

[7.21]   N. Jacobson (1985) Basic algebra, I.W.H. Freeman, New York.

8 Digital Cash

Yi Mu[1], Vijay Varadharajan[1], and Khanh Quoc Nguyen[2]

[1] Department of Computing, Macquarie University,
Sydney, Australia

[2] Gemplus Technologies Asia,
12 Ayer Rajah Crescent, Singapore

8.1 Introduction

A digital-cash system normally consists of clients, vendors, and a bank. Any legitimate client can obtain a valid digital coin[1] from a bank and anonymously send the coin to a vendor. The vendor later deposits the coin to the bank. Because of the anonymity of the client, the bank can validate the coin but cannot link the coin to the information used in the coin-issuing process. The bank and the vendor cannot trace transactions made by the client.

The first digital-cash scheme was proposed by Chuam [8.1]. The transaction untraceability proposed in Chaum's digital-cash is based on the use of zero-knowledge proofs, which is computationally expensive and is not efficient enough for any real applications. Some subsequent works [8.2, 8.3, 8.6, 8.7] have achieved various improvements on Chaum's scheme. In particular, protocols proposed by Brands [8.2] and Ferguson [8.6] achieve transaction untraceability without requiring zero-knowledge proofs.

There are several forms of digital-cash. Besides the normal digital-cash, there are two additional catalogs: divisible digital-cash and fair digital-cash.

The first divisible digital-cash scheme was proposed by Okamoto [8.7], and then two more efficient methods were proposed [8.8, 8.9]. The divisible digital-cash scheme allows a user to divide a digital coin into several even

---

[1] For convenience, we use "digital coin" to represent a monetary unit of digital cash.

pieces that can be used as normal digital coins. Fair digital-cash schemes are applied to restricting unconditional privacy of clients. In a normal digital-cash system, there is no any mechanism for banks and vendors to identify a client in a transaction without breaking the underlying number theoretic assumptions. This protection, which is desirable from client's viewpoint, is a major concern for law enforcement agencies. It was pointed out in [8.16, 8.31] that anonymous e-cash can be a "safe haven" for criminal activities that include money laundering, illegal purchases, perfect blackmailing and other attacks. This prevents the deployment of anonymous digital-cash cash systems in a large scale, where such attacks and many others are often expected. In a fair digital-cash system, a designated trusted third party can compute the identity of a client when necessary.

In this chapter, we will introduce three typical digital-cash schemes: the digital-cash scheme proposed by Brands [8.2], and the digital-cash and the fair digital-cash scheme proposed by Nguyen et. al. [8.14, 8.14].

8.2 Security Requirements for Digital Cash

Digital-cash must not be illegally forgeable and cannot be double spent. In the meanwhile, digital-cash must also have such properties as providing anonymity to clients and untraceability to digital coins. In general, Digital-cash should have the following security properties:

- Unforgeability. This is the basic requirement for digital-cash. Digital cash must not be able to be forged in a polynomial time frame.
- Untraceability. Once a digital coin is issued, it is not traceable by the bank and any other parties.
- Anonymity. The identity of the digital-cash owner should not be revealed. That is, given a digital coin, any other parties cannot find the identity of the owner.
- Double-spending detection. A digital coin can be used only once, bounded by its monetary value. Any attempt at duplication of a coin or double uses of a coin can be detected by the bank that has signed the coin.
- Fairness. In fair digital-cash, the anonymity of a coin owner is conditional. There is a trusted third party who can find the identity of the coin owner when the coin has been illegally used.

8.3 Brands' Digital-Cash Scheme

Brands proposed the first digital-cash scheme without using cut-and-choose, therefore it is much more efficient than Chaum's original scheme. In this section, we introduce Brands' scheme. Like Chaum's scheme, Brands' digital-cash scheme has four phases: opening an account, withdrawal, payment, and deposit. For simplicity of the following presentation, we have slightly modified the scheme without compromising its security.

8.3.1 The Setup

We first give some general notations to be used in Brands' digital-cash scheme.

- p: a large prime
- q: an integer satisfying $q | p - 1$
- $\mathbb{Z}_p^*$: a multiplicative group of prime order q satisfying $q | p - 1$
- $\mathbb{G}_q$: a multiplicative group of prime order q and $\mathbb{G}_q \subset \mathbb{Z}_p^*$
- $\mathbb{Z}_q$: a finite field of size q
- $\mathcal{H}(.)$: a strong correlation-free one-way hash function $\mathcal{H}(.) \in \mathbb{Z}_q$

The system consists of clients, merchants, and a bank. We denote by C a client, M a merchant, and B a bank.

B chooses $(g_1, g_2, g_3) \in_R \mathbb{G}_q^3$ as generators and a number $x \subset_R \mathbb{Z}_q$ as its private key, and then computes its public key $z = g^x \bmod p$. For simplicity, we will omit modulo p in the following protocols.

8.3.2 Opening an Account

To open an account, C and B follow the following steps:

1. The client C needs to identify himself to the bank B, when opening an account by, for example, showing his passport to B.
2. C selects a secret random number $U \in_R \mathbb{Z}_q$ and computes $I = g_1^U$ where $g_1^U g_2 \neq 1$, then sends I to B.
3. B stores C's identification information along with I. I will be used as C's account number.

The security of U is based on the difficulty of solving discrete logarithm. In other words, if C spends a digital coin related to I once, his identity U cannot be computed within a polynomial time frame.

8.3.3 The Withdrawal Protocol

To withdraw a coin from B, C needs first identify himself to B and prove his ownership of the account. The following withdrawal protocol is then performed (also see Fig. 8.1).

1. B generates a number $w \in_R \mathbb{Z}_q$ and sends $a = g^w$ and $b = (Ig_2)^w$ to C.
2. C generates three numbers $s, x_1, x_2 \in_R \mathbb{Z}_q$ and computes $A = (Ig_2)^s$, $B = g_1^{x_1} g_2^{x_2}$, and $z' = z^s$. C also generates two numbers $u, v \in_R \mathbb{Z}_q$ and uses them to compute $a' = a^u g^v$ and $b' = b^{su} A^v$. C then computes the challenge $c' = \mathcal{H}(A, B, z', a', b')$, and sends the blinded challenge $c = c'/u \bmod q$ to B.
3. B sends the response $r = cx + w \bmod q$ to C, and debits the account of C.

C accepts iff $g^r = h^c a$ and $(Ig_2)^r = z^c b$. If this verification holds, C computes $r' = ru + v \bmod q$. The withdrawn coin consists of (A, B, z', a', b', r').

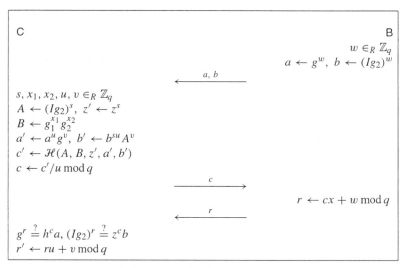

Fig. 8.1 The coin withdrawal protocol

8.3.4 The Payment Protocol

When C wants to spend his coin at V, the following protocol is performed.

1. C sends A, B, and Sign(A, B) to V, where Sign(A, B), which represents B's signature on a pair $(A, B) \in (G_q)^2$, is the tuple (A, B, z', a', b', r').

2. V computes a challenge $d = \mathcal{H}_0(A, B, ID_V, Date/Time)$ and sends d to C.

3. Upon receipt of c, C computes the responses $r_1 = du_1 s + x_1 \bmod q$ and $r_2 = ds + x_2 \bmod q$, and then sends them to C.

V accepts the coin iff Sign(A, B) is valid and $g_1^{r_1} g_2^{r_2} = A^d B$.

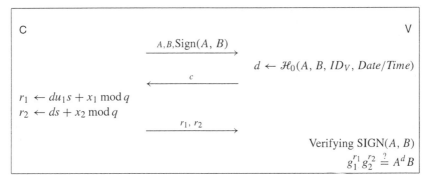

Fig. 8.2 The payment protocol

8.3.5 The Deposit Protocol

V sends the payment transcript of a coin to B. B needs to check if the coin has been stored before. If not, B stores $(A, Date/Time, r_1, r_2)$ in its database as being deposited by V, and credits the account of V. However, if the coin has been spent before, a double-spending fraud must have occurred. A double-spending can be easily detected, since the challenges are different. B can obtain a triplet (c, r_1, r_2) from the new transcript and a triplet (c', r_1', r_2') from the deposited information. B can compute $I = g_1^{(r_1 - r_1')/(r_2 - r_2')}$ and then search its database for this account number.

8.4 One-Response Digital Cash

Current offline digital-cash systems [8.1, 8.4, 8.6] tend to provide double-spending detection, client anonymity, and transaction untraceability. However, as there is always a trade-off between double-spending detection and transaction untraceability, the computational cost is often high. Even in the most efficient systems [8.4, 8.6], many discrete exponential computations are required for each digital monetary unit in order to achieve the untraceability. To design an electronic-payment system that allows small payment amounts, heavy use of discrete exponential computations must be avoided. In fact, this requirement makes all current offline cash systems economically infeasible.

In this section, we introduce an efficient approach [8.13] to offline digital-cash schemes that makes small payment amounts possible. This scheme maintains the basic features in digital-cash: client anonymity and double-spending detection. The computational efficiency achieved in this scheme is due to the use of one-way hash functions that make clients perform only *one* major computation and perform no discrete exponential computations in the payment phase. This feature leads to a significant improvement in computational efficiency in contrast to all previously proposed schemes.

8.4.1 Schnorr's One-Time Signature Scheme

Schnorr's one-time signature scheme [8.11] is used for this digital-cash scheme. Let p and q be prime such that q is a prime factor of $p - 1$. Let $g \in \mathbb{Z}_p^*$ be the multiplicative primitive, where $g \neq 1$ and $g^q \equiv 1$. Again, we omit the modulo p in our presentation.

To generate a particular pair of private key and public key, a user (say, Alice) chooses a random number s as her private key, $0 < s < q$. Alice then computes her public key v as $v = g^{-s}$.

To sign a message m, Alice picks a random number $r \in \mathbb{Z}_q$ and does the following computations:

$$x = g^r$$
$$c = \mathcal{H}(m \| x)$$
$$y = (r + sc) \bmod q,$$

where $\mathcal{H}(.)$ is a suitable collision-free one-way hash function. The signature on the message m is the pair (c, y). To verify the signature, we check: $x \stackrel{?}{=} g^y v^c$ and check if c is equal to $h(m \| x)$.

8.4.2 The One-Response Digital-Cash Protocol

We assume that each *coin* in this scheme represents a monetary unit. The face value of each coin is decided by the bank. We denote by C_i a coin with an abstract face value c_i. We also assume that the bank has a RSA public/secret key (e, d) with the composite modulo n of the product of two large prime numbers, q_1, q_2, and a number g such that $g^q \equiv 1$ and $gcd(g - 1, n) = 1$. The values of g, p, q, n, and e are public.

Account opening phase. When C wishes to open an account at B, after identifying himself to B, C uses a zero-knowledge process to obtain a blind-signature from B on $h(g^U)$ as $(h(g^U))^d \bmod n$. U is constructed as $U = I\|k$ ($0 < U < q$) by C, where $\|$ denotes a concatenation of bits, k is a random number, and I is the client identity registered with the bank (also referred as the client's bank account number). The bank should not have any knowledge about the value of k and consequently the value of U. There have been several such zero-knowledge processes[2] described in the literature; see, for instance, [8.12, 8.10].

The length of I and k should be fixed, at least 80 bits each, so that given g^U, it is feasible to obtain I. After the account's opening phase, the client has an anonymous bank certificate $Cert$ as $(h(g^U))^d \bmod n$. This certificate would remain anonymous as long as nobody is able to compute U. Extracting U from $Cert$ is infeasible unless the client double-spends under the discrete logarithms assumption (Further discussions will be given later.) After the account-opening process, C stores $Cert$ and $g_C = g^U$.

Withdrawal phase. Before withdrawing any money from the bank, the client C proves his ownership of I to B. If the client wishes to withdraw k coins, he chooses a random number c_k and computes $c_i = h(c_{i+1})$ for $\forall i \in \{1, \ldots, k-1\}$. For each c_i, C uses a blind signature technique[8.5] to withdraw an anonymous coin from B using the following protocol (see Fig. 8.3):

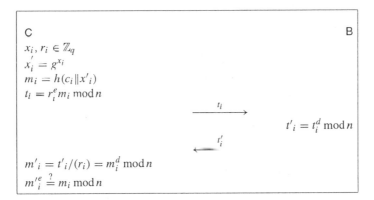

Fig. 8.3 The withdrawal protocol

---

[2] A cut-and-choose method has to be used in the proof. To avoid it, a trusted third party may be included for verifying correctness of $h(g^U)$ and signs it prior to the bank's signing.

1. C generates a random number $x_i \in_R \mathbb{Z}_q$, and computes: $x'_i = g^{x_i}, m_i = h(c_i \| x'_i)$.

2. C then uses blind signature technique [8.5] to obtain a bank signature on m_i by choosing a blind factor r_i and sending $t_i = r_i^e m_i \bmod n$ to B. B signs the value of t_i and returns the signature as t'_i. The client then removes the blind factor r_i to obtain the bank blind signature $m'_i = t'_i / r_i = m_i^d \bmod n$.

For each signature, the bank deducts the client's account by an equivalent value of a coin. After the withdrawal, C has each coin C_i with a face value of c_i in the form of $[h(c_i \| x'_i)]^d \bmod n$. It is unforgeable unless the factorisation of n is known.[8.1] For each coin C_i, C stores $[c_i, x_i, x'_i, m'_i]$.

Payment phase. When the client wants to spend the coin chain $C_1, C_2, \ldots, C_n$ to V, he must spend them in the order $C_1, C_2, \ldots, C_n$.

Without the loss of generality, we assume that C has already spent all the coins $C_0, C_1, \ldots, C_{i-1}$ in some previous payments. Now if C wishes to pay some coins to V, C must send the coins to V in the exact sequence $C_i, C_{i+1}, \cdots, C_j, \cdots$ according to the following process:

- For the first coin C_i (see also Figure 8.4):

    1. V generates a random challenge a and sends it to C. This challenge should be unique for each transaction. For example, it can be computed as $a = h(C \| V \| Date \| Time)$.

    2. C computes the response $b = x_i - Ua \bmod q$ for the challenge a and sends it along with $(Cert, g_C, b, c_i, x'_i, m'_i)$ to V. The response b is also considered as Schnorr's one-time signature on the message a, where x_i is a one-time value.

    V accepts the coin if and only if $Cert$ and m'_i are valid bank signatures on g_C and $\mathcal{H}(c_i \| x'_i)$, respectively, and $g_C^a g^b = x'_i$.

- For every coin C_j, thereafter (see also Fig. 8.5):

    C sends (x_j, c_j, m'_j) to V. V accepts the coin C_j if and only if $h(c_j) = c_{j-1}$ (where c_{j-1} was obtained from the previous coin) and m'_j is a valid bank signature on $h(c_j \| g^{x_j})$.

For the sake of convenience, let us name the first coin C_i as *signed coin* and all the other coins C_j as *normal coins*.

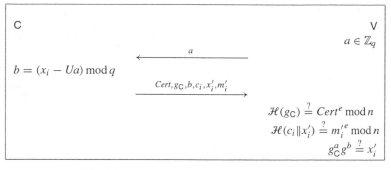

Fig. 8.4 The payment protocol for the first coin

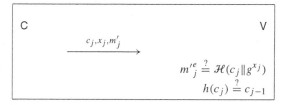

Fig. 8.5 The payment protocol

Deposit phase. In deposit phase, V deposits all the received coins at B by sending $(Cert, g_C, a, b, c_i, x_i', m_i')$ for each signed coin and (c_j, x_j, m_j') for each normal coin. B goes through exactly the same verification process as V did in the payment phase. If everything is OK, B pays V an equivalent amount of money and stores (a, b, c_i) for the first coin, (c_j, x_j) for each other coin in its coin database.

8.4.3 Discussion

In this section, we will closely examine security and efficiency features of the system, including double-spending detection, client anonymity, and efficiency.

Double spending. Double-spending occurs when C double spends some coins in the hope that B cannot detect the identity. In our protocol, double-spending is detected as follows:

When C double spends some coins, for the first double-spent coin C_i, it must be a signed coin in at least one transaction. So there are only two possibilities: C_i is spent as either a signed coin in the both transactions or as a signed coin in one transaction and as a normal coin in another transaction.

- Double spend a coin as signed coins: C spends C_i as a signed coin twice, i.e., for two different challenges a and a', B therefore has $b = x_i - Ua \mod q$ and $b' = x_i - Ua' \mod q$. B can easily find U by computing:

$$U = \frac{b - b'}{a' - a} \mod q$$

- Spend a coin as a signed coin and as a normal coin: C spends C_i twice, once as a normal coin and the other as a signed coin. B therefore has a and $x_i - Ua$ from the signed coin and x_i from the normal coin. This information is sufficient to compute U.

So in either case, the value U can be computed. After obtaining U, B extracts I and matches it with the client's ID stored in its database. Once, a match is found, B asks C to reveal the value U incorporated in his *Cert*. If this value matches the value U obtained by B from the first double-spent coin, C must have double spent the coin. The evidence is *undeniable* because U is client's secret information, which is infeasible for anyone else to compute unless the client had double spent a coin.

Anonymity. Client anonymity is protected unconditionally in this scheme. The zero-knowledge process used in the account's opening phase completely hides the identity of the client. The bank will not be able to link *Cert* to C's ID, once *Cert* is issued. On the other hand, our coins are blindly signed by the bank so the bank cannot trace any particular coin to any particular client.

During the payment process, the client only has to show *Cert*, which is an anonymous certificate and reveals $x_i - Ua \mod q$ for each signed coin and x_j for each normal coin. For two different coins, as their corresponding (x_i, x_j) are chosen at random, they are different and unlinkable. Having only a, B cannot obtain U from $x_i - Ua \mod q$ (since x_i is chosen at random).

Efficiency. The account's opening phase is a one-off process, so even though the zero-knowledge process is inefficient, it will not affect the efficiency of the system for any transaction later on.

The withdrawal phase is very efficient. To withdraw a coin, ignoring the number of hash operations, C computes only two exponentiations. The number of discrete exponentiations required in Chaum's [8.1], Ferguson's [8.6], Brands' [8.4] protocols are forty, seventeen, and ten, respectively. In contrast to these schemes, this protocol needs only two multiplication operations.

In the payment protocol, for the whole transaction, the client only has to compute a single response, i.e., $b = x_i - Ua \mod q$. This is far more efficient than all off-line digital-cash schemes known todate, especially as the response message does not involve any discrete exponential computation. Moreover, the vendor, in the payment phase, does not need to perform any complicated verification. In fact, the vendor only has to verify one RSA signature per coin plus a certification *Cert* and a Schnorr's one-time signature for each transaction.

Hence the protocol is much more efficient than other existing digital-cash schemes such as those in [8.1, 8.4, 8.6, 8.12].

8.5 Fair Digital Cash

Brickell, Gemmell, and Kravitz [8.16] proposed an escrowed digital-cash scheme to control unconditional privacy of clients, often known as *fair digital-cash*. The main feature of fair digital-cash is the existence of a trusted authority or a revocation authority that can revoke the anonymity of any given coin. A different and more efficient scheme was later proposed by Camenisch, Piveteau, and Stadler [8.27]. Both schemes require the revocation authority to be actively involved in every withdrawal and thus are not desirable.

Frankel, et. al. [8.25] and Camenisch, et. al. [8.20] respectively proposed a fair digital-cash scheme employing an off-line revocation authority. The advantage of this approach is that the revocation authority is not involved in any payment transaction. When needed, the revocation authority can be called upon to identify the owner of a coin or a transaction. The most efficient schemes to date are those by Davida, Frankel, Tsiounis, and Yung [8.24] and by Camenisch, Maurer, and Stadler [8.20]. Both of these two schemes are constructed from Brands' anonymous e-cash scheme.

In this section, we will not describe all fair-digital-cash schemes, whereas we introduce the concept of fair-digital-cash by using a typical model that uses an off-line revocation authority [8.28]. This fair-digital-cash scheme is based on Nyberg–Rueppel digital signature scheme and thus poses as an alternative to Schnorr-based fair-digital-cash schemes.

In a fair e-cash scheme, there are the following parties, a bank B, a trusted authority T, vendors, and clients. We denote by V a vendor and by C a client.

A fair e-cash scheme consists of five basic protocols, three of them are the same as in anonymous e-cash, i.e., a withdrawal protocol, a payment protocol, and a deposit protocol. The two additional protocols are conducted between B and T, *owner-tracing* and *coin-tracing* protocols.

- In the owner-tracing protocol, B gives to T the view of a deposit protocol and T returns a string that contains some specific information which allows B to identify the owner of the coin.
- In the coin-tracing protocol, B gives to T the view of a withdrawal protocol and T returns some specific information that allows B to identify the coin in the deposit phase.

These two additional protocols provide the revocation capacity and the protection against certain types of attacks. For instance, the owner-tracing protocol allows the authorities to identify the origin of dubious coins and thus eliminates money laundering. The coin-tracing protocol allows the authorities to find the destination of dubious coins and thus eliminates blackmailing.

In the following, we will first introduce a digital-cash scheme based on Nyberg–Rueppel digital-signature scheme[8.21] and then convert it to a fair version.

8.5.1 Nyberg-Rueppel Digital-Signature Scheme

The key generation protocol works as follows. Let p be a large prime and q be equal to $p - 1$ or a large integer factor of $p - 1$. Also let g be a random generator of $\mathbb{G}_q \subset \mathbb{Z}_p^*$. Each signer chooses $x \in_R \mathbb{Z}_q^*$ and computes $h = g^x \bmod p$, where (x, h) is his secret and secret-public key pair. Again, we omit the modulo p in our presentation.

To sign a message $m \in \mathbb{Z}_p$, the signer selects a random number $w \in \mathbb{Z}_q$ and computes r and s as

$$r = mg^w \text{ and } s = xr + w \bmod q.$$

The pair (r, s) is the signature of the message m. To verify the signature, we check

$$m = g^{-s}h^r r.$$

This signature scheme can be converted into a blind version using the protocol given in Fig. 8.6.

The pair (r', s') is a blind signature on message m. The correctness of the signature is shown as follows:

$$
\begin{aligned}
g^{-s'}h^{r'}r' &= mg^{-s\beta - \alpha + xr' + w\beta + \alpha} \\
&= mg^{-m'x\beta - w\beta + r'x + w\beta} \\
&= mg^{xr' - xm'\beta} = m.
\end{aligned}
$$

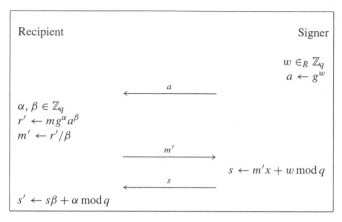

Fig. 8.6 Blind Nyberg–Rueppel digital signature scheme

The blindness holds because if α and β are chosen at random, r' and m are uniformly distributed in their respective domains. As r' and m uniquely identify s', (r', s', m) is a random triplet and independent of the signer's view.

No apparent security weakness of this protocol is known. Some security proofs of this protocol have been discussed in [8.19, 8.30]. Particularly, [8.30] shows that the view of the signer in the protocol and the signature are statistically independent, i.e., generated signatures are witness-indistinguishable.

8.5.2 The Digital Cash Scheme

In this section, we take a look at a previously proposed digital-cash scheme, which is based on the blind Nyberg–Rueppel digital-signature scheme. [8.28]

The setup protocol. On inputting a security parameter k, the bank B runs a key generation algorithm to generate:

- a large prime p and a large number q such that $q | p - 1$,
- three generators g, g_1 and g_2 of the unique subgroup $\mathbb{G}_q$ of the multiplicative group $\mathbb{Z}_p^*$,
- a randomly chosen collision-intractable hash function $\mathcal{H}(.)$ of polynomial size of k that maps its inputs to $\mathbb{Z}_q$,
- a random number $x \in \mathbb{Z}_q$ and
- $h_1 = g_1^x$ and $h_2 = g_2^x$.

B has now the secret key x and the public tuple $(p, q, g_1, g_2, h, h_1, h_2, \mathcal{H}(.))$ respectively.

The account setup. The setup phase is similar to those we studied previously in this chapter. To set up an account at B, C chooses $U \neq 0 \in_R \mathbb{G}_q$ at random and calculates $I = g_1^U$. B regards $I \neq 1$ as C's account identification and sends $z = (Ig_2)^x$ to C. Note that I is the unique link to the user's real name, while U is unknown to the bank. U can be computed by the bank only when the user double spends a coin.

The withdrawal protocol. The withdrawal protocol between C and B is given in Fig. 8.7.

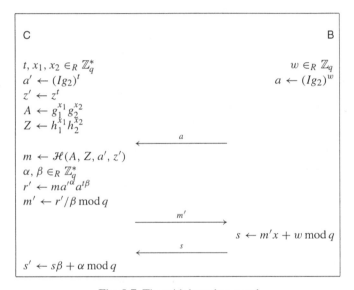

Fig. 8.7 The withdrawal protocol

The blind Nyberg–Rueppel signature scheme is essential for the anonymity of clients. Note that the base used in the protocol is not the fixed base g of the signer public key, but the base $(Ig_2)^t$ for a random number t chosen by the user. At the end of the withdrawal protocol, the client should receive the blind Nyberg–Rueppel signature $\text{Sign}(A, Z) = (A, Z, z', a', r', s')$, which is verified using the equation

$$\mathcal{H}(A, Z, a', z') = a'^{-s'} z'^{/r'} r'.$$

It is important to verify that the secret key used in the signature generation is the secret key x of the bank. Otherwise, the user can create such a signature using any secret key. This verification is described in the payment protocol.

The payment protocol. The payment protocol is run between C and V. The payment of a coin (A, Z, z', a', r', s') is described in Fig. 8.8. As for the proof of equality of

C   V

$$c \leftarrow \mathcal{H}(V\|Date\|Time\| \dots)$$

$r_1 \leftarrow c(ut) + x_1 \bmod q \quad \xleftarrow{\quad c \quad}$

$r_2 \leftarrow ct + x_2 \bmod q$

$\xrightarrow{\quad r_1, r_2, \ Sign(A,Z) \quad} \quad \mathcal{H}(A, Z, a', z') \overset{?}{=} a'^{-s'} z'^{r'} r'$

$$g_1^{r_1} g_2^{r_2} \overset{?}{=} a'^{c} A$$

$$h_1^{r_1} h_2^{r_2} \overset{?}{=} z'^{c} Z$$

Fig. 8.8 The payment protocol

discrete logarithms, for a random challenge c if

$$g_1^{r_1} g_2^{r_2} \overset{?}{=} a'^{c} A,$$
$$h_1^{r_1} h_2^{r_2} \overset{?}{=} z'^{c} Z,$$

we must have $\log_{a'} z' = \log_{g_1} h_1$. This shows that the bank's secret key $x = \log_{g_1} h_1$ was used in the generation of $Sign(A, Z)$.

The deposit protocol. V can deposit the coin $Sign(A, Z)$ at any suitable time. The deposit procedure is to send the transcript of the payment to B. B verifies the payment procedure and accepts the coin if V follows the procedure correctly and the coin satisfies all verifications as checked in the payment phase.

8.5.3 The Fair-Digital-Cash Scheme

We now convert the digital-cash scheme described previously in this section into a fair version.

The setup. The setup phase is similar to the original scheme. Here, we give only the difference. Let $x \in \mathbb{Z}_q$ be the secret key of B. The public data of B consists of tuple: $(p, q, g_1, g_2, g_3, h_1 = g_1^x, h_2 = g_2^x)$, where $(g_1, g_2, g_3) \in (\mathbb{Z}_p^*)^3$. To set up an account at B, C chooses $U \neq 0 \in_R \mathbb{G}_q$ at random and calculates $I = g_1^U$. B regards $I \neq 1$ as C's account identification and sends $z = (Ig_2g_3)^x$ to C.

The trusted authority T's secret key is $\tau \in \mathbb{Z}_q$ and his public key is the doublet $(h_{T1} = g_1^\tau, h_{T2} = g_2^\tau)$.

The withdrawal protocol. The withdrawal protocol is executed between C and B. Formally, the protocol is given in Fig. 8.9.

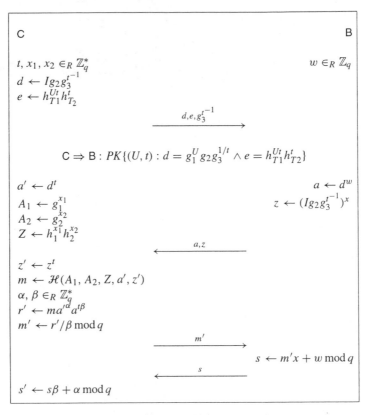

Fig. 8.9 The withdrawal protocol

The withdrawal protocol is basically the blind Nyberg–Rueppel digital signature scheme but the base is $d^t = (Ig_2)^t g_3$. At the end of the withdrawal protocol, the user should receive the blind Nyberg–Rueppel signature

$$\text{Sign}(A_1, A_2, Z) = (A_1, A_2, Z, z', a', r', s')$$

which is verified using the equation

$$\mathcal{H}(A_1, A_2, Z, a', z') = a'^{-s'} z'^{r'} r'.$$

Besides $(A_1, A_2, Z, z', a', r', s')$, the bank also stores the value e, given below, in the coin database for referencing.

In this protocol, the value A is split into two values A_1 and A_2. This is necessary to achieve owner tracing. The extra computation of (d, e) and the associate proof of knowledge

$$PK\{(U, t) : d = g_1^U g_2 g_3^{1/t} \wedge e = h_{T1}^{Ut} h_{T2}^t\},$$

will be used to achieve coin tracing, where we meant that the prover proves his knowledge on (U, t) from the given (d, e) without revealing the value of (U, t). This notation will also be used later on. The details of the proofs can be found in the Appendix.

The payment protocol. The payment protocol is run between C and V. The payment of a coin $(A_1, A_2, Z, z', a', r', s')$ is described in Figure 8.10. The payment protocol

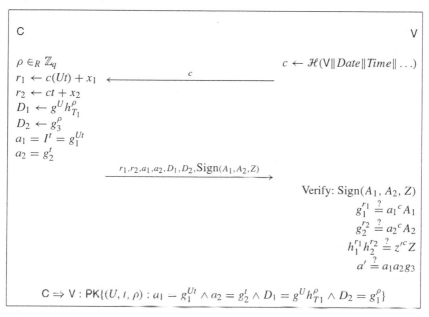

Figure 8.10 The payment protocol

is similar to the payment protocol of the original scheme, whereas C now splits a' into $a_1 = I^t = g_1^{Ut}$ and $a_2 = g_2^t$ and proves to V that

$$PK\{(U, t, \rho) : a_1 = g_1^{Ut} \wedge a_2 = g_2^t \wedge D_1 = g^U h_{T1}^{\rho} \wedge D_2 = g_1^{\rho}\}.$$

This proof is used to achieve user tracing.

The deposit protocol. V can deposit the coin $Sign(A_1, A_2, Z)$ at any suitable time. The deposit procedure is to send the transcript of the payment to B. B verifies the payment procedure and accepts the coin if V follows the procedure correctly and the coin satisfies all verifications as checked in the payment phase.

The completeness of the scheme is straightforward. As the scheme is developed using our proposed anonymous-digital-cash scheme, it is easy to show that this fair-digital-cash scheme satisfies all security requirements of the anonymous e-cash scheme, e.g., unforgeability. It remains to show that user tracing and coin tracing can be satisfied.

Anonymity revocation. There are two possible anonymity controls in this scheme. One is to identify the user in a payment transaction and the other is to identify the history, i.e., the life cycle of a coin. The former is referred to as user tracing and the latter is referred as coin tracing. In practice, T should only run these protocols under a court order. Formally, the user-tracing and coin-tracing protocols work as follows:

Client Tracing

To identify the client in a payment transaction, B brings (D_1, D_2) to T who then computes

$$D_1/D_2^\tau = g^U h_{T1}^\rho / g_1^{\tau\rho} = g^U,$$

which identifies the client.

The soundness of this protocol is due to the proof of knowledge

$$PK\{(U, t, \rho) : a_1 = g_1^{Ut} \wedge a_2 = g_2^t \wedge D_1 = g^U h_{T1}^\rho \wedge D_2 = g_1^\rho\},$$

which shows g^U is the plaintext corresponding to the ElGamal ciphertext (D_1, D_2) encrypted using T's public key for the client secret information U. In the client-tracing protocol, T simply decrypts the ciphertext and returns g^U which identifies the client.

Note that this procedure is not possible for other parties as only T can decrypt a ciphertext encrypted using T's public key.

Coin Tracing

Identifying a coin history can be done in two different ways. One is to identify the coin payment for a given coin withdrawal and the other is to identify the coin withdrawal for a given coin payment.

In the later case, B sends to T the payment transcript. Then T computes the value

$$a'/g_3^\tau = ((Ig_2)^t)^\tau = g_1^{Ut\tau} g_2^{t\tau} = h_{T1}^{ut} h_{T2}^t = e,$$

and sends the value e back to B. The anonymity revocation is done by searching for the computed value e in the coin withdrawal reference database.

In the former case, B sends to T the withdrawal reference e. Then T computes and sends to B the value

$$e^{1/\tau} g_3 = h_{T1}^{Ut/\tau} h_{T2}^{t/\tau} g_3 = g_1^{Ut} g_2^t g_3 = a'.$$

Now, the anonymity revocation is done by matching this computed value a' with the value a' in every deposited coin.

8.6 Summary

There are various digital-cash protocols having been proposed in past two decades. We can refer them to as three forms: normal digital-cash (e.g., [8.1, 8.2]), divisible digital-cash [8.7], and fair digital-cash (e.g., [8.14]). In this chapter, we have described three typical digital-cash schemes: the digital-cash scheme proposed by Brands[8.2], and the digital-cash and the fair digital-cash scheme proposed by Nguyen et. al. [8.14] We hope that these schemes give the reader an overall picture of digital-cash.

8.7 Appendix

This section gives protocols for proving the knowledge of various discrete logarithms. Some of these protocols presented in this section are borrowed from Camenisch [8.17], which gives a rigorous treatment of proofs of knowledge about discrete logarithms. The interactive versions of these protocols are known to be witness-indistinguishable and proofs of knowledge. The reader is also referred to [8.15, 8.18, 8.26, 8.29] for detailed discussions of these protocols and other variations.

In the following, we assume that $g, h_1, h_2, g_1, \ldots, g_m \in \mathbb{G}_q (\subset \mathbb{Z}_p^*)$ are generators of order q such that computing a representation of any generator with respect to other generators is infeasible.

Proving the Knowledge of Discrete Logarithms. A proof of knowledge of the discrete logarithm proves the knowledge of the secret number $x \in \mathbb{Z}_q$ from $y = g^x$. This proof is actually part of the Schnorr identification scheme. Following the the notations of [8.17, 8.18], we denote this protocol as

$$PK\{(\alpha) : y = g^\alpha\}.$$

The proof is straightforward. We omit it here.

Proving the knowledge of a Representation. The proof of knowledge of a representation proves the knowledge of a representation of y to the bases $g_1, \ldots, g_m$, which is denoted by

$$\mathrm{PK}\{(x_1, \ldots, x_m) : y = \prod_{i=1}^{m} g_i^{x_i}\}.$$

This proof is first introduced in [8.22] and is given in Fig. 8.11.

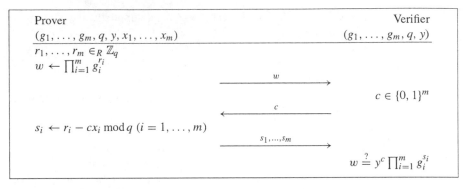

Fig. 8.11 A proof of representation of y to the bases $g_1, \ldots, g_m$

The correctness of this protocol is due to

$$y^c \prod_{i=1}^{m} g_i^{s_i} = \prod_{i=1}^{m} g_i^{cx_i} \prod_{i=1}^{m} g_i^{s_i} = \prod_{i=1}^{m} g_i^{cx_i+s_i} = \prod_{i=1}^{m} g_i^{r_i} = w.$$

The soundness is due to the fact that given a same value w, if the prover can answer two different challenges c and c' correctly, the knowledge extractor obtains two sets of $(c, s_1, \ldots, s_m)$ and $(c', s_1', \ldots, s_m')$ and extract the secret x_i as:

$$x_i = \frac{s_i - s_i'}{c' - c} \bmod q.$$

The zero-knowledge holds because a honest verifier can construct a valid view by choosing $s_1, \ldots, s_m$ and c at random and computing $w = y^c \prod_{i=1}^{m} g_i^{s_i}$.

Proving the Equality of Discrete Logarithms. This proof proves not only the knowledge of secret keys but also certain relations among them. In the most simplest form, it is a proof of knowledge and of equality of discrete logarithm of y_1 to the base g_1 and y_2 to the base g_2. This proof was first introduced by Chaum and Pedersen in [8.23]. Let us denote this protocol by:

$$\mathrm{PK}\{(\alpha) : y_1 = g_1^{\alpha} \wedge y_2 = g_2^{\alpha}\}.$$

The intuition is to run the proof of knowledge of discrete logarithm of y_1 to the base g_1 and of discrete logarithm of y_2 to the base g_2, and then $\log_{g_1} y_1 = \log_{g_2} y_2$ only if the prover can return the same answer in both cases for a random challenge chosen by the verifier. Formally, this protocol is given in Fig. 8.12.

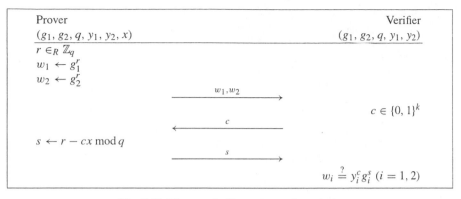

Fig. 8.12 The proof of $\log_{g_1}(y_1) \equiv \log_{g_2}(y_2)$

It is trivial to extend the proof system of equality of discrete logarithms to a proof system of equality of representations. One of such proof is the proof of knowledge of representation of y_1 and y_2 to the bases (g_1, h_1) and (g_2, h_2), respectively and that the representation of y_1 to g_1 and y_2 to g_2 are equal. This protocol, which is denoted by

$$\mathsf{PK}\{(\alpha, \beta_1, \beta_2) : y_1 = g_1^\alpha h_1^{\beta_1} \wedge y_2 = g_2^\alpha h_2^{\beta_2}\},$$

is described in Fig. 8.13. This proof introduced in [8.23] is the basic building block for many blind digital signatures and anonymous-digital-cash schemes.

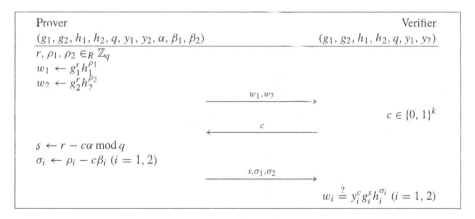

Fig. 8.13 The proof of equality of representations

Proving knowledge of inverse of discrete logarithms. In this protocol, we give the proof for: given $y_1 = g_1^t$ and $y_2 = g_2^{t^{-1}}$, Proving that $(\log_{g_1} y_1)^{-1} = \log_{g_2} y_2$. The protocol is given in Figure 8.14.

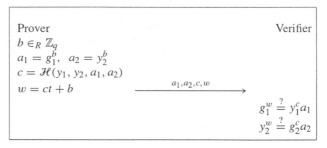

Fig. 8.14 A proof of equality of inverse of discrete logs

8.8 References

[8.1] D. Chaum, A. Fiat, M. Naor (1988) Untraceable electronic cash. In: Advances in Cryptology – CRYPTO'88. Springer, Berlin Heidelberg New York, pp. 319–327.

[8.2] S. Brands (1993) Untraceable off-line cash in wallet with observers. In: Advances in Cryptology – CRYPTO'93. Springer, Berlin Heidelberg New York, pp. 302–318.

[8.3] L. A. M. Schoenmakers (1995) An efficient electronic payment system withstanding parallel attacks. Technical Report CS-R9522, CWI.

[8.4] S. Brands (1993) Untraceable off-line cash in wallet with observers. In: Advances of Cryptology – CRYPTO'93. Springer, Berlin Heidelberg New York, pp. 302–318.

[8.5] D. Chaum (1985) Security without identification: transaction systems to make Big Brother obsolete. Commun ACM 28(10):1030–1044.

[8.6] N. T. Ferguson (1993) Single term off-line coins. In: Advances in Cryptology – EUROCRYPT'93. Springer, Berlin Heidelberg New York, pp. 318–328.

[8.7] T. Okamoto, K. Ohta (1991) Universal electronic cash. In: Advances in Cryptology – CRYPTO'91. Springer, Berlin Heidelberg New York, pp.324–337.

[8.8] T. Eng, T. Okamoto (1994) Single-term divisible electronic coins. In: Advances in Cryptology – EUROCRYPT'94. Springer,Berlin Heidelberg New York, pp. 306–319.

[8.9] T. Okamoto (1995): An efficient divisible electronic cash scheme. In: Advances in Cryptology – CRYPTO'95. Springer, Berlin Heidelberg New York, pp. 438–451.

[8.10] W. Mao (1996) Blind certification of public keys and off-line electronic cash. Technical Report HPL-96-71, HP Laboratories.

[8.11] C. Schnorr (1989) Efficient identification and signatures for smart cards. In: Advances in Cryptology – CRYPTO'89, LNCS 435. Springer, Berlin Heidelberg New York, pp. 239–252.

[8.12] Y. Yacobi (1994) An efficient off-line cash. In: Advances in Cryptology – Asiacrypt'94. Springer, Berlin Heidelberg New York.

[8.13] K. Q. Nguyen, Y. Mu, V. Varadharajan (1997) One-response off-line digital coins. In: Proceedings of Fourth Annual Workshop on Selected Areas in Cryptography (SAC'97), Canada, 1997, pp. 244–251.

[8.14] Y. Mu, K. Q. Nguyen, V. Varadharajan (2001) A fair electronic cash scheme. In: W. Kou, et al. (eds.) Electronic commerce technologies – ISEC2001, LNCS 2040. Springer, Berlin Heidelberg New York, pp. 20–32.

[8.15] S. Brands (1997) Rapid demonstration of linear relations connected by boolean operators. In: Advances in Cryptology – Eurocrypt'97, LNCS 1223. Springer, Berlin Heidelberg New York, pp. 318–333.

[8.16] E. F. Brickell, P. Gemmell, D. Kravitz (1995) Trustee-based tracing extensions to anonymous cash and the making of anonymous change. In: Symposium on Distributed Algorithms. Albuquerque, NM.
http://www.cs.sandia.gov/psgemme/

[8.17] J. Camenisch (1998) Group signature schemes and payment systems based on the discrete logarithm problems. Ph.D. thesis, Swiss Federal Institute of Technology, Zurich.

[8.18] J. Camenisch, M. Michels (1999) Proving in zero-knowledge that a number is the product of two safe primes. Technical Report RS-98-29, BRICS. An abstract version appeared in Proceeding of Eurocrypt'99, LNCS 1592. Springer, Berlin Heidelberg New York, pp. 106–121.

[8.19] J. Camenisch, J. M. Piveteau, M. Stadler (1994) Blind signatures based on the discrete logarithm problem. In: Advances in Cryptology – Eurocrypt'94, LNCS 950. Springer, Berlin Heidelberg New York, pp. 428–432.

[8.20] M. Camenisch, U. Maurer, M. Stadler (1996) Digital payment systems with passive anonymity-revoking trustees. In: ESORICS'96, LNCS 1146. Springer, Berlin Heidelberg New York, pp. 33–43.

[8.21] K. Nyberg, R. A. Rueppel (1995) Message recovery for signature schemes based on the discrete logarithm problem. In: Advances in Cryptology – Eurocrypt'94, LNCS 950. Springer, Berlin Heidelberg New York, pp. 182–193.

[8.22] D. Chaum, J. Evertse, J. Graaf (1988) An improved protocol for demonstrating possession of discrete logarithms and some generalizations. In: Advances in Cryptology – EUROCRYPT'87, LNCS 304. Springer, Berlin Heidelberg New York, pp. 127–141.

[8.23] R. Cramer, T. P. Pedersen (1993) Improved privacy in wallets with observers. In: Advances in Cryptology – Eurocrypt'93, LNCS 765. Springer, Berlin Heidelberg New York, pp. 329–343.

[8.24] G. Davida, Y. Frankel, Y. Tsiounis, M. Yung (1997): Anonymity control in e-cash. In: Proceedings of First Financial Cryptography conference, LNCS 1318. Springer, Berlin Heidelberg New York.

[8.25]   Y. Frankel, Y. Tsiounis, M. Yung (1996) Indirect discourse proofs: achieving fair off-line e-cash. In: Advances in Cryptology – ASIACRYPT'96, LNCS 1163. Springer, Berlin Heidelberg New York, pp. 286–300.

[8.26]   E. Fujisaki, T. Okamoto (1997) Statistical zero-knowledge protocols to prove modular polynomial relation.In: Advances in Cryptology – CRYPTO'97, LNCS 1294. Springer, Berlin Heidelberg New York, pp. 16–30.

[8.27]   J. Piveteau, J. Camenisch, M. Stadler (1994) An efficient payment system protecting privacy. In: Computer Security – ESORICS'94, LNCS 875. Springer, Berlin Heidelberg New York, pp. 207–215.

[8.28]   K. Q. Nguyen, Y. Mu, V. Varadharajan (1997) A new digital cash scheme based on blind Nyberg-Rueppel digital signature. In: Information Security Workshop, LNCS 1396. Springer, Berlin Heidelberg New York, pp. 312–320.

[8.29]   T. Okamoto (1995) An efficient divisible electronic cash scheme. In: Advances in Cryptology – CRYPTO'95, LNCS 963. Springer, Berlin Heidelberg New York, pp. 439–451.

[8.30]   M. Stadler (1996) Cryptographic protocols for revocable privacy. Ph.D. thesis, Swiss Federal Institute of Technology, Zurich.

[8.31]   B. Solms, D. Naccache (1992) On blind signatures and perfect crimes. Computer and Security 11(6): 581–583.

9 Digital Checks

Bo Yang

National Key Laboratory for ISN
Xidian University, Xi'an, China

9.1 Introduction

In electronic commerce, there is a need for a check-like payment system where funds are transferred from the payer's bank account to the payee's bank account at the time the transaction takes place. From the bank's point of view, it would be desirable to use existing interbank funds-transfer networks as much as possible. This chapter will introduce the foundational concept of digital check and two important electronic-check systems: NetBill and NetCheque.

9.2 Digital Check Concept

9.2.1 Digital Check's Basic Elements

As with its paper counterpart, the digital check will contain an instruction to the payer's bank to make a payment of a specified amount to an identified payee. The fact that the check is in electronic form and is being conveyed across computer networks should allow more flexibility in the handling of the check. New services can be provided, such as the ability to immediately verify funds availability. Allowing digital-signature validation can enhance security, and check payments can more easily be integrated into electronic ordering and billing processes.

The concept of digital checking can be described using Fig. 9.1. There are five parties in the system: the customer, the merchant, the consumer's bank, the merchant's bank, and clearing house, in which the clearing house processes checks among different banks. The functions described for a clearing house may be handled by a separate entity or by an existing banking system. For simplicity, we have not included the online malls.

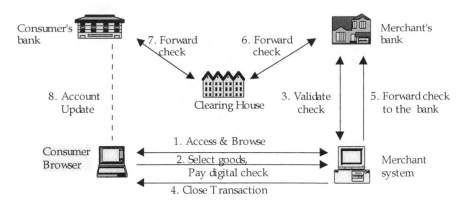

Fig. 9.1   A digital check system

The consumer uses a web browser that has access to various web servers over the Internet. The consumer views various shopping malls and storefronts at the browser. The browser has provisions for displaying the digital check formats. The banks process digital checks which are similar to paper checks.

A complete digital check transaction may consist of several basic steps outlined next. These steps are executed in three distinct and optionally separate phases. In the first phase, the consumer makes a purchase. In the second phase, the merchant sends the digital checks to its bank for redemption. In the third phase, the merchant's bank approaches the clearing house or the consumer's bank to cash the digital checks.

Phase 1: Purchasing goods

1. The consumer accesses the merchant server, and the merchant server presents its goods to the consumer.

2. The consumer selects the goods and purchases them by sending a digital check to the merchant. The check can be transported in some kind of secure envelope; the form of this envelope is outside the architecture and could be sent in a secure email or in an encrypted interactive dialogue between the two parties.

3. The merchant may validate the digital check with its bank for payment authorization, and endorses the check.

4. Assuming the check is validated.

Phase 2: Depositing checks at the merchant's bank

5.   The merchant electronically forwards the checks to its bank. This action takes place at the discretion of the merchant.

Phase 3: Clearing the checks among the banks

6.   The merchant's bank forwards the digital checks to the clearing house for cashing. The processing is identical to that undergone by any paper check today. This means that the banks involved would clear the check using the normal *automated clearing house* (ACH) or *electronic check presentment* (ECP) methods.

7.   The clearing house works with the consumer's bank, clears the check, and transfers money to the merchant's bank, which updates the merchant's account.

8.   At a later time, the consumer's bank updates the consumer with the withdrawal information.

9.2.2 Security schemes for digital checks

The security requirements for digital checks consist of authenticating the digital check, supplying the originator's public key to receiver, and securely storing the originator's private key.

Authenticity of Digital Checks

The digital check may consist of a document that is signed by the consumer's private key. The receiver (the merchant or the merchant's bank) uses the payer's public key to decrypt the digital signature. This assures the receiver that the sender indeed signed the check. It also provides for non-repudiation, such that the payer cannot deny issuing the check since it is signed by the payer's private key (that only the payer is expected to possess).

Additionally, the digital check also may require the digital signatures of the originator's bank. This step will assure the receiver that the check is written on a valid bank account. The receiver (or receiver's bank) can validate the authenticity of the originator's bank by using the public key of the originator's bank.

For large sums of money, additional security requirements may be levied.

Delivering Public Keys

The originator as well as the originator's bank must provide their public keys to the receiver. Attaching their X.509 certificates to the digital checks can provide the public keys. These certificates may use certificate chains including the signatures of the root CA. The public key of the root CA should be well publicized to avoid fraud.

Storage of Private Keys

To avoid fraud, the consumer's private key needs to be securely stored and made available to the consumer. This can be achieved by providing a smart card that the consumer can carry.

Cashier's Checks

Finally, a cashier's check may be issued by a bank as follows. The check is created by a bank and is signed using the bank's private key. The originating bank includes its certificate with the digital check. The receiving bank uses the originating bank's public key to decrypt the digital signature. In this way, the receiving bank is assured that the cashier check indeed was originated by the name of the bank indicated on the check. It also provides the receiving bank with non-repudiation such that the originating bank cannot deny issuing this check since it is signed by the originating bank's private key (that only the originating bank is expected to possess).

9.2.3 Benefits and concerns

Compared to paper checks and other forms of payments, digital checking provides the following advantages:

- **Time saved**:
  Digital checks can be issued without needing to fill out, mail, or deliver checks. It also saves time in processing the checks. With paper checks, the merchant collects all the checks and deposits them at the merchant's bank. With digital checks, the merchant instantly can forward checks to the bank and get them credited to their account. As such, digital checks can greatly reduce the time from the moment a consumer writes a check to the time when the merchant receives the deposit.

- **Deduced paper handling cost**:
  There is no need for long lines at the banks on the first day of the month, or for long lines of students paying their tuition at the university. Corre-

spondingly, it reduces the bank employees' effort to receive the checks, process them, and mail the cancelled checks to the consumers.

- **Reduction in bounced checks**:
  Digital checking can be designed in such a way that the merchant can get authorization from the customer's bank before accepting the digital check. Digital checks can be used to give gifts or make payments without the fear of being lost or stolen. If a check is stolen, the receiver can request the payer to stop the payment. On the other hand, digital cash is exposed to theft and other risks.

9.3 NetBill

NetBill is a payment system for the selling and delivery of low-priced information goods. A customer, represented by a client computer, wishes to buy information from a merchant's sever. A account server (the NetBill server), maintains accounts for both customers and merchants, linked to conventional financial institutions, A NetBill transaction transfers information goods from merchant to customer, debiting the customer's NetBill account and crediting the merchant's account for the value of the goods. When necessary, funds in a customer's NetBill account can be replenished from a bank or credit card; similarly, funds in a merchant's NetBill account are made available by depositing them in the merchant's bank account. NetBill acts as an aggregator to combine many small transactions into larger conventional transactions, amortizing conventional overhead fees.

The transfer of information goods consists of delivering bits to the customer. Users may be charged on a per-item basis, by a subscription allowing unlimited access, or by a number of other pricing models.

9.3.1 The NetBill Transaction Model

The NetBill transaction model involves three parties. the customer, the merchant, and the NetBill transaction server. A transaction involves three phases: price negotiation, goods delivery, and payment. For information goods, which can be delivered over the network, the NetBill protocol links goods delivery and payment into a single atomic transaction.

In a NetBill transaction, the customer and merchant interact with each other in the first two phases; the NetBill server is not involved until the payment phase, when the merchant submits a transaction request. The customer contacts the NetBill server directly only in the case of communications failure or when requesting administrative functions. Fig. 9.2 shows the relationships among parties in a NetBill transaction.

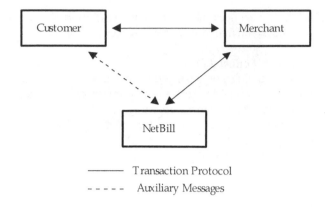

Fig. 9.2   Parties in a NetBill transaction

Transaction Objectives

NetBill transaction can obtain the following set of objectives.

a) Only authorized customers can charge against a NetBill account.
b) The customer and merchant must agree on the item to be purchased and the price to be charged.
c) A customer can optionally protect his identity from merchants.
d) Customers and merchants are provided with proof of transaction results from NetBill.

In addition, NetBill can also obtain the following objectives to support price negotiation and goods delivery.

e) There is an offer and acceptance negotiation phase between customer and merchant.
f) A customer may present credentials identifying them as entitled to special pricing or treatment.
g) A customer receives the information goods he purchases if and only if they are charged (and thus the merchant is paid) for the goods.
h) A customer may need approval from a fourth (access control) party before the NetBill server will allow a transaction.

Finally, as a general objective for all phases of the purchase process, the following objective can be added:

i) The privacy and integrity of communications is protected from observation or alteration by external parties.

To achieve these goals, the NetBill protocol provides for strong authentication and privacy, atomic payment and delivery protocol, and a flexible access control system.

In the price- negotiation phase, the customer presents evidence of their identity, and (optionally) supplemental credentials, and requests a price quote on an item. The customer may also include a bid for the item. The merchant responds with a price offer.

In the second phase, the customer accepts or declines the offer. In the case of information goods, acceptance constitutes an order for network delivery. The merchant provisionally delivers the goods, under encryption, but withholds the key.

Key delivery is linked to completion of the third phase, the payment protocol. In this phase, the customer constructs and digitally signs an *electronic payment order* (EPO), and sends it to the merchant. The merchant appends the key to the EPO and endorses (digitally signs) the EPO, forwarding it to the NetBill server. The NetBill server returns a digitally signed receipt, which includes the key, to the merchant, who forwards a copy to the customer.

9.3.2 The Transaction Protocol

We use the notation $X \Rightarrow Y$ to indicate that X sends the specified message to Y. The basic protocol involves three phases that can be divided into eight steps, where C, M, and N represent respectively customer, merchant and NetBill.

1. $C \Rightarrow M$ Price request
2. $M \Rightarrow C$ Price quote
3. $C \Rightarrow M$ Goods request
4. $M \Rightarrow C$ Goods, encrypted with a key K
5. $C \Rightarrow M$ Signed Electronic Payment Order
6. $M \Rightarrow N$ Endorsed EPO (including K)
7. $N \Rightarrow M$ Signed result (including K)
8. $M \Rightarrow C$ Signed result (including K)

The Price-Request Phase

The price-request phase consists of step 1 and step 2, which present a request/response message pair in which the customer requests a price quote of the merchant. The customer presents an identifying ticket (the identity presented may be a pseudonym) to the merchant, along with some optional credentials establishing their membership in groups which may make their eligible for a discount.

The customer passes parameters indicating a request for the disposition of the transaction. The merchant, on receiving the request for a quotation, determines a price for the user and returns a quotation.

Step 1 and 2 may be repeated as needed until customer and merchant can agree on a price.

The Goods-Delivery Phase

Once the customer and merchant have negotiated a price for the goods in question, the customer directs the merchant to deliver the goods in step 3.

In step 4, the merchant generates a unique symmetric cipher key K, encrypts the goods using this key and sends the encrypted goods to the customer, along with a cryptographic checksum computed on the encrypted goods, so that the customer will immediately detect any discrepancy before proceeding. The merchant also sends an *electronic payment order ID* (EPOID), with the goods. The EPOID is a globally unique identifier that will be used in the NetBill server's database to uniquely identify this transaction. It consists of three fields: a field identifying the merchant, a timestamp marking the time at the end of goods delivery, and a serial number to guarantee uniqueness.

The specification that the EPOID must be globaly unique is used to prevent replay attacks, in which unscrupulous merchants reuse customers' old signed payment instructions. The time stamp portion of the EPOID is used to expire stale transactions; it must be generated at the end of goods delivery because the delivery (especially for very large goods) may take longer than the payment expiration time.

Because the goods are delivered encrypted in step 4, the customer cannot use them. The key K needed to decrypt the goods will be delivered in the payment phase, which follows.

The Payment Phase

After the encrypted goods are delivered, the customer submits payment to the merchant in the form of a signed *electronic payment order* (EPO), in step 5. At any time before the signed EPO is submitted, a customer may abort the transaction and be in no danger of its being completed against their will. The submission of the signed EPO marks the "point of no return" for the customer.

An EPO consists of two sections, a clear part containing transaction information that is readable by the merchant and the NetBill server, and an encrypted part containing payment instructions that is readable only by the NetBill server.

After the customer presents the signed EPO to the merchant, the merchant endorses it and forwards the endorsed EPO to the NetBill server in step 6. The endorsed EPO adds the merchant's account number, the merchant's memo field, and the goods decryption key, as well as the merchant's signature.

At any time before the endorsed EPO is submitted to the NetBill server, the merchant may abort the transaction and be in no danger of its being completed against their will. The submission of the endorsed EPO marks the "point of no return" for the merchant.

Upon receipt of the signed and endorsed EPO, the NetBill server makes a decision about the transaction and returns the result to the merchant, who in turn forwards it to the customer.

The NetBill server makes its decision based on verification of the signatures, the privileges of the users involved, the customer's account balance, and the uniqueness and freshness of the EPOID. It then issues a receipt containing the result code, the identities of the parties, the price and description of the goods, the EPOID, and the key K needed to decrypt the goods. The receipt is digitally signed by the NetBill server, using the *digital signature algorithm* (DSA).

This receipt is returned to the merchant in step 7, along with an indication of the customer's new account balance (encrypted so that only they may read it). The EPOID is repeated in the customer-specific data to ensure that the merchant cannot replay data from an earlier transaction.

In step 8, the merchant responds to the request from the customer in step 5, forwarding the messages returned by the NetBill server in step 7.

9.3.3 Identities and Authentication

When a customer creates a NetBill account, they receive a unique User ID and generate the RSA public key pair associated with that User ID. This key pair is certified by NetBill, and is used for signatures and authentication within the system. In [9.1], the authors proposed that symmetric cryptography be used instead of using public-key cryptography for message authentication and encryption throughout the NetBill system because symmetric cryptography offers significant performance advantages. At the same time, the public key cryptography is used to alleviate problems with traditional symmetric-key Kerberos.

Kerberos uses a two-level ticket scheme; to authenticate oneself to a Kerberos service, one must obtain a service ticket, which establishes a shared symmetric session key between the client and server, and establishes that the Kerberos ticket granting server believes the client's identity. To obtain a service ticket, a client must first obtain a ticket-granting ticket (TGT), which proves the client's identity to the Ticket Granting Server. A client obtains a TGT via request from a *key distribution center* (KDC).

The Kerberos KDC/TGT arrangement introduces two significant problems that we may alleviate using public-key cryptography. First, because it maintains a shared symmetric cipher key with every principal in the system, it is an attractive target for attack; recovering from compromise of the KDC requires establishing new shared keys with all users of the system. Second, a KDC and TGT will be a communications or processing bottleneck if a large number of users present a heavy traffic load.

To eliminate the ticket granting server, we replace the TGT with a public key certificate, allowing each service to act as its own ticket granting server. That is, a user presents a service ticket request encrypted with a certified public key, called a *public key-based TGT* (PKTGT), and receives in response a symmetric-cipher-based service ticket. This service ticket is identical in form to a Kerberos service ticket. The key distribution center is replaced by a key repository.

This model can preserve the efficiency of symmetric ciphers for most communication and repeated authentication, and isolates the computational expense of public key cryptography to initial authentication between parties. This model is referred as public-key Kerberos, or PK Kerberos.

In the NetBill system, a customer obtains Kerberos tickets for the NetBill transaction server at the beginning of a session and obtains Kerberos tickets for merchants as he needs them. Merchant servers will continually maintain their own tickets for the NetBill transaction server.

Key Repository

Private keys are large, so users cannot be expected to remember them. Permanently storing private keys at a user's workstation poses security risks and restricts the user's electronic-commerce activities to a single workstation. NetBill uses a key repository to optionally store customers' private keys. These keys are encrypted by a symmetric key derived from a password known only to the customer.

- **Key validation and revocation certificates**

  A public-key-certificate scheme is used to bind User IDs to keys, with NetBill as the certifying authority. NetBill generates a certificate when a customer first proves his identity and begins using NetBill. However, allowing merchants, as services, to grant their own ticket based on these certificates poses a problem: NetBill is no longer involved in ticket-granting, and cannot prevent a ticket from being issued to a user with a compromised key. NetBill needs to invalidate compromised keys as quickly as possible. NetBill maintains a *certificate revocation list* (CRL) at its server. When a key is compromised, the owner creates a revocation certificate and places it in the key repository along with their key. Any party can check that a given key has not been compromised by examining the revocation list. Initially, it would seem that it is necessary for the customer and merchant to contact the server to check CRLs on each transaction. However, it is possible to eliminate this check by allowing the NetBill transaction server to do it when it processes the payment transaction. By delaying the CRL check to late in the protocol, we introduce some minor risks. Customers and merchants may disclose information, such as their preference for particular items or special prices to bogus peers, but there is no financial risk.

- **Pseudonyms**

  Some customers want to disguise their identities. NetBill provides two pseudonym methods to protect the privacy of the customer's identity: a per-transaction method that uses a unique pseudonym for each transaction, and a per-merchant method that uses a unique pseudonym for each customer merchant pair. The per-merchant pseudonym is useful for customers who wish to maintain a consistent pseudonymous identity to qualify for frequent-buyer discounts.

These pseudonym schemes are implemented by introducing a pseudonym-granting server to create pseudonymous for the customer.

9.3.4 Credentials and Authorizations

A restricted proxy is a ticket giving the bearer authority to perform certain operations named in the ticket. NetBill uses a similar construct to implement credentials to prove group membership (to allow merchants to provide discounts to special groups) and to implement access control mechanisms.

Credentials for Group Membership

An organization can provide a credential server that issues credential proxies proving membership in a group. In this case, the credential server is asserting a fact (membership in a group) about which it is authoritative. For example, an auto club may provide a credential server that issues credentials to the members of the club; merchants who offer discounts to the club's members will accept these credentials as proof of membership.

A credential issued to a customer may be unrestricted, or it may optionally be restricted for use on a specific account (for example, in order to prevent corporate employees from taking advantage of corporate discounts for personal purchases).

This is accomplished by passing the account number to the group server as part of the request. If the account number is appropriate for this group, the credential will be issued. The credential contains a cryptographic checksum of the account number and an *account verification nonce*, which is also returned to the customer along with the credential.

This nonce is a pseudorandom number ensuring that merchants can neither determine which different customers (or the same customer in repeated sessions) are using the same account nor easily verify guesses of the customer's account number. The nonce is passed along to the NetBill server in the encrypted part of the EPO so that the NetBill server can verify that checksum passed to the merchant (for his comparison to the credential) corresponds to the account number actually being used.

Credentials can also be used by cooperating merchants to restrict information access. In this way, merchants only sell to approved customers, i.e., those who can present a certain credential. This offers a solution for merchants who, for example, can restrict distribution of sensitive documents only to individuals whose credentials verify a need-to-know.

Access Control Mechanism

Access control can be implemented by using proxies, an account owner (such as a parent) may have a restriction on the account such that no purchases can be completed by a given customer (such as a child) without approval from an access-control server. This allows a different organization to provide access-control services. For example, both the PTA and a church group could offer competing access control services.

The NetBill protocols are robust against failures, and retain essential information to protect customers and merchants against fraud.

9.4 NetCheque System

The NetCheque system, under development at the Information Sciences Institute of the University of Southern California, is a distributed accounting service supporting the credit-debit model of payment. Users of NetCheque maintain accounts on accounting servers of their choice. A NetCheque account works in much the same way as a conventional checking account: account holders write electronic documents that include the name of the payer, the name of the financial institution, the payer's account identifier, the name of the payee, and the amount of the check. Like a paper check, a NetCheque bears an electronic signature, and must be endorsed by the payee using another electronic signature before the cheque will be paid.

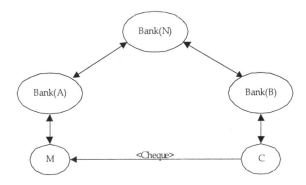

Fig. 9.3   Hierarchy of NetCheque servers

As a distributed accounting service, properly signed and endorsed cheques are exchanged between accounting servers to settle accounts through a hierarchy, as shown in Fig. 9.3. In addition to improving scalability and acceptability, clearing between servers allows organizations to set up accounts in their own in-house-accounting servers with accounts corresponding to budget lines. Authorized signers write cheques against these accounts, while the organization maintains a single account with an outside bank, integrating its own internal accounting system with the external financial system.

The NetCheque accounting system was designed originally to maintain quotas for distributed system resources, resulting in frequent transactions for small amounts. Thus, it is well suited to support small payments needed for some kinds of electronic commerce. This requirement for handling micropayments requires high performance, which is obtained through the use of conventional, instead of public-key, cryptography. This gives up some support for independent verification of payment documents at each stage in the payment pipeline.

9.4.1 Implementation Overview

The system is based on the Kerberos system [9.6]. The electronic signature used when writing or endorsing a cheque is a special kind of Kerberos ticket called a proxy. The cheque itself contains information about 1) the amount of the cheque, 2) the currency unit, 3) an expiration date, 4) the account against which the cheque was drawn, and 5) the payee or payees, all readable by the bearer of the cheque, together with 6) the signatures and endorsements accumulated during processing, verifiable by the accounting server against which the cheque was drawn. For performance, the Kerberos proxy used as a signature is based on conventional cryptography, but it may be replaced by a signature using public-key cryptography with a corresponding loss of performance.

To write a cheque, the user calls the write-cheque function, specifying an account against which the cheque is to be drawn, the payee, the amount, and the currency unit. Defaults for the account and currency unit are read from the user's chequebook file. The write-cheque function generates the cleartext portion of the cheque, obtains a Kerberos ticket that will be used to authenticate the user to the accounting server, generates an authenticator with an embedded checksum over the information from the cheque, and places the ticket and authenticator in the signature field of the cheque. The cheque is then base-64 encoded and may be sent to the payee through electronic mail, or transferred in real time as payment for services provided through an online service.

The deposit-cheque function reads the cleartext part of the cheque, obtains a Kerberos ticket to be used with the payer's accounting server, generates an authenticator endorsing the cheque in the name of the payee for deposit only into the payee's account, and appends the endorsement to the cheque. An encrypted connection is opened to the payee's accounting server and the endorsed cheque is deposited. If the payee and the payer both use the same accounting server, the response will indicate whether the cheque cleared.

If different accounting servers are used, the payee's accounting server places a hold on the funds in the payee's account and indicates to the payee that the cheque was accepted for collection. The payee has the option of requesting that the cheque be cleared in real time, though we expect there may be a charge for this service. If a cheque accepted for collection is rejected, the cheque is returned to the depositor, who can take action at that time. As a cheque is cleared through multiple accounting servers, each server attaches its own endorsement, similar to the endorsement attached by the payee.

In some cases the payee's and payer's accounting servers can settle the check directly, bypassing higher levels of the hierarchy. This is possible when the cheque is drawn on an accounting server that is trusted to properly settle accounts. Such trust might be based on certificates of insurance representing endorsement of the accounting server. In such cases, the hierarchy would still be used to settle any imbalance between credits and debits for each accounting server at the end of the day, but the cost of these transfers would be amortized over the days transactions. To determine account balances and fill out about cleared cheques, authorized users can call the statement function which opens an encrypted connection to the accounting server and retrieves the account balance for each currency unit, together with a list of cheques that have been recently deposited to, or drawn on and cleared through the account. The entire cheque is returned, allowing the user's application to extract whatever information is needed for display to the user, or for integration with other applications.

9.5 Summary

This chapter is divided into two parts, the first part describes the ways in which existing banking organizations can introduce a check-based payment system in a phased manner. The second one introduces two electronic check systems: NetBill and NetCheque.

In the NetBill system, some methods have been introduced for certified delivery, access control, user certificates, pseudonyms, and their integration. The design principle is to provide very high degrees of security and flexibility while still providing good efficiency.

The NetCheque system is a distributed payment system based on the credit-debit model. The strengths of the NetCheque system are its security, reliability, scalability, and efficiency. Signatures on cheques are authenticated using Kerberos. Reliability and scalability are provided by using multiple accounting servers. NetCheque is well suited for clearing micropayments; its use of conventional cryptography makes it more efficient than those systems based on public-key cryptography. Though NetCheque does not itself provide anonymity, it may be used to facilitate the flow of funds between other services that do provide anonymity.

9.6 References

[9.1]   B. Cox, J. D. Tygar, M. Sirbu (1995) NetBill security and transaction protocol. Technical Report, Carnegie Mellon University. http://www.ini.cmu.edu/netbill

[9.2]   M. Sirbu, J. D. Tygar (1995): NetBill: an electronic commerce system optimized for network delivered information and services. In: Proc. IEEE Compcon'95. IEEE Press, New York. http://ini.cmu.edu/netbill

[9.3]   C. Neuman, G. Medvinsky (1995) Requirements for network payment: the NetCheque perspective. In: Proc. IEEE Compcon'95. IEEE Press, New York. http://nii.isi.edu/info/netcheque/documentation.html

[9.4]   University of Southern California Chronicle (1994) The check is in the e-mail.   ftp://prospero.isi.edu/pub/netcheque/information/usc-chronicle-941107/netcheque-usc-chronicle-941107.html

[9.5]   D. O'Mahony, M. Peirce, H. Tewari (1997) Electronic payment systems. Artech House, Boston London.

[9.6]   C. Neuman, T. Ts'o (1994) Kerberos: an authentication service for computer networks. IEEE Communications 32(9).

10 Secure Electronic Transactions: Overview, Capabilities, and Current Status

Gordon Agnew

A&F Consulting, and
University of Waterloo, Ontario, Canada

10.1 Introduction

Until recently, there were two primary forms of credit card transactions:

1) Card present and,
2) Card not present or mail order telephone (MOT).

In a typical "in store" transaction, the customer presents their credit card to perform a transaction. The merchant "swipes" the card and the customer's credit card information along with the amount of the transaction is forwarded to a payment gateway. Once the credit information is verified, the payment gateway returns an authorization to the merchant and a receipt is issued to the customer. In the event of fraud on the part of a customer, the merchant is indemnified against loss since the payment gateway authorized the transaction.

In the case of a purchase made via the telephone, the customer's credit card is not physically present for verification. Generally, the merchant simply accepts the customer's card number over the phone and completes the transaction. Since no authorization was issued by the payment gateway, liability for customer fraud rests with the merchant. For some merchants, this risk is acceptable if profit margins were large enough. On the other hand many merchants have found the risks unacceptable.

In 1996, Mastercard and Visa announced their support of a developing standard for electronic credit card transactions. This replaced the competing standards that each company was pursuing independently. In 1997Visa and Mastercard pooled their resources and formed Secure Electronic Transaction LLC (SETCo) to implement the *SET Specification* [10.4].

SETCo manages the Specification, oversees SET product-compliance testing, and promotes the use of SET as a global payment standard.

The secure electronic transaction (SET) protocol, in many ways, mirrors a card-present transaction over the Internet.

In the following sections, we will examine the details of the operation of SET as well as compare its capabilities to other protocols used in electronic commerce. In addition, we will look issues related to SET's adoption and refinements to the protocol.

10.2 Protocol Stack and Capabilities

There are many functions required to implement a large interconnected network such as the Internet. To facilitate this, network functionality is usually divided into a set of layers or the *protocol stack*. Each layer "talks" to a corresponding or "peer" layer at the other end of the communications channel. Each layer works transparently with the other layers in the network. The lowest layer in the network is the *physical* layer that involves the actual means for transporting data, for example, the actual cables or fibre optics that form the network. At the highest level is the *application* layer which are the programs that are run by the user. One major advantage of such a structure is that the user does not have to be concerned with how the lower layers are implemented. The user simply runs the application and information is passed locally down through the various layers to the Physical layer. The user's data is passed to the physical layer at the destination server then back up to the corresponding application layer at the other end of the connection. In most cases, this layer transparency is realized by a process called "encapsulation;" as data is passed from a higher layer to a lower, the lower layer takes the original data and adds header and control information then passes it down to the next layer. At the destination, the process is reversed and the header/control information is stripped off as data is passed to higher layers. This process simplifies implementation of networks but introduces some interesting security issues, as we will explain below.

There are several levels at which security can be introduced to protect Internet connections. The level in which security functions are used has a strong impact on what types of security can be provided. In Fig. 10.1, three security protocols are shown as they fit into the Internet protocol stack. The three we will consider are IPSec, SSL and SET.

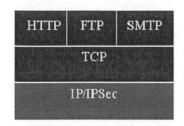

Network

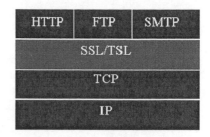

Transport

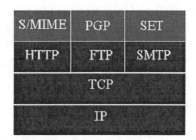

Application

Fig. 10.1 Security layers

10.2.1 Internet Protocol Security (IPSec)

As we see in Fig. 10.1, Internet protocol security (IPSec) is implemented in a relatively low layer. IPSec provides the facilities to encrypt and authenticate user's data (*payload*). If this done, an attacker can see the where the information is going (at least what IP addresses are involved) but not the information itself. In addition, IPSec has the option of taking a standard IP message encrypting it and placing it in a new IP message with a new "disguised" header. This is known as tunnel mode and allows users, for example, to set up private groups over the Internet (virtual private networks).

There are several advantages to providing security at this level:

- Security functions are transparent to the user – the user may not even be aware they are being used.
- The identity of participants can be protected as their IP addresses can be masked.

There are also disadvantages:

- The security functions only protect the IP layer and below – one data is passed to higher layers, it is not protected. If several users are on the same system, information for one user may be visible to other users.
- Identities of users can only be resolved to an IP address. It is common that many users may share an IP address thus, authentication of a particular user may not be possible.

10.2.2 Secure Socket Layer (SSL)

Secure Socket Layer (SSL) was developed by Netscape and is currently in version 3. It is the defacto standard for Internet security at this level and is implemented in most browsers and by most web servers. SSL is designed to provide security functions independent of the application. Since it works at a higher layer than IP-Sec, identities can be resolved to the level of an individual. By the same token, SSL by itself cannot prevent an observer from knowing who is communicating since IP addresses will be added at the lower layers.

SSL designates two types of participants: clients and servers. Clients always initiate a communications session with a server. The server is required to provide authentication information to the client (a certified public key) if requested. The client, however, is not required to provide a certified public key to the server. If this is the case, the applications using SSL may require some other means of authenticating the user (such as a user ID and password/PIN). Once the session has been negotiated, SSL provides a secure (encrypted) and authenticated (data-integrity checks) communications channel between the client and server.

10.2.3 SET

As shown in Fig. 10.1, SET provides security functions at the highest (application) layer of the protocol stack. As in our previous discussion, there are advantages and disadvantages to this. SET is an application and security its functions are not available to other applications. The integrity of SET relies on the ability to resolve identities to a particular individual, merchant or payment gateway (through the use of a full public key infrastructure as we will discuss in Section 10.3) as well as the ability to protect the information exchanged.

As with SSL, even though the information is protected, and observer can still glean information about the participants in a transaction.

10.3 SET Overview

In this section, we will examine the structure of SET and its related security functions[1].

There are two major parts to the SET protocol.

- Registration
- Transaction processing

10.3.1 SET Registration

The security and integrity of transactions are heavily reliant on the use of certified public keys or *public key certificates*. To create a certificate, the user presents unique identification information (ID) and their public key to a *certificate authority* (CA). Once the CA is satisfied that the user is authentic (for example, the manager of a bank may authenticate a particular customer), the CA binds the ID and public key of the user together (usually by creating a message digest[2]) then forms a *digital signature*[3] on the result. For another participant to verify the public key of a particular user, they require a trusted copy of the CA's public key in order to verify the certificate. It is assumed that a trusted version of at least on CA's public key is available to the participants.

SET recognizes three types of participants in a transaction.

- The customer (cardholder)
- The merchant
- The payment gateway.

SET then defines a hierarchical approach to creating and distributing public-key certificates for each type of participant. This is shown in Fig. 10.2. Here, the highest member of the hierarchy is the *root certificate authority* maintained by SETCo. The root authority issues public key certificates to the various payment brands. These in turn become Certificate Authorities authorized to issue certificates to their member banks.

---

[1] A full description of SET can be found in SET Specification Books [10.4]

[2] A message digest is a fixed length image of a longer message formed using a transformation that is "one-way" and unpredictable. That is, it is very easy to create but virtually impossible to find a second message that would create the same image. For a more in depth look at cryptographic functions, the reader is referred to [10.2]

[3] A digital signature is formed using the signer's private key. It can be verified using the signer's public key.

Further down the hierarchy are the certificate authorities associated with each type of participant in a transaction. The *payment card issuing certificate authority* issues public key certificates to customers. The *merchant bank* or *acquirer certificate authority* issues public key certificates to the merchants while payment gateways have their own certificate authority.

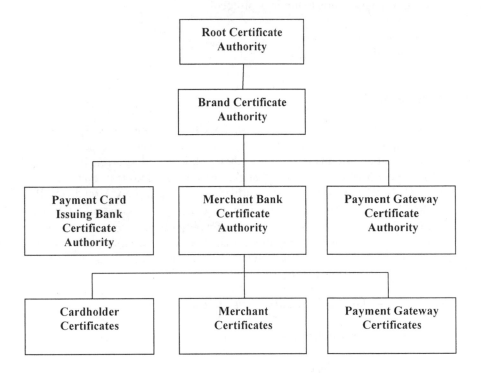

Fig. 10.2 SET certificate hierarchy

In such a hierarchy, a *certificate chain* can be used to verify any member of the hierarchy. For example, for a particular merchant, the certificate chain might include their own public key certificate issued by their acquirer CA, a certificate on the acquirer CA issued by the brand CA and finally the certificate of the brand CA as issued by the root CA. A trusted version of the root CA's public key would allow the chain to be verified. A graphic representation of a certificate chain is shown in Fig. 10.3.

Merchant's Certificate (from Merchant's Bank CA)	Merchant's Bank CA Certificate (from Brand CA)	Brand's CA Certificate (from Root CA)

Fig. 10.3 Example certificate chain for a merchant

10.3.2 Transaction Processing

There are three main phases in a secure electronic transaction:

- Purchase request
- Payment authorization
- Payment capture

An overview of the interaction among the participants in a transaction is shown in Fig. 10.4.

Purchase Request Phase

The details of the purchase request are shown in Fig. 10.5. Within the purchase-request phase, there are 5 basic steps, as we will describe.

Initiate Request

The process starts with the customer shopping, and selecting an item or items. The customer has a completed order form and has selected a particular payment card. The customer's (cardholder's) computer running the cardholder's software package (hereafter called just the *cardholder*) sends an *initiate request* (*P INIT REQ*) message to the merchant requesting the certified public key of the payment gateway.

Initiate Response

Once the merchant receives the initiate request, it assigns an unique transaction ID to the message and returns a signed version of the transaction ID, its own certificate and the appropriate (for the particular brand) payment gateway's certificate to the cardholder.

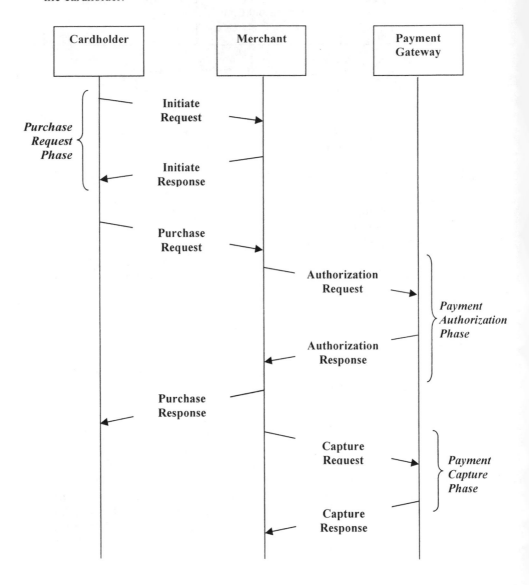

Fig. 10.4 SET overview

Cardholder Purchase Request

Once the response is received, the cardholder verifies the certificates of the merchant and gateway as well as the merchant's digital signature on the transaction information. Once this is complete, the cardholder creates two messages: an *order information* (OI) message intended for the merchant and a *payment information* (PI) message intended for the payment gateway. The PI message information such as the credit card number of the cardholder and will be concealed from the merchant. These messages both contain the unique transaction ID that the merchant assigned. This is done so that the two messages can be linked to one another.

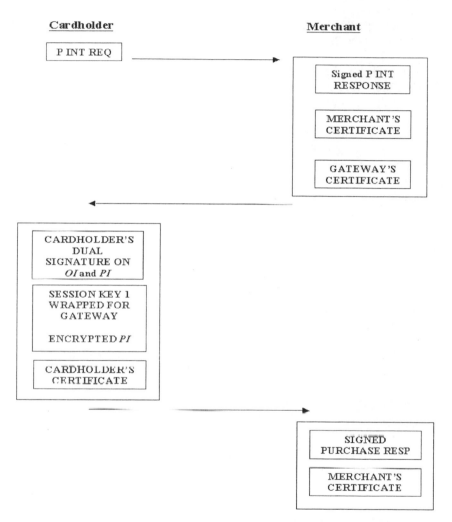

Fig. 10.5 Purchase request phase

At this point, a very elegant method is used bind the two messages together. The cardholder forms message digests of both the OI and PI. These digests are concatenated, then a third message digest is formed. This final digest is then digitally signed by the cardholder. This forms the *dual signature* on OI and PI.

The next step is used to hide the PI information from the merchant. The cardholder generates a random session key (to be used with a conventional encryption algorithm) that is used to encrypt the PI. To transport this information to the payment gateway, the cardholder combines the random session key and their account information into a message then encrypts it using the payment gateway's public key (so that only the PG can recover the account information and the session key that can decrypt the PI).

Merchant then is forwarded a message containing the PI and OI digest, the dual signature, the "wrapped" version of the PI, session key and account information and the cardholder's certificate.

The reason for the dual signature scheme is as follows: the payment gateway will only have a digest of the order information and not the order itself. The payment gateway cannot determine the purchase from that information. If a dispute arises, between the merchant and customer, the OI can be produced and the payment gateway with knowledge of the PI can regenerate the message digests and verify whose claim is correct. This is an important element in security of SET.

Merchant's Purchase Request Processing

When the purchase request is received at the merchant, it verifies the cardholder's certificate. This is then used to verify the dual signature on the OI and digest of the PI to ensure no tampering of the OI has occurred.

Once this has been verified, the merchant generates a digitally signed *purchase response* message that is returned to the cardholder.

Purchase Response

In the final step in this phase, the cardholder uses the merchant's certified public key to verify the purchase response. This is stored for future reference.

Payment Authorization Phase

This part of the protocol involves the merchant and the payment gateway. The objective is for the merchant to acquire authorization for the transaction. There are three basic steps, as shown in Fig. 10.6.

Merchant Authorization Request

The merchant starts by creating a digitally signed authorization request that includes the amount to be authorized, the transaction ID, and other details about the transaction.

The merchant generates a random session key that is used to encrypt this message. The session key is then wrapped using the payment gateway's public key.

This information is sent along with the cardholder's PI information and wrapped session key, cardholder's certificate and merchant's certificate.

Payment Gateway Processing

When the gateway receives the authorization request, it uses its private key to recover the wrapped session key. This is then used to decrypt the request. The merchant's certificate is verified then used to verify the signature on the request.

Next, the second session key and customer account information are recovered. The session key is then used to recover the PI. The cardholder's certificate is verified and the digital signature on the OI and PI is verified. As a further check, the Transaction ID's on both parts of the message are compared to ensure that they are the same.

The next operation involves the payment gateway creating a message for the issuing bank. This is done over the private financial network.

If the purchase is authorized, then a digitally signed response message is generated by the payment gateway. This message is encrypted with a new random session key that is wrapped using the merchant's public key, then forwarded to the merchant.

Merchant Response Processing

When the response is received by the merchant, the payment authorization is recovered and the signature is verified. A copy of this authorization is kept by the merchant.

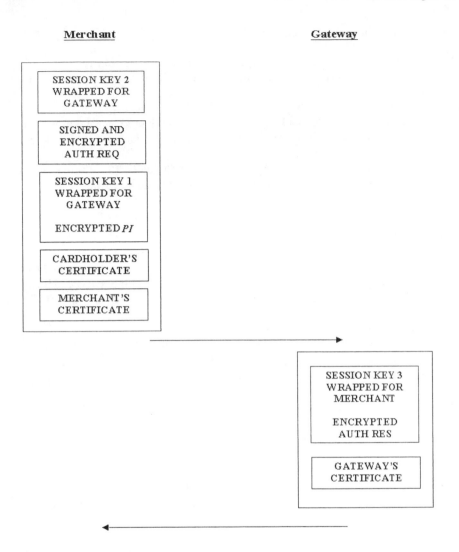

Fig. 10.6 Payment authorization phase

Payment Capture Phase

The final phase in the SET protocol is payment capture. In this phase, the Merchant requests payment from the payment gateway. This phase may occur sometime after the transaction has occurred and involves three basic steps, as shown in Fig. 10.7.

Merchant Payment Capture Request

The merchant creates a digitally signed payment request that includes the final transaction amount, the transaction ID, and other transaction information. This is encrypted using a new random session key that is wrapped using the payment gateway's public key. The encrypted message is sent to the payment gateway along with the merchant's certificate.

Payment Gateway Capture Processing

Upon receipt, the payment gateway recovers the session key, capture request then verifies the merchant's certificate and signature on the request

The payment gateway generates a digitally signed and encrypted response message that is forwarded to the merchant along with the gateway's certificate.

Merchant Processing of Response

This is the final step in the protocol. The merchant recovers the session key and the capture message and verifies the gateway's certificate as well as the digital signature on the message. This is stored by the gateway for reconciliation for payment from the issuer.

10.4 SET Performance

From the description of the SET protocol, it is apparent that SET provides a high level of security and privacy for the participants. This is mainly due to the extensive use of public key certificates and digitally signed and verified messages. This has several important implications. Trust in the system relies on the deployment of a full public key infrastructure. If SET is to be used on a wide-scale basis, certificates have to be issued to all users. This is an enormous and expensive task. On the other hand if the PKI is not in place, then SET will not be used by a large number of users.

In version 1.0 of SET, RSA is specified to implement the public key operations. At present a minimum of 768-bit RSA is required for security, preferably 1024-bit. Public key operations (signing/verifying, wrapping/unwrapping) are computationally intensive, and certificates are large in size and require significant bandwidth to transmit.

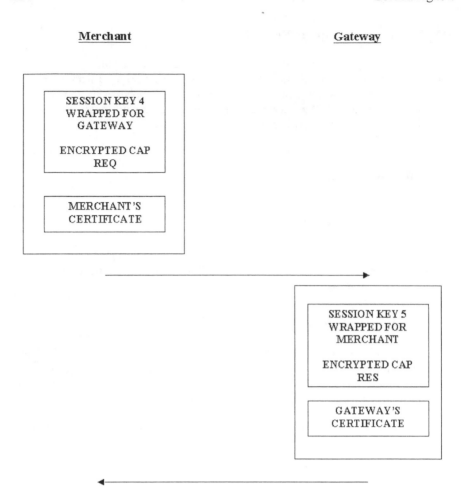

Fig. 10.7 Payment capture phase

In the case of the cardholder using a typical desktop computer, the computational load is not significant. If, on the other hand, the cardholder is not bound to a particular machine, then the cryptographic functions may be implemented in a portable token, such as a smart card. Implementing RSA on smart cards usually requires the smart card to have a cryptographic co-processor that raises the cost of the card.

There is also the issue of conducting e-commerce transactions using wireless handheld devices, such as cell phones or PDAs. In these situations bandwidth and processing power are at a premium and supporting SET may be difficult.

The GartnerConsulting Group did an extensive evaluation of the performance of SET [10.1]. In the study, it was anticipated that merchants could expect in the order of 10,000 transactions per day while a large payment gateway may approach ½ million transactions per day. In this case, software implementations of the public-key system may not be able to perform operations quickly enough; hardware accelerators may be required (adding to the cost of the infrastructure). They also examined the advantages of using other public key cryptographic systems. In their report, *elliptic curve cryptosystems*[4] (ECC) were considered and shown to have significant advantages in terms of bandwidth and processing overhead.

Sans and Agnew [10.3] present the results of an extensive study of the communications and processing overhead for SET. They show some alternative methods for processing transactions that reduce the overhead incurred using SET.

10.5 What Lies Ahead

There are a number of companies currently offering support for SET. These include IBM, Verisign, CyberTrust, Verifone, Sterling Commerce, Terisa, Netpay and GlobeSet.

SETCo lists more than 40 countries that have adopted SET in one form or another [10.4].

A proposal for SET 2.0 incorporates alternative asymmetric key cryptographic systems (specifically, elliptic curves) and SET 2.0 will also support the use of debit cards by allowing personal identification numbers (PINs) to be encrypted and included in the payment message [10.5]. In addition, a smart-card-based version known as chip-secured SET (C-SET) is being developed to allow smart cards to perform cardholder authentication and transaction security functions (encryption and signatures).

10.6 Summary

In this chapter, we have presented a detailed outline of the SET protocol. The capabilities and shortcomings of SET have been compared to other Internet security protocols.

Currently, SSL is the most widely deployed and used security protocol. It is relatively fast and provides transparent security to the user. It does not, however

---

[4] The reader is referred to www.certicom.com for a more complete review of ECC technology.

provide the mutual authentication and digital signature capabilities that are required for truly secure e-commerce.

SET, on the other hand, is a very robust protocol that provides a high level of security and trust. The major impediments to widespread deployment and use of SET are the current lack of a comprehensive public key infrastructure and the large overhead required to run the SET protocol. Improvements in processing power and the use of alternative public key cryptosystems such as elliptic-curve-based systems (ECC) may help to overcome some of these obstacles.

10.7 References

[10.1]   GartnerConsulting: SET comparative performance analysis. www.setco.org/download/setco6.pdf
[10.2]   A. J. Menezes, P. Oorschot, S. Vanstone (1997) Handbook of applied cryptography. CRC Press, New York.
[10.3]   O. Sans, G. Agnew (2001) An efficient multiple merchant payment protocol for secure electronic transactions based on purchase consolidation. In: W. Kou, et al. (eds.) Electronic commerce technologies – ISEC2001, LNCS 2048. Springer, Berlin Heidelberg New York.
[10.4]   www.setco.org/set_specifications.html
[10.5]   www.setco.org/extensions.html

11 Credit Card-Based Secure Online Payment*

Johnny W. Wong[1], Lev Mirlas[2], Weidong Kou[3], and Xiaodong Lin[1]

[1] University of Waterloo
Waterloo, Ontario, Canada

[2] IBM Canada Ltd.
Warden Ave., Markham, Ontario, Canada

[3] University of Hong Kong
Pokfulam Road, Hong Kong

11.1 Introduction

The credit card is a popular payment method for the purchase of goods and services. Traditionally, credit cards are used by buyers to purchase merchandise from
brick-and-mortar stores. Transactions are carried out face-to-face. Typically, the
merchant first obtains authorization from the credit card company regarding the
transaction. If the transaction is authorized, the buyer is asked to sign for the purchase, and a paper receipt stating the terms of the sale will be issued to the buyer.
The merchant also verifies that the buyer's signature matches the cardholder's signature at the back of the card, and that the card has not expired.

Shopping by phone, by mail, or by fax are convenient alternatives to shopping
at a brick-and-mortar store. The buyer sends the order information to the merchant
by phone, mail, or fax, together with the credit card information such as the credit
card number, cardholder ID, and expiry date. The order information contains the
goods or services to be provided by the merchant and the agreed price. Upon receiving the order, the merchant first obtains authorization of the transaction from
the credit card company. The merchant then ships the merchandise and charges
the buyer through his/her credit card. For purchase by mail or by fax, the merchant
has the buyer's signature on the order form. The buyer's signature is not available
to the merchant when the order is by phone. To obtain a record of the order, the

---

* This work was supported by the IBM Centre for Advanced Studies and an IBM Faculty
Partnership Award.

merchant records the phone conversation with the buyer when the order was placed.

Shopping over the Internet is another alternative to shopping at a brick-and-mortar store. In this case, the order information and credit card information are transmitted over the Internet, which may not have the same level of security as phone, mail, or fax. Methods to ensure secure online payment by credit card are therefore important to the success of shopping over the Internet. This chapter is concerned with online payment methods based on the existing credit card payment infrastructure. We first provide an overview of online payment by credit card, and then discuss the trust issue related to this payment method. To overcome the trust problem, we introduce a new payment protocol using a trusted third party. This protocol can be viewed as a special case of online payment by credit card, which addresses the trust problem that the current credit-card-based online payment systems have.

11.2 Online Payment by Credit Card

When making a purchase over the Internet using a credit card, procedures for secure communication are needed to authenticate the parties involved, to ensure confidential transmission of order and payment information, and to protect the integrity of the transaction. The current approach to achieving secure communication is to use the secure sockets layer (SSL) [11.1].

As briefly discussed in Chap. 10, SSL is a protocol designed to provide secure communication. It performs server authentication, and, optionally, client authentication. With SSL, private information is protected through encryption, and a user is assured through server authentication that they are communicating with the desired website and not with some bogus website. In addition, SSL provides data integrity, i.e., protection against any attempt to modify the data transferred during a communication session. The main exchanges in an SSL session [11.5-11.6] are shown in Fig. 11.1, and the detailed descriptions for each exchange are provided in Sect. 11.6.1, Appendix A. The use of SSL has led to an improvement in the buyer's confidence when making payments by credit card over the Internet.

A credit card transaction involves five main parties: buyer, merchant, merchant bank, issuer, and acquirer. The merchant has a contract with the merchant bank to enable them to accept credit card payments over the Internet. The issuer is a financial institution such as a bank that issues a credit card to the buyer. It is responsible for the cardholder's debt payment. The acquirer, on the other hand, obtains credit card transactions from the merchant and processes them for payment. The acquirer provides authorization to the merchant that a given account is active and that the proposed purchase does not exceed the cardholder's credit limit. The acquirer also makes payments to the merchant's account, and is then reimbursed by the issuer. The merchant bank may function as the acquirer.

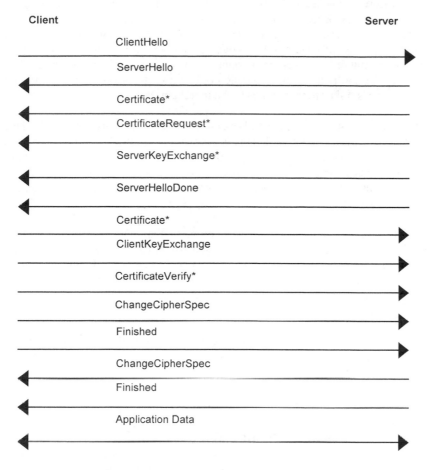

* Indicates optional or situation-dependent messages that are not always sent.

Fig. 11.1 The main SSL exchanges

We now describe the steps involved in handling payments by credit card over the Internet. The transaction starts with the buyer deciding to place an order online from a web page at the merchant's website. The merchant's commerce application prompts the buyer for payment information (i.e., credit card number, cardholder ID, and expiry date) along with other information such as shipping address. The buyer then enters payment information into a form secured using SSL. With the secured form, the payment information is protected as it is sent to the merchant.

Upon receiving the order, the merchant server sends the payment information to the acquirer processor for authorization, using dedicated and secure lines. The authorization is a request to hold funds for the purchase. The acquirer will verify that the credit card has sufficient funds to cover the amount of the transaction. The acquirer either authorizes a certain amount of money or declines the transaction. Each authorization reduces the available credit only, it does not put a charge on the cardholder's bill or transfer funds to the merchant.

After the transaction has been authorized, the merchant charges the authorized amount to the buyer's credit card. This is known as "capture." According to bank card association rules, the merchant is not allowed to capture a transaction until the ordered goods can be shipped, so there may be a time lag between authorization and capture. If the buyer cancels the order before capture, a "void" is generated.

Captures are accumulated into a batch and settled automatically at regular time intervals, e.g., at the end of each day. This settlement can be viewed as a transaction between the acquirer and the merchant. When a batch is submitted, the merchant's payment-enabled web server connects with the acquirer to finalize the transactions and transfer the corresponding amounts to the merchant's bank account.

At the issuer, a monthly statement is sent to the cardholder for the purchases made since the last statement.

11.3 Trust Problems in Credit Card Payments

The issue of trust in the payment process is one of the most critical aspects that determines the acceptability of a payment method. Clearly, if the parties participating in a payment transaction cannot be assured of the correctness of the transaction, then they are unlikely to conduct the transaction in the first place.

In a payment transaction, trust is engendered through the following assurances:

The buyers must be assured that:

- The transaction will result in them paying exactly the specified amount and being billed only for the item they bought at the agreed price.

- The payment information they provide will not be stolen or abused for extracting unauthorized payments from them.
- They will receive the goods that they have purchased.
- In the case of a dispute they have in their possession enough evidence to prove whether or not the payment took place.

The merchants must be assured that:

- The transaction will result in them being paid exactly the agreed amount.
- In the case of a dispute they have in their possession enough evidence to prove whether or not the payment took place.

A "good" payment protocol assures these trust points for both the buyer and the merchant. These trust points are easily met in credit card transactions at a brick-and-mortar store. Since the transaction is face-to-face, the merchant can verify the buyer's signature against that on the back of the credit card. The amount of the transaction and goods purchased can readily be confirmed. There is no danger in payment information being stolen if the buyer is dealing with a trustworthy merchant. In the case of a dispute, each party has a signed copy of the receipt which can be used as evidence that the transaction took place.

The issue of trust becomes more complicated when credit-card payments are made over the Internet. The use of SSL may not address all the trust points mentioned above. A common concern is that some of the traditional assurances of integrity of the payment transactions can become compromised. Consider the assurance mentioned above in the context of online transactions.

The issues at the buyer side are:

- The buyers would like to be assured that they are paying exactly the specified amount. In general, there is a lack of trust in online systems. As a result, there is no guarantee that the amount charged is the same as the amount requested.
- The buyers would like to be assured that the payment information provided cannot be stolen or abused for extracting unauthorized payments from them. The online security of trusted data has been compromised many times, and such events have been highlighted in the media. It seems that the task of keeping trusted data, such as credit card numbers, safe from intruders in an online site is not trivial. However, merchants who collect this data are typically not technically savvy, and do not have the resources to institute the kind of secure and trusted computing base necessary to constantly guard against possible intrusion and data theft attempts.

- The buyers would like to trust that they will receive the goods that they have purchased. This depends on the track record and reputation of the merchant.
- In the case of a dispute the buyers would like to have in their possession enough evidence to prove whether or not the payment took place. In the online world, the buyers generally do not get much protection. Sometimes a merchant will give a "transaction reference number," though this number merely indicates that a transaction has taken place, without proving the time or amount involved. Merchants have started sending e-mails confirming payment transactions, and in some cases e-mail has been accepted as evidence in court. However, there is no guarantee that the e-mail will actually be sent and, moreover, even if sent, e-mail systems have been known to lose or be unable to deliver some documents.

The best assurance that the buyer has in this area is to deal with a large and well-established company. If the transaction amount is relatively small compared to the total business done by the company, then the company will not compromise its reputation over a small dispute. However, this is not always true, and may not apply if the transaction amount is large.

The issues at the merchant side are:

- The merchants would like to be assured that they are being paid exactly the specified amount. This issue is not a concern from the perspective of the merchant.
- In the case of a dispute the merchants would like to have in their possession enough evidence to prove whether or not the payment took place. The assurance is weak because there is little evidence that the buyer has agreed to pay the specified amount. For example, the buyer may call the credit card company and claim that the transaction never took place. The merchant has little evidence to argue on. The only evidence is if the buyer has registered at the site in a way that proves their identity, and somehow signed for the purchase. In this case, one has to prove that the registration site has good password security, and even then the buyer may claim that his/her password was stolen, or given away by the merchant.

As mentioned earlier, user authentication, privacy of information, and data integrity can be assured by using SSL. However, SSL is only part of the solution to the security of online credit card transactions. It does not address all the trust issues between the buyer and the merchant. An effective approach to ensure trust is to use a *trusted third party* (TTP), who is trusted by both the buyer and the merchant.

11.4 Trusted Third Party and a Payment Protocol Using a Trusted Third Party

Long before the invention of online commerce, people resorted to the use of trusted third parties to assure transaction integrity. For example, a notary public certifies documents for correctness, which gives such documents extra weight as court evidence. Another classic example is buying a house, which is a transaction performed "in trust" by the lawyers of the buyer and the seller. In this case, the lawyers act as "trusted third parties" on behalf of their clients.

In the online world, we believe that transactions should be similarly notarized by a trusted third party, and such notarization assures both parties of the integrity of the transaction. In this section, we describe a new payment protocol that uses a trusted third party, which can be used for credit card payments and other types of payments. This protocol has several advantages over existing protocols, e.g., SET, as described in Chap. 10. These advantages are discussed below:

- There is no sharing of payment instrument between the buyer and the merchant. This results in improved protection for both parties.
- There is no need for the buyer to register with any payment service (some protocols, such as CyberCash or PayPal, require this type of registration). As a result, buyers have increased flexibility and convenience in the choice of payment service.
- The protocol is designed as a HTTP-style request-response message protocol [11.4]. This approach reduces the complexity in implementation. For example, there is no need at any point to transmit a message to two destinations and expect the receiving parties to synchronize with each other. Instead, each step in the protocol involves a single message from the sender to the receiver, and a corresponding response back from the receiver to the sender.
- The protocol is robust in the sense that recovery is possible at any point in the case of a failure; hence the protocol protects both the merchant and the buyer from insufficient or excessive charges due to communication or system failures.
- The protocol can be used with any existing payment instruments, e.g., credit cards and debit cards. This offers increased versatility in terms of supporting a variety of payment methods.
- Supporting evidence is provided to the buyer and to the merchant regarding the nature of the transaction in case dispute resolution is required. This is accomplished by sending only a digest of the details of the transaction to the TTP.
- A single TTP may be used by both the buyer and the merchant. Alternatively, the buyer and the merchant can each be represented by their own TTP.

11.4.1 Description of the New Payment Protocol

In this section, the new payment protocol for the case of one TTP is described. The protocol requires the availability of a public-key certificate authority. Any certificate authority can be used, such as Pretty Good Privacy (PGP) or commercial providers, such as VeriSign.

The basic steps of our protocol are shown in Fig. 11.2. For each step, any message transfer (if required) is secured using cryptographic technology, such as SSL.

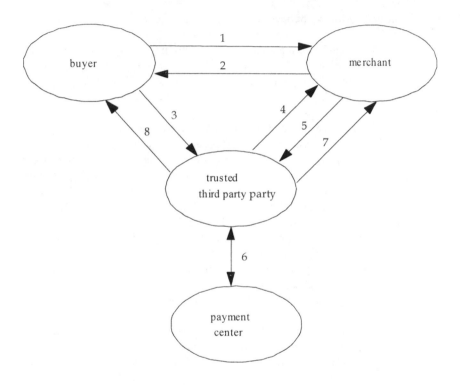

Fig. 11.2 Payment protocol with one TTP

There are eight steps in the protocol (detailed information on each step is provided in Sect. 11.6.2, Appendix B).

(1) The buyer sends an "order" message to the merchant.
(2) The merchant, upon receiving the order message, returns a "payment request" message to the buyer.

(3) The buyer, after verifying the merchant's signature, proceeds by sending a "payment" message to the TTP.

(4) The TTP, after verifying the buyer's signature, requests a confirmation from the merchant by sending a "confirmation request" message to the merchant.

(5) The merchant, upon receiving the confirmation request message, verifies the transaction ID and amount, and sends a "transaction confirmed" message to the TTP.

(6) The TTP obtains authorization from the payment center.

(7) The TTP sends a signed "merchant receipt" message to the merchant.

(8) The TTP sends a signed "buyer receipt" message to the buyer.

In these steps, all three parties, namely, the buyer, the merchant, and the trusted third party have each provided evidence of the transaction (a signed request or receipt). In the case of a dispute, the buyer has a signed payment request from the merchant and a signed receipt from the TTP. The merchant has a signed receipt from the TTP. The TTP has a signed payment from the buyer and a signed confirmation from the merchant. The signed information is sufficient for dispute-resolution purposes.

11.4.2 Extension to the Case of Two TTPs

For the case of a single TTP, the TTP could have a conflict of interest in the case of a dispute because it would be representing the interests of both the buyer and the merchant. For this reason, examples of candidates for trusted third parties are typically organizations, such as major banks or major credit card companies, which have no obvious vested interest in supporting either dispute party in a transaction.

In some cases, however, buyers and merchants may want to be represented by a trusted third party that is more active in supporting their concerns, and perhaps is targeted specifically at providing a service for their needs. In such a case, a conflict of interest can be avoided if two TTPs are involved, one for the buyer (referred to as TTP-B), and the other for the merchant (referred to as TTP-M). In the case of a dispute, TTP-B and TTP-M will be involved in dispute resolution, protecting the interests of the buyer and merchant, respectively. In addition, such a protocol with two TTPs has the potential to allow more types of organizations to assume the role of the trusted third party.

The payment protocol can readily be extended to the case of two TTPs. The basic steps are illustrated in Fig. 11.3.

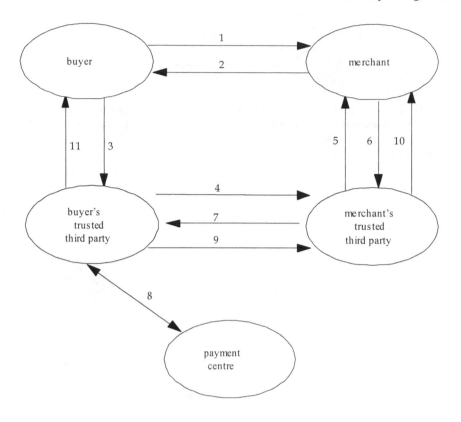

Fig. 11.3 Payment protocol with two TTPs

These steps are:

(1) The buyer sends order information to the merchant.
(2) The merchant requests payment from the buyer (message from the mer-
    chant to the buyer also contains the address of TTP-M).
(3) The buyer sends the payment information and the amount of the payment
    to TTP-B (this message also contains the address of TTP-M).
(4) TTP-B sends a message to TTP-M, requesting a confirmation from the
    merchant.
(5) TTP-M checks with the merchant to get a confirmation of the transaction
    and the amount of the payment.
(6) The merchant returns a confirmation to TTP-M.
(7) TTP-M forwards the confirmation to TTP-B.
(8) Message exchange between TTP-B and the payment center regarding the
    payment authorization.
(9) TTP-B sends a receipt to TTP-M, confirming the payment.
(10) TTP-M forwards the receipt to the merchant.

(11) TTP-B sends a receipt to the buyer.

The message contents, together with the actions taken by the buyer, the merchant, TTP-B, and TTP-M at the various steps are straightforward extensions of those for the case of one TTP (see Sect. 11.6.2, Appendix B), and will not be presented.

11.4.3 Discussion

It is important to trace the business reason for the viability of this payment protocol.

Typically, once a buyer gives the payment information to the merchant, it is the merchant's responsibility to ensure that payment is captured from the corresponding financial institution. Note that in some cases the financial institution may insure the buyer against fraudulent use of the payment information. This is the case with credit cards, where most issuers do not hold buyers responsible for payment of unauthorized transactions on their cards. The cost of this insurance is imposed on the merchants, who must pay an increased fee for online transactions.

With our protocol, some of the burden of transaction insurance is shifted to the trusted third party. The buyer's TTP provides assurance to the buyer that the correct amount of payment will be collected and passed to the merchant. At the same time, insurance against unauthorized transactions may now be split among the financial institution and the TTP, depending on the service agreement.

The merchant's TTP must provide assurance to the merchant that the buyer's payment instrument will be charged, and funds transferred to the merchant. This had been the merchant's responsibility, but is now a burden carried by the TTP.

Clearly, for the protocol to be successful there needs to be a business case to operate a buyer or merchant TTP service. The following are sample business cases:

- The TTP charges the merchant a transaction fee (similar to current credit card transaction fees), and carries the entire weight of the fraudulent transaction insurance. Typically, credit card companies charge a large premium for Internet-based transactions. By charging merchants a fixed or transaction-based service fee, the TTP would fund the insurance. In this scenario, the TTP is effectively competing with credit card companies for a portion of the payment transaction fees.

- The buyer's TTP charges the buyer a fixed service fee, or a transaction fee. The buyer would use the service because it results in more trusted transactions, with extra security provided by the TTP, as well as the TTP's enhanced insurance policy.

- The TTP charges the merchant a fixed service fee. The merchant uses the service to attract buyers who demand the use of a trusted payment protocol.

- A financial institution provides a single TTP service, to stimulate online commerce by engendering trust, and hence potentially increase its transaction revenue.

11.5 Summary

In this chapter, an overview of credit card-based online transactions is presented, including payment authorization, capture, and settlement. The issue of trust between buyers and merchants is analyzed. We have also described a new protocol for secure online payment. This protocol allows a buyer to avoid sharing key payment method information with merchants, by moving the burden of payment assurance to a trusted third party. The protocol supports privacy because the order information is not sent to the trusted third party. The buying operation is simplified because there is no need to register with a payment service.

11.6 Appendices

11.6.1 Appendix A: the Main SSL Exchanges

In this section, we provide detailed information on the main exchanges in an SSL session.

To establish an SSL session between an SSL client and server, they need to agree on the SSL protocol version to be used, select cryptographic algorithms, optionally authenticate each other, and use public-key encryption techniques to generate and exchange shared secrets. The main exchanges between the client and the server during the establishment of an SSL session are described as follows:

ClientHello and ServerHello messages: These two messages are used to establish security enhancement capabilities between the client and the server. The attributes of the two messages include:

- Protocol version
- Session ID
- List of cryptographic options
- Compression method
- Random number

Server certificate: The server sends its certificate, if it is to be authenticated. The certificate format generally follows the X.509.v3 standard [11.7].

Server key exchange message: This is optional. It is required for certain circumstances, for example, if the server has no certificate, or if its certificate is for signing only. The attributes include a key exchange algorithm and associated parameters (e.g., RSA algorithm with RSA modulus and exponent).

ServerHelloDone message: This message indicates that the hello-message phase of the handshake is complete. After sending this message, the server will be in a mode to wait for a client response. The client verifies that the server provided a valid certificate if required and checks that the ServerHello parameters are acceptable.

Client key exchange message: This message has different formats, depending on which public-key algorithm has been selected between the ClientHello and the ServerHello messages. Once again, similar to the Server key exchange message, the attributes include a key exchange algorithm and associated parameters.

ChangeCipherSpec message: This is not a handshake massage. After this message is sent, the pending CipherSpec is transferred into the current CipherSpec.

Finished message: This message is always sent immediately after a ChangeCipherSpec message to verify that the key exchange and authentication processes were successful.

11.6.2 Appendix B: Steps of the Payment Protocol for the Case of One TTP

In this section, we provide the detailed steps of the payment protocol for the case of one TTP.

The following notation is used in our description:

CERT$_j$	j's certificate (j = b for buyer, j = m for merchant, j = t for TTP)
H(x)	Cryptographic digest of x
S$_j$(y)	Signature on information set y using private key of j (j = b for buyer, j = m for merchant, j = t for TTP)
*	Optional field

Step 1. The buyer sends an "order" message to the merchant.

The "order" message contains the following information:

> order = items to be purchased, shipping information, *previously quoted price, *time stamp

The previously quoted price is an optional field. The time stamp is an optional field included to prevent a replay attack. An intruder performs a replay attack by intercepting a protected message, and replaying it at a later time. The timestamp contained in a received message can be used to determine whether this is a replay of a previously received message or not.

Step 2. The merchant, upon receiving the order message, returns a "payment request" message to the buyer.

The "payment request" message contains the following information:

> payment request = transaction ID, amount, order, validity period, CERT$_m$, *purchase agreement, S$_m$(transaction ID, amount, order, validity period, CERT$_m$, *purchase agreement)

The transaction ID is generated by the merchant and used by the merchant and the TTP to keep track of all the transactions. The order information is the same as that provided by the buyer. The validity period specifies the time during which the payment must be confirmed. The merchant's certificate can be used by the buyer to verify the merchant's signature. The purchase agreement is an optional field which contains information such as refund policy, product quality, warranty, etc. A digital signature is included as part of the payment request message.

Step 3. The buyer, after verifying the merchant's signature, proceeds by sending a "payment" message to the TTP.

The "payment" message contains the following information:

> payment = payment information, amount, merchant, transaction ID, $CERT_b$, *timestamp, S_b(payment information, amount, merchant, transaction ID, $CERT_b$, *timestamp)

The payment information field contains information such as the credit card number, credit card holder, and expiry date. Besides credit cards, other payment instruments such as debit cards can be used. The transaction ID is the same as that provided by the merchant. The buyer's certificate can be used by the TTP to verify the buyer's signature. Again, an optional time stamp may be included to prevent a replay attack. A digital signature is included as part of the payment message.

Step 4. The TTP, after verifying the buyer's signature, requests a confirmation from the merchant by sending a "confirmation request" message to the merchant.

The "confirmation request" message contains the following information:

> confirmation request = transaction ID, amount, status, S_t(transaction ID, amount, status)

This message contains the transaction ID, amount, and payment status. A digital signature is included as part of the confirmation request message.

Step 5. The merchant, upon receiving the confirmation request message, verifies the transaction ID and amount, and sends a "transaction confirmed" message to the TTP.

The "transaction confirmed" message contains the following information:

> transaction confirmed = transaction ID, amount, status, S_m(transaction ID, amount, status), *H(transaction ID, amount, order, validity period, *purchase agreement), S_m(H(transaction ID, amount, order, validity period, *purchase agreement))

This message contains the transaction ID, amount, and payment status. As an option, a cryptographic digest of the transaction details (namely the transaction ID, amount, order, validity period, purchase agreement), as contained in the payment request message in step 2, may be included. This digest is useful for dispute-resolution purposes. A digital signature is included as part of the transaction-confirmed message.

Step 6. Obtain authorization from the payment center.

Upon receiving the transaction-confirmed message, the TTP requests the authorized amount from the payment center. The payment center returns an approval to the TTP.

Note that any payment method can be used in this step. Note also that the requirement for payment approval is tied to the TTP's policy. It is possible that in some cases (e.g., for preferred customers) the TTP would not wait for credit approval, but would process the payment immediately. In this case, the TTP, rather than the payment center, would be taking on the responsibility for the payment.

Furthermore, different TTPs may have different policies on handling unknown or delayed credit approval requests. For example, if the approval request times out, the TTP may either refuse to process the payment, or may take the risk of processing it. Similarly, even if the payment center rejects the request, the TTP may still process it, taking on the payment responsibility as described above.

Step 7. The TTP sends a signed "merchant receipt" message to the merchant.

The "merchant receipt" message contains the following information:

> merchant receipt = payment ID, transaction ID, amount, S_t(payment ID, transaction ID, amount)

Step 8. The TTP sends a signed "buyer receipt" message to the buyer.

The "buyer receipt" message contains the following information:

> buyer receipt = payment ID, transaction ID, amount, S_t(payment ID, transaction ID, amount)

After step 8, the TTP captures the payment and transfers the funds to the merchant. This step happens offline and involves the actual payment settlement.

Note that the above steps are sequential in nature. The transaction is not complete until the last step (step 8) is performed. A timer is used at each step to protect against unusual situations where one of the parties (buyer, merchant, or TTP) is not proceeding to the next step within a predetermined time interval. For steps 1 to 6, if the timer expires the transaction is assumed to be aborted. Any subsequent messages regarding this transaction will be ignored. Therefore, up to this point, any party can abort the transaction by simply not continuing with the next step.

At step 7, if the merchant does not receive a receipt within a time-out period, the merchant attempts to obtain the receipt by sending a request message to the

TTP. If a receipt is not received after a predetermined number of attempts, the transaction is assumed to be aborted. In this case, the buyer will not receive the order, but he/she can contact the TTP to request a refund.

At step 8, if the buyer does not receive a receipt within a time-out period, the buyer may request a receipt from the TTP at a later time. This would not affect the transaction because the order will be shipped by the merchant as long as the merchant has received the receipt.

11.7 References

[11.1]   A. O. Freier, P. Karlton, P. C. Kocher: SSL 3.0 protocol specification. http://home.netscape.com/eng/ssl3/index.html.

[11.2]   MasterCard International Incorporated, Visa International. The SET specification. http://www.setco.org/set_specifications.html.

[11.3]   D. Eastlake, B. Boesch, S. Crocker, M. Yesil (1996) CyberCash credit card protocol version 0.8. Internet RFC1898.

[11.4]   R. Fielding, J. Gettys, J. Mogul, H. Frystyk, L. Masinter, P. Leach, T. Berners-Lee (1999) Hypertext Transfer Protocol – HTTP/1.1. Internet RFC2616.

[11.5]   X. Lin, J. W. Wong, W. Kou (2000) Performance analysis of secure web server based on SSL. In: Proceedings of ISW2000, J. Pieprzyk, E. Okamoto, J. Seberry (eds.), LNCS 1975. Springer. Berlin Heidelberg New York, pp. 249–261.

[11.6]   A. O. Freier, P. Karlton, P. C. Kocher (1996) The SSL protocol version 3.0. http://wp.netscape.com/eng/ssl3/ssl-toc.html

[11.7]   W. Ford, M. Baum (1997) Secure electronic commerce: building the infrastructure for digital signatures and encryption. Prentice-Hall, Englewood Cliffs New York.

12 Micropayments

Amir Herzberg

Security Consultant
Israel

12.1 Introduction

Open data networks, such as the Internet and the wireless data networks, allow low-cost delivery of content (information) and services to a huge population (market). The production costs of content and services are often small and largely independent of the number of customers. Therefore, producers of content and services provided to many customers often want to charge very small amounts – if the payment system allows it (with reasonable overhead). Payment by credit cards, which is the common method for online consumer purchasing, involves substantial minimal fee per transaction, e.g., 20 cents, and therefore is not applicable for charging smaller amounts. This provides one definition of the micropayments, as charging amounts smaller (or close to) the minimal credit card transaction fees (of about 20 cents). There are other difficulties in using credit cards for low-value transactions, namely, substantial delay and user involvement, and the potential for disputes resulting in refunds, chargebacks, and substantial handling costs.

This creates a difficulty for many existing and potential applications and services on the Internet[1], which need a source of income to cover their costs and generate profits while the amount they can charge (for one use) is too low to justify a credit card transaction. Currently, most of the deployed services and applications are funded only by advertising or by charging substantial amount in advance for multiple purchases (e.g., subscriptions). A direct-payment mechanism could be an important alternative or complementary source of funding, especially to facilitate smaller vendors and applications where advertising cannot be used (e.g., due to lack of appropriate display, and in particular when services are consumed by automated agents without any advertising potential). This motivates the development and introduction of *micropayment* schemes and systems.

In this chapter, we focus on providing micropayment services with acceptable (low) transaction cost. This is the basic requirement from a micropayment system, namely, that it can be used to charge sufficiently low amounts, in particular, below

---

[1] We only mention the Internet but the discussion applies to most open networks.

credit card minimal fees (of about 20 cents). The minimal amount to be supported may be considered as a parameter of the system, or there may be a specific requirement. In particular, when considering payments that involve a manual decision element (by a person), it seems that a minimal amount of about one cent may be sufficient, as the cost of the decision process itself is probably worth about a cent, and smaller-value items should probably not require specific user decision and action (otherwise, a lower-denomination coin would have been introduced). When considering payments by a software agent of the user, e.g., to pay for the actual communication services, there may be room for payments of amounts even significantly smaller than one cent.

In Section 12.3 below we analyze the different cost factors for online payments, and in Section 12.4 we elaborate on different mechanisms used to reduce each of the significant cost factors. But first, in the next section, we provide an overview of micropayment systems.

12.2 Overview of Micropayment Systems

There are different motivations for developing new payment mechanisms. We focus on micropayments mechanisms that are operated by one or more payment service provider (PSP), allowing merchants to charge small amounts from customers. There have been many different definitions, goals, and proposals for micropayment mechanisms, including low-value offline payments (using a device rather than coins), anonymous payments (digital cash), and systems where the merchant charges a large amount once but allows the customer to use it incrementally over many small purchases (merchant acting also as a micropayment service provider).

Our focus is on the most common interpretation, namely, many payments of small amounts (micropayments) from customers to merchants, over open-data networks, such as the Internet, made by using one or more payment service providers. A PSP maintains a long-term relationship with customers and merchants, receiving payments of aggregated (large) amounts from customers and passing aggregated payments to the merchants, as illustrated in Fig. 12.1. This model assumes that consumer relationships with merchants are sporadic rather than long-term, and that a major role of the PSP is to provide facilities for efficient and secure transactions by using its relationships with the parties.

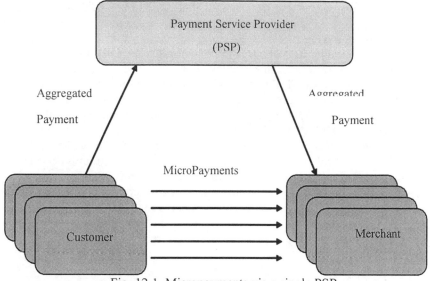

Fig. 12.1 Micropayments via a single PSP

Fig. 12.1 shows the payment relationships between the parties: sporadic micropayments from consumers to merchants, and long-term, usually periodic, payments of aggregated amounts from customers to PSP and from PSP to merchants. This does not describe the flow of messages for a micropayment transaction; we will describe different protocols, with different message flows. Payment protocols include mechanisms for *payment approval* by the customer, where the customer agrees to pay, as well as *payment authorization* by the PSP, where the PSP indicates that there are funds to cover the payment.

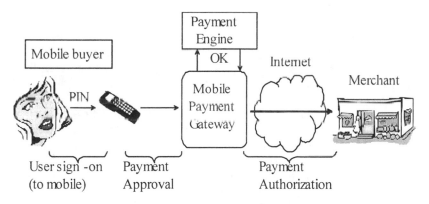

Fig. 12.2 Payments via the PSP

Payment approval and payment authorization may be integrated or separated. Separation of the payment-approval process from the payment-authorization process is appropriate, in particular, in scenarios where the PSP is (or controls) a gateway between the customer and merchant, as illustrated in Fig. 12.2. The customer approves the payment to the PSP, and then the PSP sends an *authorized payment order* (PO) to the merchant. This scenario is applicable whenever the PSP is also providing the communication services to the consumer or is in close alliance with the communication providers. In particular, this scenario is appropriate when the PSP is also the consumer's ISP or a mobile-communication provider, or when the ISP or mobile provider are cooperating with the PSP to improve the user interface for payments. In this case, the payment authorization is, naturally, always online and involves only the PSP and the merchant. Furthermore, payment authorization can be completely independent from the payment approval process between the consumer and the PSP, and certainly from the login process (if any) between the consumer and their computer or device. In particular, in this scenario we can take advantage of existing security mechanisms between the consumer and their ISP or mobile gateway to validate that the consumer approved the payment. For example, a mobile gateway usually can identify the handset, e.g. using a shared key, and the handset may identify its user, e.g., using PIN, voice recognition, or any other identification technology.

In other scenarios, the PSP is not "on the path" between the consumer and merchant, and therefore either consumer or merchant should contact it to request authorization for payment when required. This is typical, e.g., for web browsing, when the PSP is not the ISP (or in alliance with the ISP). In most micropayment systems, the consumer contacts the PSP to approve the payment and to request the PSP to authorize the PO. For technical reasons, namely, allowing the PSP to operate as an efficient server application, the PSP sends the authorized PO as a response to the consumer, who forwards it to the merchant. The merchant will later (offline) deposit the PO, often in a batch process with many other payment orders, to receive the aggregated payment.

Fig. 12.3 presents a high level illustration of the online payment process in this scenario (payment invoked by the consumer), as implemented by most currently-deployed micropayment systems, e.g., by Qpass, iPin, and TrivNet. We will later also discuss systems where the merchant is requesting the authorization from the PSP, or where there is no online payment authorization.

So far, we have discussed only a single PSP providing service to both customer and merchant. The single-PSP solution is simple and efficient. However, currently, there is no dominant single PSP for micropayments. Indeed, there are a substantial number of competing PSPs for micropayments, and we can expect more PSPs to emerge as the demand for micropayments grows and the market matures. In fact, the expected financial returns from a micropayment system may not be high enough to justify a sufficient effort by a single PSP, or even a small number of PSPs, to gain market dominance (in contrast to the $2 \sim 3$ major credit card brands). We would therefore expect that there will be multiple PSPs offering micropayment services.

It is unrealistic to expect all customers and all merchants to have accounts with multiple PSPs. Instead, we expect that micropayment systems will need to support interoperability among multiple PSPs, each with its own customers and merchants, with aggregated payments and long-term relationships between the PSPs, allowing customers of one PSP to make purchases from merchants of the other PSP. A simple architecture with two PSPs is illustrated in Fig. 12.4.

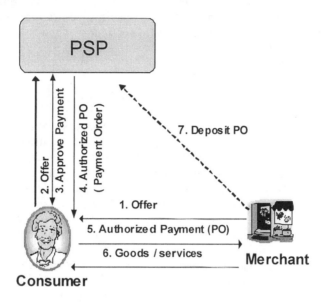

Fig. 12.3 Online payments invoked by consumer

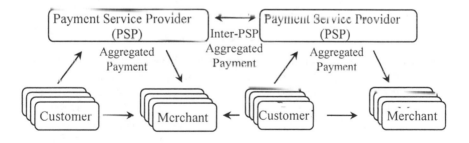

Fig. 12.4 Micropayments via two interoperating PSPs

12.3 Cost Factors for Online Payments

In order to allow economical charging of small amounts, we need to consider the different cost factors that, by affecting the payment service provider, affect the merchant directly and indirectly. Indeed, from the merchants' perspective, it may be enough to use a PSP without the substantial minimal-fee requirement of existing credit cards; but these costs are not pure profit, and the PSP needs to have a viable business case. In order to design a mechanism with substantially reduced costs, as compared to credit cards, we need to consider (and minimize) at least the most significant cost factors.

In the following sections, we consider three major categories of costs:

- **Disputes, chargebacks and their processing cost:** Many payment systems, and even certain laws, allow the customer to dispute charges, or otherwise not to pay, usually under certain circumstances. In some or all of these cases, the PSPs may *reverse* the transaction, requiring the merchant to return the funds (*chargeback*). In particular, payment orders received electronically, without a signed authorization, are often reversible. Indeed, disputes and subsequent chargebacks are substantially more common for Internet transactions than for face-to-face transactions that have been authorized with the signature of the customer. The costs here include the actual refund amount, as well as substantial processing cost (for the PSPs and the merchant) and possible penalty payments (by the merchant). The processing costs of credit card payment service providers are estimated at about $50, with penalties payments for merchants with frequent disputes of about $100 [12.34]. This is probably the most critical cost factor for micropayments, and much of the work on micropayment systems is targeted at reducing the expenses associated with it (see Section 12.4).

- **Customer acquiring and support costs:** These are the costs of encouraging customers to deploy the new service (open an account, install a wallet, etc.), and later assisting customers. These expenses may be substantial, especially compared to the small value of the transaction. The main mechanism to reduce these costs is to use simple procedures and user interface. In particular, it is highly desirable to offer an easy-to-use, "click and pay" user interface for micropayments. On the other hand, to minimize installation and support costs, the customer should be able to use standard software tools (e.g., a browser) rather than installing customer software (wallet) on the consumer's machine. Finally, PSPs should be interoperable, namely, the customer of one PSP should be able to buy from a merchant of another PSP, as shown in Fig. 12.4, so that multiple

PSPs share the customer acquiring and support costs (See more details in Section 12.5).

- **Equipment, processing, and communication costs:** These are the costs of the necessary hardware, software, and communication for processing the payments by customer, merchant, and PSP. These costs are a function of the processing and communication requirements of the payment protocol, including the dependency on online involvement of the PSP, requiring high availability. Indeed, most of the research on micropayments, and several of the deployed systems, focus on minimizing the processing and/or communication costs. In particular, many efforts have focused on reducing the processing costs by avoiding public-key operations. Another area that received a lot of attention is reduction in communication requirements, and in particular, allowing offline or semi-offline payments (in particular, "stored value" offline payments, where the merchant and browser are in direct connection but disconnected from the PSP. See more details in Section 12.6).

There are several additional cost factors, which are less significant or easier to deal with, such as:

- **Bookkeeping and auditing costs:** Many payment systems have substantial bookkeeping and auditing mechanisms and costs. It is tempting to suggest that these costs can be eliminated by simply not logging and auditing micropayments, or keeping only very partial and temporal logs. However, accurate logging and auditing is often required by law, and may also be necessary to provide non-repudiation for efficient dispute resolution and to detect fraud. Bookkeeping and auditing costs may be reduced by secure automated *record aggregation* mechanisms, e.g. [12.13], whereby the customer signs a single document, which is archived instead of multiple separate documents (similarly to the presentment of a monthly statement by utilities). Record aggregation may reduce, also help, to protect the privacy of the customer by not keeping track of individual transactions for long. Other approaches try to protect the privacy of the buyer even further, by preventing the PSP from identifying payments of a particular customer, using one of the many anonymous (digital) cash protocols, e.g. [12.3]. Some, e.g. [12.1], believe that anonymous payments would also be less expensive, by avoiding bookkeeping (almost) entirely and preventing disputes and chargebacks.

- **Point-of-sale integration costs:** These are the costs for a merchant for setting up merchandise for sale, and for publishing information and services. These costs can be reduced by simple, automated tools for the merchants (for small merchants, and for initial phases), hosting services by the PSP may also be desirable. However, these are one-time expenses and should usually be rather insignificant in the long run.

- **Credit risk:** When the customer is charged for the aggregated payments only after the purchases are made, the customer may refuse to pay their PSP. Often, PSPs eliminate this risk by requiring funds to be deposited in advance. This problem also appears when interoperating between multiple PSPs, where one PSP ends up owing the other PSP; in this case, prepayment is rarely a solution, since usually both PSPs may end up owing the other PSP. This becomes a risk-management issue, with associated costs of estimating and containing the risk.

12.4 Disputes and Chargebacks

As noted above, disputes and chargebacks, and in particular, their processing costs, are of the most significant expense factors for online credit card purchasing. In credit card purchasing, and to some extent in any remote purchasing, such as through the Internet, there are laws protecting consumer's right to dispute and reverse transactions that were not approved by the consumer, and often to some extent also transactions that were not properly fulfilled. This creates a difficult challenge to the designers of micropayment systems. In general, disputes and chargebacks for electronic payments fall into four main categories.

- **Disputes on whether payment was approved by consumer**: Consumer claims that they did not *approve* the payment.
- **Unauthorized overspending chargebacks:** PSP claims that it did not *authorize* the payment, and that there are not sufficient funds in the customer's account to cover it (in systems where the merchant should receive authorization from the PSP for each payment).
- **Disputes on delivery and/or quality**: Consumer claims that the merchant did not *deliver properly* the goods or services as ordered.
- **Chargebacks due to consumer default**: PSP claims that the consumer *defaulted,* and did not provide necessary funds.

We now discuss each of these categories for disputes and chargebacks, beginning with the last two, which we believe should simply be disallowed for micropayment systems. But first let us consider an example.

12.4.1 Example: First Virtual Payment System

A simple example is the First Virtual payment system, illustrated in Fig. 12.5, which was of the earliest payment systems proposed [12.36]. One of First Virtual's goals was to offer lower fees for small charges (compared to credit cards) and avoidance of chargebacks. First Victual's system used two (non-cryptographic) security mechanisms for each purchase: a secret "first virtual account number" (FV#) provided by the consumer to the merchant and forwarded to the First Virtual Net server (on the Internet), and an email approval request, sent from the First Virtual Net server to the consumer and approved (or declined) in a message from the consumer back to the First Virtual Net server. Only after the consumer approves the payment, the merchant's account with First Virtual is credited, the merchant is informed that the payment was cleared. A credit card transaction is performed (immediately or periodically) to collect the funds from the customer's credit card account, whose details were kept in a separate First Virtual "Credit Card Server".

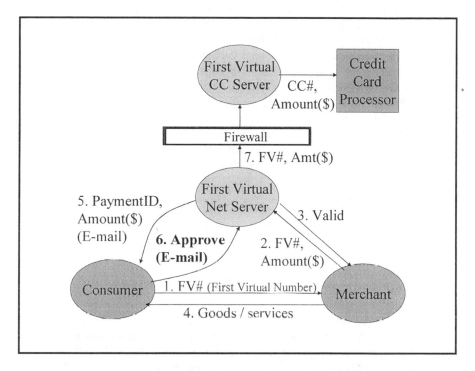

Fig. 12.5 First Virtual's centralized PSP based on email confirmation

The payment-approval process of First Virtual is subject to attacks, since standard Internet email is not secure; this makes the entire authorization process insecure. It is particularly easy to inject e-mail messages with incorrect source identification; First Virtual protects against this attack by including a random payment transaction identifier in the approval-request email message (PaymentID). However, the attacker may be able to intercept the email message in transit to the consumer, and then send the approval response with the correct PaymentID. To protect against this, First Virtual suggested that consumers may use available secure email software to digitally sign their payment approval responses.

12.4.2 Consumer Default and Disputes on Delivery/Quality

We believe that micropayment systems should not allow disputes on product delivery or quality or on chargebacks due to consumer default. The basic reason is
that there may not be a long-term relationship between the buyer and the merchant. Therefore, the merchant can hardly manage such risks, e.g., the risk of the
consumer defaulting on its payment obligations to its PSP.

In particular, consider disputes about whether the purchased product or service
was in fact delivered, or about the quality of the product or service. Some proposed and deployed systems attempt to avoid disputes on product delivery, by using a trusted third party as an "escrow agent" that ensures delivery of product (to
buyer) and payment (to merchant). Most of the deployed systems, e.g., [12.6,
12.21], focus on escrow of high-value physical products (or legal title, e.g., to real
estate), and in particular involve minimal fees of several to dozens of dollars. Proposals have also been made for escrow for digital content (for efficiency, the actual escrow is often of a key to decrypt the content, see [12.4]), which may seem
applicable to micropayments. However, it is impossible to completely automate
the resolution of disputes regarding quality of (most) products and services. Therefore, the third party will require manual intervention for every dispute, making the
process rather expensive, and inappropriate for micropayments. Therefore, micropayment service providers should prohibit this kind of dispute.

By disallowing disputes related to proper delivery/quality and chargebacks due
to consumer default, micropayment systems can focus on disputes related to payment approval (by the customer) and payment authorization (by the PSP).

12.4.3 Unauthorized Overspending Chargeback

In some payment systems, a customer may overspend, i.e. approve more payments
than the funds available in her account. In this case, the PSP may wish to refuse to
pay (or chargeback) the merchant. Some micropayment systems allow this, claiming that merchants can accept this risk, since the amounts are small, and especially
for selling information (with negligible cost for the merchant for each extra transaction).

However, since merchants do not have a long-term relationship with consumers, they often require secure *payment authorization* from the PSP, such that payments properly authorized by the PSP cannot be reversed. Micropayment schemes
often focus on reducing the overhead required for payment authorization, especially on the PSP, by adopting different strategies. The overhead for payment authorization has two major elements: communication and computation.

First, consider the computational overhead, and in particular, whether the PSP
must perform computationally-intensive operations such as public key signature

for each payment. Public key signatures are the main technique for achieving non-repudiation. For large amounts, and when the merchant does not trust the PSP, the merchant may require non-repudiation of the payment authorization from the PSP, to make sure that the PSP is committed to transfer the funds for the payment. In particular, in multi-PSP scenarios as illustrated in Fig. 12.4, the merchant may require non-repudiation from the customer's PSP. In Section 12.6, we discuss techniques for achieving non-repudiation with reduced computational requirements, compared to digitally signing each payment authorization.

When the transaction amounts are small relative to the value of the PSP-merchant relationships, then the merchant may not demand non-repudiation for every (micropayment) transaction, and agree to receive only secure payment authorization from the PSP (not signed). When the aggregated amount of authorized (but not signed) payments exceeds some merchant-specified threshold, the merchant may require the PSP signature authorizing the total, aggregated amount (providing non-repudiation). By not signing (and validating) every micropayment authorization, the PSP (and merchant) may save some computations.

Consider now the communication required for the PSP to authorize payments. Several micropayment schemes support *offline payment authorization*, i.e., transactions where the client communicates with the merchant, without involving the customer's PSP to authorize the payment. Offline transactions can be used where communication with the PSP during the purchase process is impractical, e.g. for payment using direct communication between consumer and merchant, without requiring connectivity and communication with the PSP. Usually, the PSP will require the merchant to return funds in case of double spending; but sometimes PSPs may assume limited liability, usually when the consumer is using a tamper-resistant hardware that authorizes the payments on behalf of the PSP (and keeps track of the available funds in the consumer's account). The PSP may pre-authorize payments up to a predefined amount for a particular merchant, but this is rarely useful (since it is hard to predict purchases) and indeed rarely used.

Therefore, whenever communication with the PSP during the purchase process is feasible, micropayment schemes should use it to perform *online payment authorization*. Sometimes, as in Fig. 12.2, all communication between the consumer and the merchant flows through the PSP (or a gateway associated with it), in which case the online payment authorization does not add substantial overhead. In other cases, the customer or the merchant must contact the PSP to request payment authorization. When possible, it is preferable for the customer to request the (online) payment authorization, so that, after local validation, the merchant can respond to the purchase request from the customer immediately without having to keep the connection with the customer open while requesting authorization from the PSP.

12.4.4 Disputes on Whether Payment Was Approved by Consumer

We now focus on the most important (and common) type of disputes and charge-backs, where the customer claims they did not approve the payment transaction. To understand this problem better, consider the common mechanism of perform-ing credit card transactions over the Internet (or phone), by sending the credit card details to the merchant. Usually, the credit card details are encrypted on transit us-ing SSL/TLS [12.27-12.28], as illustrated in Fig. 12.6. Since payment approval is only by inclusion of the credit card number, at any tome in the transaction, an at-tacker with access to the card number may invoke an unapproved transaction. As a result, there are many disputes in Internet transactions, which are much larger than proportion to all credit card transactions. The dispute rate in Internet transac-tions was so high that it caused losses to credit card issuers, and in the first years of Internet commerce, the rate grew rapidly (for example, see practical experience in [12.34]). The rate of disputes was considerably reduced with the introduction of substantial penalties to merchants with high dispute rates[2]. Many disputes were due to unauthorized purchases by a third party that somehow got hold of the cus-tomer's details, by exposure in Internet or non-Internet transaction, or otherwise. In addition, there are disputes made by customers denying payments they actually approved, knowing that there is no way to distinguish between them and unap-proved transactions, namely, that there is no non-repudiation.

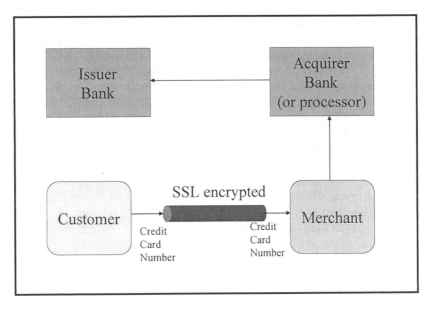

Fig. 12.6 SSL credit card payments

---

[2] Typical penalties for disputes: merchants with over 2.5% disputes among their transac-tions, pay 100$ per dispute [34].

Due to the high cost of dispute resolution and chargebacks, there have been several proposals to improve the security of the consumer approval process for credit card payments over the Internet. This has resulted in the iKP protocol [2], which evolved to the SET credit card payment standard [12.33, 12.20], and later in other proposals, such as 3D Secure and secure payment application (SPA) [20]. Most of these proposals attempt to emulate "face to face" transactions, where the customer physically signs a payment order (and presents a physical card with the same signature), often by using digital signatures. The goal is to reduce the number of disputes by preventing unauthorized use and preferably ensuring non-repudiation.

Reducing the number, and associated cost, of disputes resulting from claims of payments that were not approved by the consumer is even more critical for micropayment systems, where the average transaction amount is several orders of magnitude below the reported cost of handling a dispute in the credit card business. In the rest of this section, we discuss three major approaches to reducing the number of disputes and chargebacks due to consumer denial of approving the payments, and the associated costs.

The first approach is to perform a *secure payment approval* process, confirming to the PSP that the consumer approves the transaction. This would prevent an attacker from initiating transactions without consumer approval, which the consumer would later dispute. It also allows the PSP to detect when a consumer is disputing a properly approved transaction, although the PSP may not be able to "prove" to a third party that the transaction was properly approved, as long as non-repudiation is not provided. Possibly, the agreement between the consumer and the PSP may indicate that the consumer is willing to accept the records kept by the PSP of transactions approved by the consumer, and not to dispute them.

The second approach takes another step and provides not only secure payment approval, but also *non-repudiation* of the payment approval. Namely, whenever the PSP authorizes a transaction, it will retain a proof that allows it to convince a third party that the consumer, indeed, properly authorized the transaction. The proof will usually be in the form of a payment order digitally signed by the consumer. When complemented with an appropriate agreement with the consumer, accepting the digital signature or other proof as sufficient evidence to the consumer's approval of the transaction, this may be sufficient to prevent disputes. The agreement may also require the consumer's signature only when the aggregated amount of approved payments exceeds some predefined threshold, thereby amortizing the computational overhead over several micropayments.

The third approach takes a somewhat radical view, namely, that the only legally-acceptable way to refuse to reverse a transaction is when the PSP is technically *unable to reverse transactions*, since the necessary records do not exist. We call such payment instruments *bearer certificates*, since the payment is done by passing a message (*token, bearer certificate*) to the merchant, who deposits it at the PSP, but the message does not indicate the identity of the consumer. Designs that try to ensure irreversible transactions sometimes use *anonymous payment* ("digital cash") mechanisms, such as blinded signatures.

We discuss each of these approaches in more detail in the following sections.

Secure Payment Approval

Secure payment approval is relatively simple between two parties with a long-term relationship, such as the customer and their PSP. In this case, the payment approval is by an authenticated message from the customer to the PSP. Often, end-to-end authentication of the payment approval message from customer to PSP is possible (typically, when the customer communicates directly with their PSP, as in Fig. 12.2 or Fig. 12.3). Such end-to-end authentication of the payment approval requires only standard, pre-installed software components. The payment-approval process, when invoked by the consumer using only standard browser, as illustrated in Fig. 12.3, has the following steps:

1. The merchant presents the offer of goods or services to the consumer. In the usual browsing scenario, the offer is in a regular or special hypertext link, sometimes called a *per-fee link,* invoked by the consumer to pay, and encoding the payment details necessary to create the payment order. Inside the per-fee link, and possibly also outside it, the merchant provides the *offer description,* which is text and/or graphics describing the offer and presented to the consumer. We discuss some standardization efforts for the offer and per-fee link later on.

2. Typically, the browser displays the offer description. The customer invokes the payment process, typically by pressing the per-fee link. This results in passing the per-fee link parameters to the PSP, providing it with the payment offer details.

3. At this point, in most cases, the consumer has already been presented with the payment details in the description sent with the per-fee-link. However, a malicious merchant could have provided a description that differs from the payment details sent to the PSP. Therefore, the PSP has to validate that the consumer has actually approved the payment details. This is usually done by sending a payment approval request, e.g., as a web page. The user approves (or declines) this request. The approval process should be authenticated to ensure secure authorization.

4. Once the PSP has validated that the consumer properly approved the payment, then the PSP issues an authorized payment order (PO) sent to the consumer. The PO is often authorized by being signed by the PSP or

authenticated using a key shared between the PSP and the merchant. If the payment order as sent to the consumer might be "stolen" by an attacker and used to obtain goods and/or services for the attacker, this communication may be encrypted, e.g., using SSL.

5. The consumer's browser usually automatically processes the authorized PO by sending it as a request to the merchant. When a dedicated payment wallet is used by the consumer, it may modify the PO before sending it to the merchant, e.g., adding the consumer's signature or otherwise "validating" the payment order.

6. The payment order should be validated by the merchant, checking that it was properly authorized by the PSP. This may be done using a MAC key shared between the PSP and the merchant, or by the PSP's public key signature. Once the payment order has been validated, the merchant should provide the ordered goods or services to the consumer.

7. In an offline, "batch" process, the merchant deposits the payment orders and receives the funds.

Alternatively, and in particular, when the customer does not communicate directly with the PSP, but only via the merchant, then the customer can authenticate the payment approval by appending a message authenticator to it. The authenticator may be message authentication code (MAC), using a secret key shared between the PSP and the customer, or a digital signature, using the customer's private signature key and validated using the customer's public key. This may require dedicated payment software (*wallet*) in the customer's computer. We discuss this issue in Section 12.5.

Non-repudiation for Payment Approval

The solutions discussed so far provide different levels of security for the payment approval from the consumer. However, they do not completely prevent fraud; hackers may guess, steal, or otherwise expose passwords and keys, email may be misrouted, hackers may expose cookies in transit, and other users of the same computer may expose keys and passwords. In particular, all of the mechanisms above are vulnerable to a software virus in the consumer's computer or device (although many existing mobile devices may not be susceptible to viruses, due to limited functionality). Furthermore, the process depends completely on the trustworthiness of the PSP; a corrupted PSP (possibly hacked by an employee or third party) could claim that transactions were authorized, and in particular, compute any authenticators and authentication keys, as all such keys (if used at all) are also known to the PSP's computer. Definitely, therefore, non-repudiation is not achieved. Hence, consumers may still dispute their transactions, claiming unauthorized use, rightfully or possibly to avoid payment (without justification). In addition, of course, customer may dispute a transaction claiming dissatisfaction with the service or merchandise, as discussed earlier; but we focus on disputes claiming unauthorized use.

Some micropayment systems, e.g., First Virtual [12.36], solved the remaining disputes problem simply: they automatically refunded each dispute, and in this case did not pass the funds to the merchant. In fact, to completely protect First Virtual, they simply did not pay the merchants until the dispute period expired, thereby making additional profit from the float as well as avoiding the dependency on the merchant to actually pay them back. Considering the credit card experience showing the disputes are largely due to problematic merchants and merchant practices, there is some justification to this policy. Yet, it is clearly open to abuse by consumers, and raises a substantial business risk for merchants. Indeed, one might suspect that if a payment product adopting such a fully automated refund will become widely popular, then cheating may become commonplace. We therefore focus on systems that do not automatically accept all disputes. As noted above, we discuss only disputes claiming unauthorized transactions.

Many micropayment systems take the opposite approach, and simply forbid any disputes claiming unauthorized use (and therefore, usually, any form of dispute with the PSP). Often this is done simply by requiring the customer to agree to accept the record of transactions kept by the PSP. However, in many cases this mechanism may be unacceptable and possibly even illegal, especially when consumers are not fully protected against unauthorized charges. It appears that in order to completely disallow disputes, it is highly desirable that the PSP is able to prove to a third party that the consumer actually authorized each payment. This requires *non-repudiation.*

Non-repudiation may be achieved by using digital signatures, such as RSA to sign the payment approval from the consumer computer or device to the PSP. The customer must also agree in advance that payment orders digitally signed using their private key are to be considered as signed and authorized directly by the customer. The private signing key will be installed by the customer in their signing software, service and/or device.

There is, unfortunately, one serious pragmatic problem with digitally signing payment orders by the customer's computer or device: digital signing is *not* a standard, easy-to-use feature of widely-deployed[3] operating systems, browsers, or mobile devices. This should be compared with the solutions in the previous section, which do not offer non-repudiation, but on the other hand, do not require any new software in the consumer's computer or mobile device, or any complex operation for a consumer wishing to use them.

---

[3] Digital signing functionality is available in some versions of the Netscape browser, e.g. 4.04, as well as in some mobile devices.

An obvious solution is to require the consumer to install digital-signing software. Indeed, digital-signing functionality is often one of the main roles of a *wallet* utility installed on the consumer's machine. Wallets can perform other useful functions, such as payment management and logging, but their deployment is difficult and expensive. We discuss this important issue, and some possible solutions, in Section 12.5.

Another concern is that digital signing technology is relatively computationally intensive. A large amount of work on micropayment systems is focused on providing non-repudiation while minimizing or avoiding completely the use of public-key operations; see Section 12.6.

Irreversible Transactions and "Bearer Certificates"

We now discuss the third approach for preventing disputes, which takes a somewhat radical view: Design the micropayment system in such way that it will be technically infeasible to reverse payments, rather than relying on the consumer's agreement that properly authorized (or digitally signed) payments cannot be disputed. In this approach, the micropayment system operates in such a way that the PSP would not maintain track of individual payment transactions and would therefore be *unable to reverse transactions*. This kind of payment order is often referred to as *bearer certificates*, since the payment is done by the customer passing a message to the merchant, who deposits it at the PSP, but this bearer-certificate payment-order message does not indicate the identity of the consumer [12.12, 12.1]. More specifically, a bearer-certificate payment involves two separate phases:

1. Customer "buys" bearer-certificates from PSP (payment approval or withdrawal phase).
2. Customer pays merchant by providing the bearer certificate (payment authorization phase).

The PSP does not keep records of the identity of the customer who received each bearer certificate. In some proposals, the bearer certificates are provided during withdrawal, in a "blinded" manner, that does not allow the PSP to identify which bearer certificate was sent at which withdrawal. For more details on such blinded withdrawal and digital cash, see Chapter 8. In other systems, weaker anonymity is used, and the PSP simply does not maintain the records linking from the bearer certificate to a particular customer.

Bearer certificate systems should ensure that an attacker cannot "steal" the bearer certificate in transit from the PSP to the customer, from the consumer to the merchant, or from the merchant to the PSP. When the consumer is using standard, available browser software, and the bearer certificate is forwarded to the merchant exactly as sent from the PSP, the communication may be protected by using browser-provided encryption (usually SSL/TLS). In some cases, this may be avoided by requesting a bearer certificate specific to the requirements of this particular consumer. However, this may conflict with the requirement that bearer certificates cannot be linked to a particular consumer and purchase (to make it impossible to dispute transactions).

When the consumer uses dedicated wallet software, then the wallet may "activate" the bearer certificate it receives from the PSP. A bearer certificate that the wallet did not activate is not considered valid. Therefore, the attacker will not gain anything from a copy of the bearer certificate in transit from the PSP to the consumer. This activation may be as simple as attaching a random number x to the bearer certificate, where on payment approval the consumer provided to the PSP with the result of a cryptographic, a one-way hash function $h(x)$ is applied to x, and the bearer certificate is linked to $h(x)$, e.g., by including the PSP's signature on $h(x)$.

In any case, using a "bearer certificate" it should be impossible to link back from the payment order to the identity of the customer or to the withdrawal transaction in which the customer bought the bearer certificate. Therefore, the PSP simply has no way to reverse a payment done using the bearer certificate. Therefore, disputes are technically impossible. Proponents of this approach [12.12, 12.1] argue that bearer certificates are the only way to avoid disputes, since consumer-protection laws may overrule any limitations on disputes included in the agreement between the consumer and the PSP. On the other hand, using a bearer-certificate, the consumer does not receive a receipt of having paid from the payment system. This could be a substantial disadvantage for some applications.

Even if bearer certificates are used, it seems that for the goal of avoiding disputes, it may be acceptable for the PSP to know the linkage between the customer and the bearer certificate at the time of the withdrawal. This seems acceptable, as long as the PSP always erases this information later and does not provide a proof of it to the consumer. Clearly, such a solution is much simpler than the techniques used for digital cash.

12.5 Customer Acquiring and Support Costs

Businesses often spend large amounts to acquire new customers and to retain and support existing customers. Micropayments services have very small revenues per transaction and per customer. Therefore, it is especially critical to minimize the average amortized costs of customer acquiring and support efforts. In the following sections, we discuss three techniques for minimizing costs and maximizing the number of payment transactions, together ensuring low amortized costs per transaction.

1. Enable a simple-to-use, intuitive "click and pay" mechanism for payment approval. This has the dual impact of encouraging usage (more payments) and reducing support and acquiring costs (easier to use, i.e., fewer questions, easier to sell).

2. Support customers without requiring installation of a PSP-provided and supported local wallet application. This can reduce the substantial costs of providing wallet applications and supporting them (for multiple platforms), as well as the costs of convincing customers to install the local wallets.

3. Allow interoperability among the PSPs, namely, a customer of one PSP can pay a merchant of another PSP (as shown in Fig. 12.4).

12.5.1 Click and Pay Using Per-Fee Links

Micropayment systems are designed for low-value transactions. As such, it is important that the user interaction will be as natural, convenient, and quick as possible – ideally, click and pay. In fact, if the customer is not willing to pay much for a product or service, they may also not be willing to waste a lot of time and energy in the payment process. An easy, convenient and fast click-and-pay process also reduces costs for customer acquiring and support. The click-and-pay payment process becomes a natural extension of the familiar web surfing interface: To buy information or service, the user just clicks on *per-fee link*, much like clicking on a normal hyperlink.

We must ensure that the user pays only intentionally, i.e., the seller cannot trick the user into pressing a per-fee link without the user being willing to pay the price charged. For example, the IBM Micro Payments system [12.17, 12.11] provides per-fee-links which appear very similar to regular hyperlinks, by adding cues for payment. Specifically, when the cursor is over the per-fee link, the shape of the cursor changes to either a dollar sign (if the amount is over a user set threshold) or a cent sign (if the amount is under the threshold). Furthermore, the exact price is indicated in message/status area of the browser (where it normally writes the URL of the hyperlink); and the customer can specify a maximal amount for "click and pay", such that over this a pop-up box will require confirmation.

There are multiple ways for implementing per-fee links. The Web consortium developed a proposal [12.24] for per-fee-link syntax (this proposal was suspended since there were only few implementations). The proposal supported several ways for specifying and displaying per-fee-links, as <Embed>, <Applet> or <Object> elements; all of these require extensions to the standard browsers to display the per-fee-link, such as a plug-in, ActiveX control, or an applet. This requires installation of "wallet" software on the customer's machine.

It is sometimes also possible to provide per-fee link using only a standard browser to display the price simply as added text to the link. Consider Fig. 12.2, where the communication between the customer and the merchant flows through the PSP or a gateway associated with the PSP. In such scenarios, the PSP may modify the per-fee-link on its way from the merchant to the customer, and indicate the purchase details information (in particular the price) by adding the description of the payment details as textual and/or graphical hypertext link as part of the hypertext content sent to the consumer. For example, when using HTML:

<A HREF="*url*">click here to receive the song [5cents charge]</A>

The price information ([5cents charge]) was inserted or validated by the payment gateway (so that the displayed amount will be identical to the charged amount). The consumer indicates agreement by simply selecting (clicking on) this link. The transformation of the page sent from the merchant is especially natural in mobile scenarios, where the mobile gateway often creates the encoding (HTML or otherwise) appropriate to the consumer's device display capabilities.

Some caution is necessary, however, when using a regular hypertext link with the price added to the textual message as shown above, to prevent a merchant from invoking payment from a seemingly free (or less expensive) link. Namely, the PSP must accept as approval only requests that result from the consumer following the link it modified; the risk is that the merchant will insert in a page sent to the consumer a link invoking the payment procedure in the PSP but different (seemingly free) text.

To avoid this threat, the PSP may filter the hypertext to remove any fraudulent per-fee links inserted by the merchant. Another technique to prevent such fraud is to customize the per-fee links, e.g., by encoding in the hypertext link (the HREF attribute) an authenticator such as $MAC_k(price, description, clientID, time, requestID)$. The key k used in calculating the authenticator is known only to the PSP. The *price* and *description* fields ensure that the purchase conforms to what the customer approved. The *clientID*, *time* and *requestID* fields prevent the merchant from copying the authenticator field from a previous request (where *time* is used for a stateless server and *requestID* for a server who can remember states).

In addition, the gateway should validate that the page, as sent to the consumer's computer or device, does not contain script that may modify the page presented to the consumer (e.g., changing the description presented to the consumer). See [12.14] for techniques to validate that a web page is not modified by a script contained in it.

12.5.2 Local Wallets and Server Wallets

Acquiring customers, and helping them when they encounter difficulties, is difficult and expensive. It is difficult to convince customers to sign up with the system, open an account, and do any additional operations such as installation of a wallet (if necessary). Acquiring customers may therefore require substantial investment in the form of advertising and incentives, and even then, it usually takes substantial time to convince a small fraction of the potential customers to try the system.

When customers use the system, the costs of answering customer inquiries, which could be technical, financial, or administrative, can be significant. Customers are usually expecting financial service providers, including micropayment PSPs, to provide highly available and free customer support. The average cost per customer call is substantial and far exceeds the typical cost of micropayment transactions, not to mention the fees. These costs may exceed the thin profit margin per transaction, especially of a micropayment service provider.

Customer acquiring and support costs depend significantly on whether the customer has to install and use dedicated *local wallet* software to authorize micropayments, or whether the customer can use pre-installed, general-purpose mechanisms, such as the browser and/or e-mail utilities, with the payment functionality provided by a *wallet server* in the network. Dedicated, local-wallet software, running on the customer's computer or device, can provide better user interface and functionality, e.g., provide transaction log. Most importantly, dedicated wallet software can perform public-key digital signatures for payment orders, providing non-repudiation of the fact that that customer authorized the payment, and possibly avoiding dispute resolution and chargebacks.

However, it is important to realize that a malicious local user, or program, can often bypass local wallet software. In particular, when running insecure operating systems such as Windows, any malicious program (e.g., a virus) or any other user of the computer will be able to perform unauthorized signatures. Therefore, even a local, dedicated wallet cannot completely prevent unapproved payments.

Furthermore, it is substantially harder to motivate customers to download and install dedicated wallet software, compared to opening an account using purely pre-installed, general purpose mechanisms (e.g., a browser). Furthermore, dedicated, locally installed wallet software requires substantially more support costs, e.g., to resolve installation issues, and to support different operating systems. As a result, wallet software results in high customer acquiring and support costs, and a lower adoption rate. Another problem for local wallets is that consumers may use multiple devices and computers, e.g., at home, office, and while mobile, resulting in coordination problems between multiple wallet installations of the same consumer. Indeed, as shown in [12.19], there have been only failures so far in efforts to introduce wallet software, for micropayment as well as for credit card and other payments, and essentially all existing deployments support a wallet server.

However, a server wallet operated by the PSP has some significant drawbacks as well, in particular, in forcing the consumer to completely trust the PSP, which may necessitate dispute resolution with its associated high costs. In order to support micropayments without allowing disputes, the PSP may find it necessary to offer the customer control over the payment authorization, possibly as an option.

The Future: Multiple and Third-Party Wallets

We expect that in the future, PSPs will offer their customers to either use the PSP's server wallet, in which case they agree to trust it completely, or to use local-wallet or third-party operated server wallet that provides digitally-signed payment orders to the PSP, in which case non-repudiation is achieved by the public key signature. The PSP would offer local wallet software that signs the payment orders. Alternatively, the PSP may allow the customer to use third-party provided wallets to sign the payment orders, where the third-party wallets may be local or server-based. The third parties will offer the wallets as a productivity aid and often as part of a larger money-management or personal information management software or service, e.g., as part of the services offered by a portal. If some of the operations are especially sensitive, then the PSP may even require approval by more than one of the wallets of the same customer, providing additional protection against unauthorized use (but this additional complexity is probably not necessary for micropayments). By offering customers the option of using local wallets and third-party operated wallets, the PSP should be able to avoid dispute resolution process entirely, and therefore maintain low operational costs.

In Fig. 12.7, we show such an architecture, where the PSP allows the customer to use the PSP's wallet server, a local wallet provided by the PSP, or a third-party-provided wallet server or local wallet. The customer may authorize payments from their own computer or another computer, or from any of a variety of devices (different wallet servers may support different devices). This architecture requires protocols for managing an account and authorizing transactions from multiple wallets (software agents of the consumer), ensuring that the entire log of transactions is available to one or more wallets as needed. For such protocols also supporting record aggregation, see [12.13].

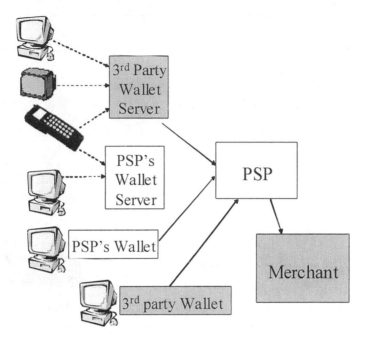

Fig. 12.7 Multiple wallets, devices, and computers for the same account

To invoke a wallet server, the merchant usually includes a link to it in the web page, with text describing the offer. It is possible for a single per-fee link to invoke one of multiple wallet servers as needed; this is achieved by the merchant including a link to a special "PSP directory" site. The PSP directory can try to detect automatically the identity of the customer's PSP, e.g., using a cookie stored in the browser and sent automatically to the PSP directory (see Fig. 12.8).

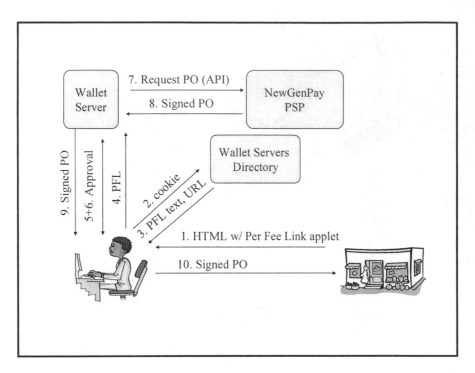

Fig. 12.8 Automated wallet server selection from directory

12.5.3 Building Critical Mass and Acceptability by Interoperability Among PSPs

For a micropayment system to be profitable, it is critical to have a large number of transactions, customers, and merchants. This is required both to reduce the amortized cost of fixed expenses (such as software development), and to make it easier to acquire customers and merchants (since customers and merchants prefer systems where they can transact with most merchants and customers, respectively).

Many micropayment service providers approach this problem by simply planning (or hoping) to become the dominant micropayment PSP, providing services to most customers and merchants. However, in an open, competitive market, it will probably require a very large investment in order to become the dominant PSP, and there is a substantial risk of failure to meet this goal.

An alternative approach is for multiple PSPs to cooperate, allowing customers of each PSP to pay merchants of each of the PSPs. This approach of cooperation between competitors is well established in many other areas of the modern, global economy. Indeed, there are several large networks connecting competitors and allowing them to interoperate, particularly, in payments, e.g., the credit card networks, clearing networks between banks, ATM networks, and others. It is therefore reasonable to expect a similar global network will handle micropayments.

It is difficult and expensive to establish trust among competitors, and even more so among many competitors. However, trust is required for allowing an interoperable payment network, where a merchant can receive a payment authorized by different PSPs. Existing, deployed payment networks handle this problem in one of two ways:

- **Centralized solution:** The payment network is "owned" by a single entity, usually called a *brand*. The brand sets up rules of operation for all the participating PSPs, possibly including technical means, such as communication protocols, and audits their operation. The recipient of payment trusts only the brand (and possibly their PSP). The major credit card systems, e.g., Visa and MasterCard, operate in this way. This solution could be appropriate for micropayments as well, if a very small number (say under five) of dominant micropayment brands would become dominant. However, substantial investment is necessary to establish a dominant brand. Such investment may not be economical for establishing a brand for micropayments where the expected fees are low.

- **Offline clearing solution:** The other approach minimizes any assumptions about global trust or organization. This is the approach normally used to deposit checks from remote, unknown banks. Namely, funds are available to the depositor (e.g., the merchant) only after the depositor's bank has received the funds from the payer's bank. This solution has two problems that seem to make it unsuitable for electronic payments (and in particular micropayments):

  o   The merchant must wait very long to know if the payment is valid.

  o   A corrupted intermediary bank (PSP) may deposit the check, receive the funds, but keep the funds to itself while claiming to the depositor that the payment was rejected. With physical checks, the merchant usually receives back the check in case of failure to prevent this attack (and for other remedies).

We conclude that, to provide interoperability among PSPs, it is desirable to ensure security without requiring global trust in all PSPs, as such, global trust will require central management and ownership (which may not exist).

Open, Decentralized Payment Network

We now describe the design of open, decentralized payment network, as presented in [12.17, 12.11, 12.16]. This design is based on two principles:

- **Minimal trust requirements – only between PSP and its account owners:** All account-based payment systems require trust between the party
  maintaining the account (e.g., bank or PSP) and the account owner (customer, merchant, or another PSP). This trust allows the account owner to
  deposit money and received payment orders in the account, trusting that
  the PSP will properly credit the account and that the funds will be
  available to the account owner and used only according to the account
  owner's instructions. Similarly, the PSP may trust the account holder to
  provide funds to cover any debt due to credit payments from the account.
  Such direct trust between the PSP and the owners of the accounts kept by
  the PSP is unavoidable, on the other hand, it is relatively easy to manage,
  as it involves only two parties with long-term relationship. However, no
  other trust relationships should be required. By avoiding any `global` trust
  requirements we make it easier and cheaper to manage risks and avoid
  fraud, thereby reducing costs.
- **Automated dispute resolution between PSP and account owners:** By
  specifying the exact terms for any transaction related to the account, we
  can completely automate the resolution of any disagreement between
  them.

The main mechanisms for achieving these goals are two digitally signed messages: the *payment order* and the *payment routing table* (PRT). Consider the simple scenario with two PSPs, A and B, illustrated in Fig. 12.9. In this scenario, the
customer C accepts an offer (flow number 3) from the merchant M, and pays for it
by sending to the merchant a payment order signed by PSP_A (flow number 6).
The merchant can immediately validate the payment order. The merchant can then
deposit the payment order, as in flows 7 and 8. Deposit can be immediate or delayed; the merchant (and intermediate PSP_B) may wait some time for possible
batching with other deposits for efficiency. The immediate, local validation, without online communication by the merchant, is possible using information that the
merchant received from PSP_B in the payment routing table signed by PSP_B, in
an offline process before the purchase, in flow 2.

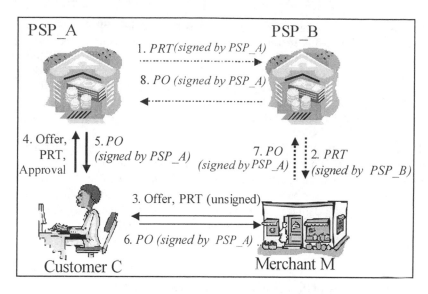

Fig. 12.9 Interoperability between two PSPs

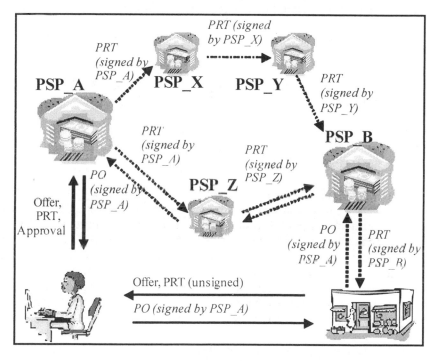

Fig. 12.10 Interoperable PSP network (example)

The payment routing table is sent in advance, e.g., daily, from each PSP to all of the entities keeping an account with this PSP and which may receive payment orders for deposit. In Fig. 12.9, PSP_A sends (e.g.. daily) PRT to PSP_B, and PSP_B sends PRT to the merchant. For a more complex scenario, consider Fig. 12.10, where we show five PSPs. Normally, each PSP will send a PRT message periodically to all of its merchants and to all of the PSPs keeping an account with it (namely, to every entity that may deposit a payment in this PSP). For efficiency, a single PRT message may contain payment routing entries for multiple issuing PSPs (i.e., for payment orders issued by different PSPs).

The PRT contains all the information necessary to allow the merchant to process a payment order signed by PSP_A. The PSP sending the PRT will always sign it with its private key (e.g., PSP_B). Payment service providers construct their outgoing PRT messages, based on the incoming messages, and on local policies (e.g., for limiting the damage if a particular PSP does not keep its commitments, or for maximizing revenues via adjustment of fees). The PRT, signed by PSP_B, will include the following details for every PSP from which PSP_B agrees to receive payment orders:

1. The identity of the account holder (merchant M).

2. The public key of the PSP issuing the payment order (e.g., PSP_A).

3. The maximal total amount of payments from this PSP allowed (until the next PRT).

4. The fees applied to deposits of payment orders from this PSP (e.g. maximum between 5 cents and 2%). The merchant receives the amount in the payment order minus these fees (no additional, "hidden" fees).

5. Minimal deposit time, in which deposits will be honored only if made before this time.

6. Acceptable proof of transmission identifies what is a sufficient proof of transmission of a message and of the time of transmission. This proof allows automated resolution of disputes on whether payments were deposited in time or expired. Typically, the proof will be either the transmission log of the PSP, or a signed receipt from one or more trusted third parties store-and-forward servers. The store-and-forward servers allow the depositor (merchant or PSP) and the PSP to resolve disputes due to failure of communication between them; as long as the total pending payments amounts are not very large, the PSP log files may be acceptable.

7. The path of PSPs through which the payment orders will be deposited. In the scenario in Fig. 12.9, this will only include the identity of PSP_B. In the scenario in Fig. 12.10, this may include the path {PSP_B, PSP_Y, PSP_X} or the path {PSP_B, PSP_Z}.

8. The validity period during which the PSP issuing this PRT (e.g., PSP_B) is committed to the terms specified in it. Later deposits may not be honored, unless covered by a new PRT.

9. A unique identifier for this PRT (e.g., counter).

10. Few other technical details may be added to ensure that there are no disagreements, see [12.16].

The Payment Order (PO) contains the precise details of the payment, including:

1. The amount to be paid (and currency).

2. The path of PSP's through which this PO is to be deposited.

3. The expiration time (the issuer will not pay for the PO after this time – it will become void).

4. The identifier of the PRT that this payment is applied to.

5. The issuing time of this PSP and a serial number of PO issued at this time (for detecting replays).

6. Possibly, additional conditions on the validity of this PO, such as a hash $h(x)$ sent by the customer, such that the payment order is valid only if the customer attaches to it the pre-image x.

The merchant also sends a (simplified) version of the PRT to the customer, and the customer may send it to her PSP (PSP_A). This allows the customer to choose the best route (and possibly currency) to use in the payment order.

12.6 Equipment, Processing, and Communication Costs

In this section, we discuss schemes to reduce the cost of the equipment necessary for the micropayment system, and in particular the cost due to the processing and communication requirements. Computational and communication requirements are reasonably well defined, and minimizing them is an obvious goal, easily measured, and similar to problems of minimizing communication and processing complexities in many other algorithms. Therefore, it is not surprising that much (or most) of the academic research on micropayments has focused on minimization of processing and communication costs. However, while these techniques are of algorithmic interest, we caution that the actual impact on cost and performance may be insignificant in many cases, as processing and communication costs are often a negligible compared to the other expenses (and delays) in the system.

Most of the efforts in reducing complexities and requirements focused on one of the following areas:

1. *Avoiding or reducing the use of public key cryptography* (digital signatures), since it is relatively computationally intensive.

2. *Allowing offline (or semi-offline) payments*, where the PSP is not involved during the process of payment (or most payments, respectively). An important form of offline payments are *stored-value payments*.

We now discuss offline (and semi-offline) payments and then techniques to avoid or reduce the use of public key cryptographic operations.

12.6.1 Reducing Communication Costs – Offline (and Semi-Offline) Payments

As discussed in Section 12.4, most micropayment systems require secure authorization of every transaction by the PSP, to assure the merchant that the payment is final and that the PSP will not refuse to pay, claiming that the customer spent more than the maximal amount allowed (overspent). Usually, this requires the PSP to authorize each payment online. In many cases, the online authorization is easy and inexpensive, as the PSP controls a gateway on the communication path between the consumer and the merchant, as in Fig. 12.2. However, in other cases, the PSP is not on the communication path; in order to involve it, the merchant must contact it (as in Fig. 12.5) or the customer must contact it (as in Fig. 12.3). This requires additional appropriate communication capabilities and capacities by the PSP and merchant or customer, in particular:

- The PSP must have sufficient capacity to handle the maximal number of concurrent payment authorization requests expected at peak time.

- Either merchant or buyer (or both) must have communication capabilities to the PSP online (during payment process). This is usually the case when paying using communication devices, such as mobile phones or computers connected to the Internet. In fact, in many applications, it is feasible and cheap to add communication capabilities to either the payer or payee (e.g., add a GSM module to a vending machine). However, there are scenarios where both payer and payee are disconnected and where it is not reasonable to require one of them to add communication capabilities, e.g., payments between two handheld devices.

In this section, we look at mechanisms for avoiding or reducing the online authorization requirements from the PSP, thereby eliminating or reducing the costs of the communication (messages) and of the necessary communication capabilities.

Micropayment schemes are called *offline* if the PSP is *never* involved during the payment process and *semi-offline* if the PSP is involved only in few payment transactions. Both offline and semi-offline payment schemes may reduce the load on the PSP, and in particular avoid bottlenecks at peak hours. Offline payments may further allow applications where payments are between a (low-cost, mobile) device carried by the customer and a (low-cost, fixed or mobile) point-of-sale device, without any network connectivity to the PSP.

The main approaches to providing offline and semi-offline payments are:

- **No authorization:** A trivial way to avoid online authorization is not to require any authorization by the PSP at all. The risk of overspending is borne by the PSP or the merchant, depending on the agreement between them. However, this requires the PSP or merchant to cover the cost of overspending by customers, which may be an unacceptable risk and expense.

- **Random or threshold authorization:** To reduce the number of authorization requests from the PSP, while limiting the risk to the merchant of a payment being cancelled due to overspending, the merchant can decide on whether online authorization by the PSP is required for each transaction. When using randomized or threshold authorization, either the merchant or the consumer wallet can request the authorization; requesting by the merchant is more direct as the merchant decides on the need for online authorization, but requesting indirectly by the consumer's wallet allows a simple, efficient client/server design for the merchant. In early versions of IBM Micro Payments [12.11, 12.17] we used threshold authorization, where the merchant requests payment authorization from the PSP when reaching a threshold amount (of that particular transaction or of all transactions pending authorization by that buyer). However, we later changed to online authorization, since we found that the its overhead is negligible, that merchant servers may spend considerable resources to keep track of total purchasing per customer, and that merchants are alarmed and confused by the possibility of unapproved payments being cancelled later. We also considered using random authorization, as proposed (independently) in Agora [12.9], where the merchant requests authorization randomly and the PSP identifies and blacklists any overspending customers. However, maintaining and distributing the blacklists may become a bottleneck and open the system to denial-of-service attacks, while on the other hand the overspending is still possible (until detected and until blacklist is updated). This, combined with the simplicity of opening multiple micropayments accounts, makes this solution impractical.

- **Pre-authorization:** The PSP may authorize the customer payments up to a pre-defined limit to a *specific* merchant. Overspending is then limited to multiple payments to that specific merchant, which the merchant can easily detect (e.g., using sequence number). When the PSP pre-authorizes payments (up to some limit, for a given merchant), it actually delegates it authority to the customer, who provides the final payment authorization directly to the merchant or point-of-sale (e.g., vending machine). The customer may digitally sign each payment authorization, or use one of the techniques described below to authorize the payments with reduced computational requirements. Pre-authorization is a semi-offline technique, as the customer needs to request pre-authorization for each specific merchant.

- **Stored Value Payments:** Taking one-step further than pre-authorization, the PSP can avoid online authorization completely by delegating its authority to authorize payments to a *tamper-resistant module trusted by the PSP,* e.g., a smartcard provided by the PSP. The module keeps track of the spending by the consumer, and authorizes payments only as long as the customer does not overspend. In a sense, the funds (value) which the customer can legitimately spend are stored in the device; hence, the name *stored value.* Stored value solutions depend on the temper-resistance of the module, to prevent duplication of money. Tamper resistant modules seem to require hardware (there are some efforts to create tamper-proof software, by *obfuscation,* but recent negative results seem to indicate that this is difficult or impossible). This introduces significant installation costs. Even tamper-resistant hardware is often subject to attacks. Therefore, stored-value protocols should limit the damage due to exposure of the keys of a limited number of modules. To limit the damage, most stored-value systems use a different key for each module and blacklist over-spending modules (but this requires identification of over-spending modules and informing all merchants, a non-trivial undertaking). Some authors claim that stored-value payment devices have the advantage of a total limit to the value lost if the card/device is stolen and abused. However, such a limit is easy to achieve with an account-based solution, simply by setting a limit to the amounts that the customer can spend using a given key.

12.6.2 Reducing Computational Complexity due to Public Key Operations

As discussed in Section 12.4, non-repudiation of payment approval is highly desirable, as it can help to reduce disputes and detect consumer fraud. The main cryptographic tool for achieving non-repudiation is public key digital signature, typically using the RSA or DSA algorithms [12.30, 12.5]. However, most public-key cryptographic mechanisms, and in particular digital signatures, are computationally intensive operations, compared to hash functions and shared-key cryptographic mechanisms. The ratios in the processing times depend, of course, on specific functions and implementations, but ratios of 100 and even substantially more are quite common. Much of the research on micropayment systems focused on reducing this computational burden by designing micropayment protocols and systems that avoid the use of public key cryptography, use only a very small number of public-key operations, or use more special, efficient public-key cryptographic mechanisms. In this section, we review some of these techniques.

We comment, however, that while the goal of avoiding or minimizing the use of (computationally intensive) public-key operations is natural and interesting, the actual cost of their processing time may be negligible compared to other costs and overheads in a practical micropayment system. The computation of an RSA digital signature [12.30], on typical desktop machines, takes only very few milliseconds; validation usually takes even less (when a small public exponent is used). The DSA algorithm [12.5] is about as efficient (but with computation faster than validation). Hardware accelerators can further substantially reduce the overhead. Therefore, it seems that for most realistic micropayment applications, computation, and validation of a digital signature on the payment order is not a significant cost factor. We therefore believe that techniques to avoid or reduce the use of public key operations and, in particular, of digital signatures and their validation, should only be used in special circumstances, and only when they do not result in a more substantial increase in other expenses. For example, a situation where it may be important to avoid digital signatures by the buyer is when the buyer is using inexpensive mobile devices for payments, such as a key-chain gadget or smart card.

The main techniques for avoiding or minimizing the computational burden due to public-key cryptographic operations are:

- Use authentication mechanisms that do not provide non-repudiation, such as (shared-key) message authentication code (MAC). This is appropriate between two parties with a long-term relationship, such as customer and their PSP or merchant and their PSP, and as long as the total amounts are not too high. However, this is not recommended between two parties with a sporadic, ad-hoc relationship, such as customer and merchant, or when the total amounts become larger than the value of the relationship. The possible savings in computation time may become smaller than the added risks and operational costs due to dispute resolution and customer support. Proposals for micropayment systems using MAC instead of digital signatures include NetBill [12.4] and MilliCent [12.23, 12.8].

- Use public-key signature algorithm that is substantially more efficient than [12.30] or [12.5]. There were several proposals of significantly more efficient public-key signature schemes, e.g., [12.31]. However, none of these schemes has yet gained sufficient adoption, and the amount of cryptanalysis effort to break them are, so far, limited, therefore their use is not recommended for sensitive and high-value signatures or where it may lead to disputes.

- Use an online/offline signature scheme as proposed in [12.7]. With these schemes, the payment is signed (online) using a one-time (or limited-use) public key digital signature scheme, which is substantially more efficient than regular, unlimited use public key signature schemes such as [12.30] and [12.5]. The public-key of the one-time scheme is signed in advanced (offline), using a regular digital signature scheme. This reduces the number of computations required online (during the payment process). By using an appropriate limited-use scheme, it may also be possible to reduce the average computational load. These schemes are easily adopted for semi-offline payments where the PSP pre-authorizes the one-time signature scheme for a particular merchant and a specific maximal amount, and the consumer applies the one-time signature to authorize a specific amount (up to the maximal).

- Use one-way hash functions, which are much more efficient than public-key signatures. These techniques fall into the following two categories:

  o *Hash chains* and *Hash trees:* this technique uses digital signatures for non-repudiation, but only once for multiple purchases between the same customer and merchant. Often, all purchases must be of the same amount. The customer or PSP digitally signs one (pre-) authorized payment order for the merchant, which the customer uses to authorize multiple purchases. We can therefore use this technique for semi-offline pre-authorized payments, where the PSP pre-authorizes the payment and the customer provides the final authorization. The (pre-)authorized, signed payment order includes a value y, which is the result of repeatedly applying l times a one-way hash function h to randomly chosen seed x. Namely, $y=h^{(l)}(x)$. The signature also includes a monetary value per pre-image, say c. To pay ic (e.g., i cents, when c is declared to equal one cent), the customer sends the authorized payment order together with a value x_i such that $y=h^{(i)}(x_i)$, namely, y is the result of applying i times the one-way hash function h to the value x_i. As long as $i \leq l$ it is very easy for the customer to compute this since he knows x. Therefore, repeated payments of the same amounts to the same merchant require only few computations from consumer and seller. This scheme is useful when the consumer buys repeatedly from the same merchant (and usually for the same amounts). Proposals based on hash chains include PayWord [12.29], micro-iKP [12.15] and others. Some variants use the natural extension of the hash-chain idea into a *hash-tree*, e.g., [12.18], for improved performance and flexibility.

o *MicroMint* [12.29]: This scheme is unique in requiring the PSP to perform a "hard" cryptographic operation, i.e., an operation that is assumed to required huge computational resources, but is easy to verify. This is justified by performing many such operations together, which is substantially more efficient *per operation* than performing only a single "hard" operation or relatively few operations, as can be expected of an attacker. Rivest and Shamir [12.29] suggest as "hard" operation to find a *k-way collision* for a collision-resistant hash functions, namely, values $(x_1, x_2, .. x_k)$ such that $h(x_1)=h(x_2)= ... =h(x_k)=y$. It is easy to see that, indeed, if searching for collisions by exhaustive search, the overhead *per each k-way collision* is much smaller if a large number of collisions are collected together. The scheme has several variants, including identifying the buyer and possibly even the seller (e.g., by producing only strings where specific bits are the buyer/seller identity), non-repudiation (e.g., by signing a common prefix to all produced coins), and others.

• Probabilistic payments: This is another hybrid technique, where the merchant receives one signed payment order for a substantial maximal amount, but with additional messages defining the actual amount paid, thereby allowing the same pre-authorized payment to be used for many micropayments. However, in this case, the micropayments are not done by gradually increasing the value (as with hash trees), but by gradually raising the *probability* of payment of the maximal (total) amount. Therefore, each micropayment is done by increasing the expected value that the merchant will receive – but the amount that the merchant actually receives is always either zero or the maximal amount. See such techniques in [12.26 , 12.22].

12.7 Summary

When the buyer and seller are in physical proximity, it is easy to pay small amounts (micropayments) using cash. There is a substantial number of such transactions, however their total value and importance is quite limited. However, remote micropayments, over a network, are an important challenge. On the one hand, we cannot physically transfer cash (or other object); and alternative existing payment mechanisms involve substantial fees, impractical for small amounts. On the other hand, there are critical needs in e-commerce for micropayments, in particular to pay for information, evaluations and services.

There have been many efforts to enable micropayments, however none has succeeded yet. To understand what makes micropayments so difficult, we reviewed the cost factors involved in payment transactions. Most of the research on micropayments focused on reducing processing costs, and in particular, avoiding the use of (computationally intensive) public key operations; we discussed some of the techniques, but also noted that in reality, the processing costs of (reasonably-efficient) implementations are not one of the most significant cost factors, even when using public key signatures.

The two most important cost factors, in practice, are (1) disputes, charge-backs and their processing, and (2) customer acquiring and support. The best way to deal with disputed micropayments is by providing secure payment authorization, and refusing to reverse the (properly-authorized) micropayments. We discussed some of the challenges of this approach, including legal and marketing issues which are beyond the scope of this work.

Finally, we discussed ways to minimize customer acquiring and support costs. We argue that these costs could be minimized in one of two opposing approaches: (1) having one or two dominant providers of micropayment services, reducing competition and associated expenses while allowing relatively high profit margins, or (2) coopetition in a network of many interoperable micropayment service providers, using appropriate secure protocols. We presented the principles of an appropriate protocol for interoperability between competing micropayment providers.

12.8 References

[12.1]   A. Back (1999) Bearer = anonymous = freedom to contract. Cryptography mailing list, Feb. 1999.
         http://www.privacy.nb.ca/cryptography/archives/cryptography/html/1999-02/0108.html.
[12.2]   M. Bellare, et al. (2000) Design, implementation and deployment of the iKP secure electronic payment system. J Selected Areas in Commun 18 (4): 611–627.
[12.3]   D. Chaum (1992) Achieving electronic privacy. Scientific American, August Issue, pp. 96–101.
[12.4]   B. Cox, J. D. Tygar, M. Sirbu (1995) NetBill security and transaction protocol. In: Proceedings of the First USENIX Workshop on Electronic Commerce.
[12.5]   National Institute of Standards and Technology (1994) Digital signature standard (DSS). FIPS PUB 186, US Department of Commerce.
[12.6]   Escrow.com (2002) Escrow payments: process overview.
         http://www.escrow.com/solutions/escrow/process.asp.

[12.7] S. Even, O. Goldreich, S. Micali (1996) On-line/off-line digital signature. J Cryptol 9: 35–67.

[12.8] S. Glassman, M. Manasse, M. Abadi, P. Gauthier, P. Sobalvarro (1995) The millicent protocol for inexpensive electronic commerce. In: 4th WWW Conference Proceedings, O'Reilly, New York, pp. 603–618.

[12.9] E. Gabber, A. Silberschatz (1996) The Agora electronic commerce protocol. In: Proceedings of 2nd Usenix Conference on Electronic Commerce.

[12.10] P. M. Hallam-Baker (1995) Micro payment transfer protocol (MPTP). W3C Working Draft WD-mptp-951122.

[12.11] A. Herzberg (1998) Safeguarding digital library contents – charging for online content. Digital Library Magazine, January Issue.

[12.12] R. A. Hettinga (1998) A market model for digital bearer instrument underwriting (manuscript). http://www.philodox.com/modelpaper.html.

[12.13] A. Herzberg, I. Mantin (2002) Secure transactions with multiple agents (manuscript).

[12.14] A. Herzberg, D. Naor (1998) Surf'N'Sign: client signatures on Web documents. IBM Sys J 37(1): 61–71.

[12.15] R. Hauser, M. Steiner, M. Waidner (1996) Micro-payments based on iKP. IBM Research Report 2791.

[12.16] A. Herzberg, E. Shai, I. Zisser (2000) Decentralized electronic certified payment order (US patent application).

[12.17] A. Herzberg, H. Yochai (1997) Mini-pay: charging per click on the Web. In: Proceedings of the 6th WWW conference.

[12.18] C. Jutla, M. Yung (1996) Paytree: amortized signature for flexible micropayments. In: Proc. 2nd USENIX Workshop on Electronic Commerce, pp. 213–221.

[12.19] K. Böhle (2001) Access is king: about the bright future of server-based e-payment systems. ePSO Newsletter, No. 6. http://epso.jrc.es/newsletter.

[12.20] L. Loeb (1998) Secure electronic transactions: introduction and technical reference. Artech House, Boston London.

[12.21] O. T. Lee (2001) Trust and confidence with escrow payment service to DRIVE Internet/eCommerce transactions. CommerceNet Singapore (CNSG) eSecurity and ePayment Seminar. http://www.cnsg.com.sg/archive/eSecurity%20Stratech%20011017.pdf.

[12.22] R. J. Lipton, R. Ostrovsky (1998) Micro-payments via efficient coin-flipping. In: Proceedings of Second Financial Cryptography Conference, LNCS 1465. Springer, Berlin Heidelberg New York, pp. 72–82.

[12.23] M. S. Manasse (1995) The Millicent protocols for electronic commerce. In: First Usenix Workshop on Electronic Commerce.

[12.24] T. Michel (ed.) (2000) Common markup for micropayment per-fee links. W3C Working Draft. http://www.w3.org/TR/Micropayment-Markup/.

[12.25] M. Peirce, D. O'Mahony (1995) Scaleable, secure cash payment for WWW resources with the PayMe protocol set. In: Proceedings of the Fourth WWW Conference.

[12.26] R. L. Rivest (1998) Electronic lottery tickets as micropayments. In: R. Hirschfeld (ed.) Financial Cryptography: FC'97, LNCS 1318. Springer, Berlin Heidelberg New York, pp. 307–314. http://citeseer.nj.nec.com/rivest98electronic.html.

[12.27] E. Rescorla (2000) SSL and TLS: designing and building secure systems. Addison-Wesley, New York.

[12.28] T. Dierks, C. Allen: The TLS protocol: version 1.0. Network Working Group, Internet Engineering Task Force (IETF). http://www.ietf.org/rfc/rfc2246.txt.

[12.29] R. L. Rivest and A. Shamir (1996) PayWord and MicroMint--two simple micropayment schemes. In: 1996 RSA Security Conference Proceedings.

[12.30] RSA Laboratories. PKCS#1 – RSA cryptography standard. http://www.rsasecurity.com/rsalabs/pkcs/pkcs-1/.

[12.31] A. Shamir (1993) Efficient signature schemes based on birational permutations. In: D. R. Stinson (ed.) Proceedings of CRYPTO'93, LNCS 773. Springer, Berlin Heidelberg New York, pp. 1–12. http://citeseer.nj.nec.com/shamir93efficient.html.

[12.32] O. Steeley (2001) Guaranteed transactions: the quest for the "Holy Grail." ePSO Newsletter, No. 10. http://epso.jrc.es/newsletter

[12.33] MasterCard and VISA: Secure Electronic Transactions. http://www.setco.org/set.html.

[12.34] T. Schurer (2001) Largest German credit card issuer on massive reduction of charge backs. ePSO Newsletter, No. 10. http://epso.jrc.es/newsletter.

[12.35] L. Tang, S. Low (1996) Chrg-http: A tool for micropayments on the World Wide Web. In: Proceedings of the Sixth Usenix Security Symposium, pp. 123–129.

[12.36] D. New (1995) Internet information commerce: First Virtual approach. In: Proceedings of the First Usenix Workshop on Electronic Commerce.

13 Industrial E-Payment Systems and Solutions*

Zheng Huang [1], Dong Zheng [1], Zichen Li [2], and Weidong Kou [3]

[1] Shanghai Jiao Tong University
   Shanghai, China

[2] Tsinghua University
   Beijing, China

[3] University of Hong Kong
   Pokfulam Road, Hong Kong

13.1 Introduction

As e-commerce over the Internet is taking off, online payment (or e-payment) has become an essential piece of the e-commerce puzzle. To support e-commerce, a variety of industrial e-payment systems and solutions have been developed and deployed in many countries. These e-payment systems and solutions enable transactions for people to trade goods or services for money. It is not our desire to cover the entire e-payment industry in a single chapter. Rather, we prefer to select a few e-payment solutions and introduce them to the readers as real-life e-payment examples, or, to some extent, as e-payment case studies. In this chapter, we select three e-payment solutions for discussion, including Visa Cash, iPIN, and PayPal. For each of them, we describe design goals, features, functions, and security mechanisms. In addition, in the appendices of the chapter, based on the available information, we selectively present the architecture of these payment systems.

13.2 Visa Cash

Visa Cash is the first e-payment system and solution that we have chosen for discussion [13.1]. The reason for selecting Visa Cash is that it is a global brand.

---

* Supported by the National Natural Science Foundation of China (Grant Nos. 90104032, 90104005, and 60173032).

Visa Cash is an electronic purse. It is a card that works like cash. A microchip is embedded in each card to store a specific amount of money and do some cryptography calculation. The Visa Cash system is a secure application module (SAM)-based system. With Visa Cash, one can pay for everyday necessities without having to carry around a pocket full of change. It is a fast, easy, convenient method of payment, which can be used for small purchases such as pay phones, cinema tickets, parking machines, or public transportation. Visa Cash can be used either in the real world or in cyberspace over the Internet.

Since its launch in 1995, Visa Cash has been widely used worldwide, including Argentina, Australia, Brazil, Canada, Columbia, Hong Kong, Ireland, Israel, Japan, Mexico, Norway, Puerto Rico, Russia, Spain, Taiwan, the UK, and the US.

13.2.1 Design Goals of Visa Cash

The design goals of Visa Cash are:

- Provide a payment product that is more convenient than cash, particularly in small-value transactions.
- Support a multi-currency capability and currency exchange.
- Supporting multi-applications on a single Visa Cash card.
- Offer similar convenience to cardholders wherever they are, traveling around the world or staying at home.
- Offer merchants a means to serve both domestic and traveling cardholders for the payments.
- Enable card issuers and acquirers to offer internationally acceptable electronic-purse services to cardholders and merchants.
- Work consistently within the existing financial environment.

13.2.2 Features of Visa Cash

Visa Cash has the following features:

- Easy to use:
  To use a Visa Cash card, one can simply insert it into the merchant's Visa Cash card reader. Visa Cash card's current balance will be displayed to let the cardholder know in advance how much Visa Cash they have to spend. The cashier will enter the amount of the transaction which is displayed to the cardholder. When the cardholder presses the "accept" button on the card reader, the amount of the purchase is automatically deducted from the Visa Cash card balance. The Visa Cash card's new card balance is then displayed.

- Anonymous:
  Compared with a Visa credit card, Visa Cash provides anonymity by not requiring the user's ID at the time of payment.

- Flexible card types:
  Visa Cash provides two types of cards, namely, disposable cards and reloadable cards. Disposable cards are loaded with a predefined value. They come in denominations of local currency, and make use of low-cost memory cards to store Visa Cash money. When the value stored in a card is used up, one can discard the card and purchase a new card. A reloadable card comes without a predefined value. This type of card can be loaded with value through specially configured devices, such as ATMs and other load devices. When the value is used up, the cardholder can reload the card. In terms of implementation, these two types of cards can be implemented based on either a proprietary or an open platform.

- Wireless supports:
  Visa Cash cards can be loaded through GSM networks.

13.2.3 Functions of Visa Cash

Visa Cash cards provide convenient and fast means for the cardholders and enable them to always have exact change. The cardholders can perform the following functions:

- Load: transfer money from a bank account to the Visa Cash card,
- Unload: the inversion of load,
- Currency exchange,
- Purchase,
- Purchase reversal,
- Incremental purchase,
- Cancel last purchase,
- Personalization: storing some personal information,
- On-line updates to the card application data.

Visa Cash can be used in many places, such as quick-serve restaurants, convenience stores, vending machines, gas stations, transportation, sundries stores, cinemas, newsstands, parking garages, grocery stores, department stores, taxis, parking meters, cafeterias, and video stores.

The most successful application of Visa Cash may be electronic tickets for the public transportation systems of Madrid and Barcelona, Spain. In these cities, Visa Cash is not only used in the public transportation system, but also used for car parking, public telephones, etc. Up to now, there have been at least 50 million Visa Cash cards issued in Spain.

13.2.4 Security of Visa Cash

The security of Visa Cash is based on the tamper-resistant property of smart cards. The security requirement is mainly authentication between each party in a Visa Cash system. In offline transactions, the smart card and merchant's terminal must perform mutual authentication using asymmetric cryptography. The authentication is a type of dynamic authentication (challenge/response).

In order to authenticate a smart card, it must be loaded with the following keys:

- Symmetric MAC (message authentication code) key,
- Card secret key,
- Card public key certified by the issuer with their private key,
- Issuer public key certified by a certification authority with their private key,
- Certification authority public key.

In order to authenticate the merchant's terminal, the terminal must be loaded with the following keys:

- PSAM (purchase secure application module) secret key,
- PSAM message authentication codes (MAC keys),
- PSAM public key certified by the acquirer with its private key,
- Acquirer public key certified by a certification authority (the same certification authority as that of the card) with its private key,
- Certification authority public key.

These keys stored in smart cards and merchant's terminals are protected by a hardware-security module. There are multiple certification authorities (CA) in the Visa Cash system and they are organized into different levels (international level, country, or region level).

13.2.5 Architecture and Workflow of Visa Cash

Participants in a Visa Cash system include: (1) the cardholder who holds a Visa Cash card; (2) the merchant whose terminal contains a card reader to read the user's card and a SAM smart card, to execute a transaction and to receive the transferred cash value; (3) the acquirer who collects and possibly aggregates transactions from several purchase devices for delivery to one or more system operators; (4) the card issuer who is responsible for the provision and distribution of integrated circuit cards, and who also authenticates load requests and transaction records, and provides cardholders with customer services. In addition, there may be a load acquirer through whom a load transaction and currency exchange transaction is initiated.

The typical workflows of a Visa Cash system include generic load transaction, processing a transaction between a cardholder and a merchant, and clearance. The descriptions for each of these three workflows follow.

Workflow for Generic Load Transaction

In this transaction, the cardholder loads money to the Visa Cash card from a linked account. The linked account is the cardholder's account at the card insurer.

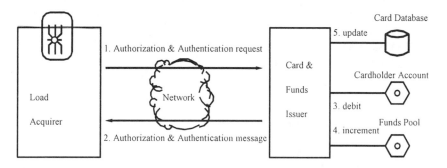

Fig. 13.1 Load workflow

(1) The load acquirer sends a combined authorization and authentication request to the card-and-funds issuer via the network.
(2) The card-and-funds issuer sends the positive combined authorization and authentication message to the load acquirer via the network. The electronic purse card is loaded.
(3) The card-and-funds issuer debits the cardholder account.
(4) Increments the funds pool of the currency loaded.
(5) The card-and funds issuer updates the card database.

Transaction Workflow between a Cardholder and a Merchant

The cardholder places their Visa Cash card into the merchant's card reader. Then the Visa Card and the merchant's purchase secure application modules (PSAM) interact as follows (see Fig. 13.2):

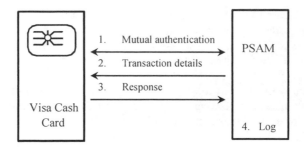

Fig. 13.2 Offline transaction workflow

(1) Mutual authentication to ensure that the Visa Card is valid and the PSAM is not a fraud.
(2) PSAM constructs the correct cryptographic details about the transaction and sends the details to the customer's card to activate the Visa Cash card to do the transaction.
(3) Visa Cash card sends a response to the PSAM and the PSAM verifies the response from the Visa Cash card to ensure that funds were deducted.
(4) PSAM produces the transaction log entry.

Workflow for Clearance and Settlement

The offline transaction between the cardholder and merchant has been done. The merchant wants to get back the money that the cardholder paid (see Fig. 13.3).

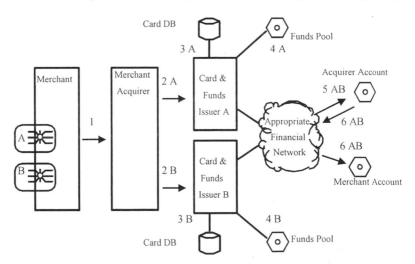

Fig. 13.3 Clearance and settlement workflow

(1) The merchant sends the transactions to the merchant acquirer.

(2) The merchant acquirer sends the transactions to the card issuer via the respective networks.

(3) The card issuer updates their card databases.

(4) The card issuer's funds pool of the transaction currency is decremented and the merchant acquirer's account is credited via the respective networks.

(5) The merchant acquirer's account is debited through the appropriate financial network.

(6) The merchant's account is credited through the appropriate financial network.

13.3 iPIN E-Payment

iPIN is an e-payments company headquartered in Northern California's "Silicon Valley" [13.2]. It also has offices in North America, Europe, and Asia. iPIN provides e-payment solutions for Web and wireless purchase transactions. It also offers e-payment solutions to telecommunications operators, financial institutions, automotive OEMs, and ISPs who want to provide their consumers with choices in paying for digital and hard goods across access devices, alternative payment options, and multiple networks and standards. We chose iPIN as the second example for e-payment systems and solutions because it is a premier provider of e-payment software worldwide, and because it has experience in the banking, credit card, telecommunications, software, and Internet industries.

13.3.1 Design Goals of iPIN

The iPIN e-payment solution is a platform to support payment across vertical markets in both the virtual and physical world. With iPIN, banks, telecommunications companies, and other partners can offer their customers the next generation of online and wireless payment products. Consumers can make payments for their purchases from any Internet-enabled device by selecting the payment method. For example, the consumers can make their payment by direct debit, credit cards, or prepaid cards.

By authorizing companies to take advantage of iPIN e-payment solutions, customers can now build their own payment networks, interconnect with industry leaders and merchants across the globe, or simply make their existing e-commerce and m-commerce initiatives more productive.

13.3.2 iPIN E-Payment Features

The features of the iPIN e-payment solution include:

- The ability to support multiple access devices: handsets (wireless devices), personal digital assistants, and Internet appliances.
- Multiple payment options enabled by iPIN's multiple payment instrument (MPI) module. An electronic MPI is similar to a physical wallet in that the consumers can select from several options in their billfold, i.e., debit cards, credit cards, stored value cards, etc., to make purchases.
- The iPIN e-payment solution is able to operate interchangeably across global networks and standards.
- The iPIN e-payments solution can be adapted to fit customers' needs by plugging into one of the add-on iPIN e-payment modules. In addition, business rules and security measures can be customized to meet specific requirements. The modular applications allow iPIN to more closely match customers' needs.

13.3.3 iPIN E-Payment Functions

iPIN e-payment provides the following functions:

- Account management: users are able to view their transaction history and change their security settings.
- Person-to-person payment (P2P).
- Payment with direct debit account.
- Payment with pre-paid/stored value.
- Bill aggregation.
- Exceptions processing.
- Sales and remittance reporting.
- Payment with any Internet-enabled PC, PDA, or mobile phone.
- Roaming freedom: layered authentication allows users to cross devices anytime, anywhere.

13.3.4 Security of iPIN

The security of iPIN e-Payment includes the following components:

- Data segregation:
  When a consumer initiates a purchase, they are redirected to the iPIN e-payment solution platform residing behind the partner's firewall for

authentication, account selection, and authorization. Once authorized, the partner sends an authorization message to the merchant.
- Message integrity:
All messaging between consumers, merchants, and partners is digitally signed using private keys, and encrypted using SSL.
- Authorization timeouts.
- Anti-robot and anti-spoof mechanisms.
- Transaction and spending limits.
- Non-payment account suspension.

The iPIN security mechanism is scalable. The customers using the iPIN e-payment solution are able to select the level of the security that is required as well as the method that will be used in the purchase. For example, in the purchase authentication, the iPIN payment platform may simply read the terminal ID for a US$ 0.50 purchase of information to be placed against a monthly bill, and require no other form of authentication. At the other end of the spectrum, a $150 purchase could be authorized against a private credit line or a checking account that may require the customer to authenticate via a digital certificate, a biometric parameter, password, and/or secret questions and answers.

Using the standard implementation of the iPIN security system, the sensitive account information is never electronically transmitted to the merchant when making a purchase, so iPIN customers are assured of the end-consumers' security.

13.3.5 Architecture and Workflow of iPIN

The iPIN e-payment architecture shown in Fig. 13.4 is comprised of the following components:

- Transaction acquisition,
- Transaction processing and real-time accounting,
- Clearing and settlement,
- Customer and merchant care.

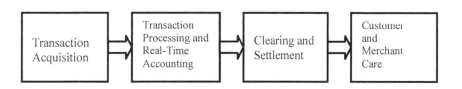

Fig. 13.4 iPIN e-payment function and architecture

Transaction Acquisition

The transaction acquisition allows the secure capture and authorization of a user transaction across multiple electronic channels. The functions include (see Fig. 13.5):

- Transaction authorization and confirmation,
- Multi-level user authentication,
- Transaction connectivity and routing.

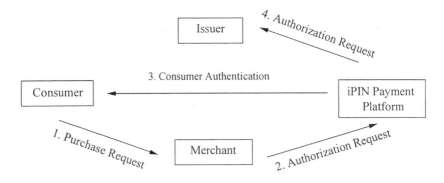

Fig. 13.5 Transaction acquisition

Transaction Processing and Real-Time Accounting

The functions of this component include transaction accounting, consolidation, revenue sharing, and transaction fee calculation and reporting (see Fig. 13.6).

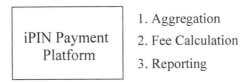

Fig. 13.6 Transaction processing and real-time accounting

Clearing and Settlement

This component facilitates the management of accounts receivable, accounts payable, and general ledger interfaces to financial systems. It includes the following four interfaces (see Fig. 13.7):

- Interface for accounts receivable and accounts payable,
- Interface to treasury management,
- Interface to financial management,
- Interface to settlement network.

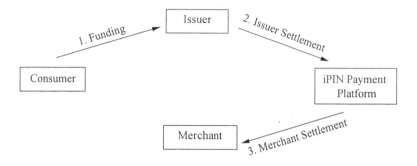

Fig. 13.7 Clearance and settlement

Customer and Merchant Care

This component provides the following tools about which the customer and merchant care (see Fig. 13.8):

- iPIN customer tools:
  Administrative tools, activity reporting, customer support.
- End-consumer tools:
  Payment panel, account management, and self-care.
- Merchant tools:
  Activity reporting, exception, and dispute handing.

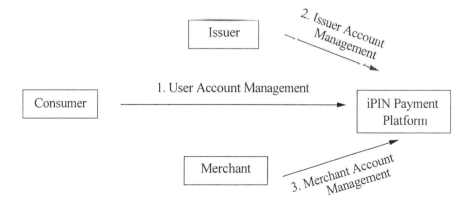

Fig. 13.8 Customer and merchant care

13.4 PayPal

PayPal is designed for handling payments and money transfers for small businesses, online merchants, individuals, and others currently poorly served by traditional payment mechanisms. The PayPal network extends the existing financial infrastructure of bank accounts and credit cards and creates a global payment solution. PayPal enables any business or consumer with an email address to securely, conveniently, and cost-effectively send and receive these payments. Any business or consumer with an email address can send and receive payments online instantly.

Paypal is now offering services to users in 38 countries including the US. It has over 16 million registered users, including more than 3 million business accounts.

13.4.1 Design Goals of PayPal

E-Commerce Services for Businesses and Individuals

PayPal [13.3] enables quick and easy payment processing for websites, classified ads, auction sites, and email (i.e., anywhere a person wants to collect payments online). PayPal supports the following functionality:

- Accept credit card and/or bank account payments for single or multiple item purchases.
- Sell products to PayPal users in 38 countries outside the US.
- Collect subscription or recurring payments.
- Gather donations or "tips."
- Get instant notification when you receive payments.

Online Auction Services

PayPal also supports online auction services. One can

- Insert PayPal logos into any number of listings automatically.
- Notify winning bidders instantly.

Person-to-Person Payment Services

PayPal makes person-to-person payment easy without the headache of the traditional person-to-person payment process involving checks, stamps, and envelopes. With PayPal one can:

- send money online from a credit card or bank account,
- request money from an individual or group,
- use a virtual debit card for safe and easy online shopping.

13.4.2 Features of PayPal

Paypal has the following features:

- Three types of accounts:
  PayPal offers three types of accounts according to the different needs. These are personal, premier, and business accounts.
- No service fee or low service fee:
  For a personal account, sending money and receiving money is free. For premier and business accounts, sending money is free of charge, while for receiving money the fee is very low.
- The PayPal VISA credit card account will be governed by the Providian, which protects customer privacy and handles customer information in a secure and confidential manner.
- It allows customers to pay anyone who has an email address.
- Over 33,000 websites accepted PayPal at the time of writing.

13.4.3 Functions of PayPal

There are two main functions in the PayPal system, namely, "send money" and "request money."

Send Money

"Send Money" allows the customer to pay anyone who has an email address. One can make the payment by just entering the recipient's email address and the amount that one wishes to send. The payment can be made either using a credit card or through a checking account.

Request Money

"Request Money" offers the customer an organized method to request and track funds. To send an auction invoice or a personal bill, one just needs to enter the recipient's email address and the amount that one wishes to request.

13.4.4 Security of PayPal

PayPal stores credit card and bank account information only in encrypted form on computers that are not connected to the Internet. PayPal restricts access to the customer's personally identifiable information to employees who need to know that information in order to provide products or services to the customer.

Secure Web Sites

When customers log into their PayPal accounts, customers will always be on a secure web site. Whenever entering sensitive personal information (such as checking account or credit card numbers) onto the secure web site, the web site encrypts the information that the customer sends to and receives from the site.

Data Security and Encryption

PayPal automatically encrypts the confidential information in transit from the customer computer to PayPal using the secure sockets layer protocol (SSL) with an encryption key length of 128 bits. Before a customer even registers or logs on the PayPal site, the server checks that the customer is using an approved browser, that is, one that uses SSL 3.0 or higher. Once the customer information reaches PayPal, it resides on a server that is secured both physically and electronically. The servers sit behind a secure firewall and are not directly connected to the Internet, so that the customer's private information is accessible only to the authorized computers.

PayPal's Identity Verification System

Verification provides the customer with some more information about the people with whom the customer transacts through PayPal, so that the customer may make more informed decisions.

There are several ways to take advantage of PayPal's verification process and decrease customer-fraud risks:

- When the customer receives a payment:
  After logging into the customer's account, the customer can go to the "History" sub tab of the "My Account" tab, find the payment in question and choose the status link (e.g., "Pending") in the Status column. This will take the customer to a payment details page. Next to the sender's name, the customer will find their verification status (verified, unverified, or international).
- When the customer sends a payment:

As the customer is sending a payment, on the "Send Money: check the details of your payment" page, a reputation link is provided where the customer may view the recipient's status (verified, unverified, or international).

Additional Verification

If PayPal cannot verify the information that the customer provides, or if the customer requests a withdrawal by check to an address other than the customer-verified credit card billing address, PayPal asks the customer to send additional information to PayPal by fax (such as the customer's driver's license, credit card statement, and/or a recent utility bill or other information linking the customer to the applicable address), or to answer additional questions online to help verify the customer's information.

13.4.5 Architecture and Workflow of PayPal

Workflow of PayPal Email Payments

The PayPal email payments system allows the user to send money instantly and securely to anyone with an email address. The workflow of PayPal email payments is shown in Fig. 13.9. The description of the workflow is as follows:

(1) The payer signs up and enters bank account information, the payee's address, and the dollar amount to PayPal.
(2) The payment is transferred from the payer account to the payee account.
(3) The payee gets an email notification with a link.
(4) The payee follows the link to sign up.
(5) The payee withdraws money or mails it to others.

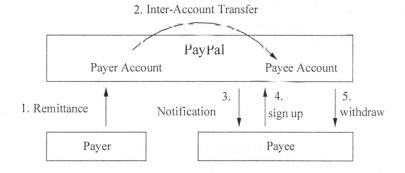

Fig. 13.9 Workflow of PayPal email payments

Workflow of PayPal Mobile Home Banking

Paypal mobile home banking allows peer-to-peer payments via wireless PDAs or web phones and allows money to be transferred from a credit card account to the recipient's PayPal account. The workflow of PayPal mobile home banking is shown in Fig. 13.10.

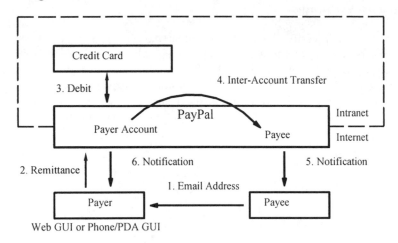

Fig. 13.10 Workflow of PayPal mobile home banking

The description of the workflow in Fig. 13.10 is as follows:

(1) The payee sends the payee's email address to the payer.
(2) The payer signs up and enters the credit card (or bank account) information, the payee's address, and the dollar amount to PayPal.
(3) Using the credit card, the payment is deducted from the payer's credit card.
(4) The payment is deducted from the payer's PayPal account and the payment is credited to the payee's PayPal account.
(5) The payee receives an email notification.
(6) The payer receives an email notification.

13.5 Summary

In this chapter, we have discussed three e-payment solutions: Visa Cash, iPIN, and PayPal. Visa Cash is an electronic purse, and it belongs in the digital cash payment category. iPIN provides e-payment solutions for Web and wireless purchase transactions. It supports various payment methods. For example, with iPIN e-Payment solutions, the consumers can make their payments by direct debit, credit card, or prepaid card. PayPal conducts payments through email. With PayPal, any business or consumer with an email address can send and receive payments online instantly.

13.6 References

[13.1]   Visa Cash. http://international.visa.com/ps/products/vcash/ and http://international.visa.com/fb/paytech/vcash.jsp.
[13.2]   iPIN. http://www.ipin.com/.
[13.3]   PayPal. http://www.paypal.com/.
[13.4]   M. H. Sherif (2000) Protocols for secure electronic commerce. CRC Press, Boca Raton London New York Washington DC.
[13.5]   P. Wayner (1997) Digital cash (2nd ed.). AP Professional, Boston New York London.

14 Challenges and Opportunities in E-Payment

Weidong Kou

University of Hong Kong
Pokfulam Road, Hong Kong

14.1 E-Commerce Challenges: E-Payment Security and Privacy

The rapid growth of online business transactions indicates that e-commerce over the Internet is an irreversible trend. Based on various reports from leading international consulting firms such as Forrester Research and International Data Corporation, it is predicted that B2B e-commerce will be worth as much as 7 trillion of US dollars in a few years, and B2C will also be worth over hundreds of billions of US dollars in the United States alone.

Although e-commerce has huge potential, there are challenges for people in adopting e-commerce in their daily life. For example, in Hong Kong it was found that only 4% of Hong Kong Internet users bought goods or services or traded securities online, according to a recent survey conducted by the Census and Statistics Department of Hong Kong. In the United States, according to E-Stats released by the Department of Commerce, retail e-sales were $10 billion US dollars in the fourth quarter of 2001, about 1.2% of total retail sales in that quarter. In Europe, according to Datamonitor, the size of the European online market in 2001 is about $3.23 billion US dollars.

What are the barriers that prevent e-commerce from reaching the mass market? A recent survey report shows that payment security is a major concern for online shopping. Consumers are not willing to expose their credit card numbers online if they are not certain whether the numbers are securely transferred and saved.

Another important issue is privacy. Currently, online merchants usually require consumers to fill in detailed private information, including address and credit card information. Consumers do not like to have their shopping activities easily traceable. Consumers want easy access to premium content without the hassle of disclosing personal credit card information to unknown sites, or going through a tedious registration and authorization process.

A recent survey on merchants shows that they are concerned that B2C e-commerce may not be cost-effective if there are not enough Internet buyers and that the cost of setting up and operating a payment-enabled Web storefront is high. These concerns contribute to the slow growth of online merchants.

In fact, both consumers and merchants face one common problem from different perspectives, that is, the lack of a secure, reliable, cost-effective, and easy-to-use online payment solution. There are some electronic payment systems for B2C e-commerce commercially available. These systems are not flexible enough to handle different payment methods. Some systems have captured the US market share, and some have captured small segments of the European and Asian markets. However, until now none of these payment systems has been able to achieve the critical mass required for B2C e-commerce to take off across the entire globe.

14.2 E-Payment Systems Supporting Multiple Payment Methods

By analyzing the current business problems in B2C e-commerce, it is found that these problems can be looked at from the three participants' perspectives:

- Consumers' concern about privacy, payment security, and convenience.
- Merchants' concern about the number of online buyers, payment options, and high cost of setting up payment-enabled Web storefronts.
- E-payment service providers face the problem of not having enough consumers and merchants.

To address these problems and meet the challenges of e-commerce, there is a need to develop an e-payment system that supports multiple payment methods including credit/debit cards, prepaid cards, and a variety of smart cards. It also supports payment through an account with a telephone company or an ISP.

Through this e-payment system, the above problems are addressed from three perspectives:

- From the consumers' perspective, to enhance payment security and provide multiple payment options, such an e-payment system should include a strong privacy protection mechanism. This will increase consumers' confidence in online shopping and payment.
- On the merchants' side, through the multiple payment options, merchants will be exposed to more Internet users thus enlarging their customer base. Consumers will also benefit from a large merchant network.

- With multiple payment options, strong security, and proper privacy protection, payment service providers will benefit from increased numbers of online consumers and merchants.

One of the key requirements of the e-payment system is to provide a privacy protection mechanism. To ensure the protection of consumers' privacy, a secure scheme should be included in the system to protect consumers' privacy and anonymity in e-commerce. The system can be designed in such a way that no single party knows the details of the entire shopping transaction. The transaction can be traced only if three parties (the merchant, the payment gateway, and the payment service provider) are working together under a court order. The idea is that the merchant does not have to know the customer identity; the merchant does not need to access any account information that is private to the customer; the bank does not need to know the order information to authorize the payment from the customer's account as long as the customer has enough money to cover the transaction.

The privacy protection scheme is based on blind signature techniques. A blind signature is a regular digital signature with the following features:

- The signatory does not know the content of the message that they are signing, as the message has been blinded before reaching them.
- From the signed blinded message, the signature on the message can be recovered by the party who blinded the message in the first place.
- After the message and the signature are revealed to the public, the signature can be verified, but the signatory cannot trace who blinded the message in the first place.

Blind digital signature has been studied for sometimes [14.1]. The objective is to design and implement the e-payment system with privacy protection and secure payment, based on a blind digital signature.

To protect consumers' privacy, the following design requirements have to be met: First, it is not acceptable for any single party in the system to know every detail of an online transaction, for example, the consumer's identification, the product that the consumer is buying, the quantity, and the price. Second, the merchant needs to have the payment authority's confirmation so that the merchant is guaranteed to be paid. Third, the payment authority must be comfortable with providing such a confirmation without knowing the transaction details. Here, the payment authority can be either a payment service provider or a billing company such as an ISP. The existing blind-signature protocols do not support the above design requirements.

To protect the consumer, the merchant will provide the consumer with a receipt of payment for the products purchased. The receipt contains a digital signature of the merchant and the purchase date and time. The exchange or refund can be arranged with this receipt according to the purchase agreement between the merchant and the consumer. Such an agreement can be included in the receipt. For example, the "final sale" products cannot be refunded or exchanged; or some products can be exchanged within 7 days after the purchase; or some products can be refunded provided that they are not opened or have a defect.

14.3 Smart Cards and Digital Cash

Smart cards provide a means of storing and processing value for digital cash. In particular, reloadable smart cards have become very popular nowadays. For example, a number of cities around the world are using or plan to use smart cards in their public transportation systems. Such cities include Washington DC, San Francisco, San Diego, Montreal, London, Singapore, Hong Kong, and many others. The Washington metropolitan transit pilot using smart cards was launched in 1999. It has 210,000 smart cards in circulation. As much as $200 US can be loaded onto the cards. Among these examples, the best one is the Octopus card in Hong Kong, as it has become a necessity for people's daily travel needs. With an estimated 10 million passenger journeys each day on Hong Kong's wide variety of public transportation services, the Octopus card provides evidence for the potential success of digital cash payment.

It was reported recently that the Octopus card is expanding its business into a variety of applications apart from public transportation, including 7-Eleven convenience stores, ticketing for the Broadway cinema chain, fast-food shops, such as Café de Coral, Maxim's, Starbucks, and even the giant hamburger chain McDonald's.

To examine the success of the Octopus card, in addition to what was discussed in Chapter 5, the following factors are crucial:

- Anonymity: no customer information is carried on the Octopus card and when using the Octopus card to make a payment, no privacy information is involved in the transaction.

- Risk is small as most people typically only load less than $200 Hong Kong dollars (or US$ 25.64) onto the card. If the card is stolen or lost, it is not a big concern to people.

- It is easy to reload the card with cash. There are many places in Hong Kong where people can reload their Octopus cards with cash, for example, at MTR (subway) stations or 7-Eleven convenience stores.

The Octopus card is an excellent candidate payment method for e-commerce applications over the Internet. However, there is a major issue that has to be resolved before the Octopus card can become popular as the preferred e-payment method over the Internet, that is, how to read from and write to an Octopus card using PCs, PDAs, pocket PCs, cellular phones, or other pervasive devices, as currently most PCs or pervasive devices are not equipped with an Octopus card reader. It is not realistic to ask every owner of a PC or pervasive device to purchase such a reader. In addition, there are issues of security and reliability related to the Octopus card readers.

14.4 Micropayment Issues and Solutions

Micropayment is particularly applicable to e-commerce over the Internet. Micropayment deals with a very small payment, typically in the range from one cent to a few dollars. Sometimes, the payment can be even a fraction of one cent. The applications for micropayment include "pay per click" for an image, a piece of music (or video), online gaming, an online report, or a piece of online information. The business justification for micropayment is the huge online customer base even if each transaction value may be tiny. The popular credit card-based online payment method may not be appropriate for small-value transactions because there is a minimum credit card charge, usually about a quarter (US$ 0.25) or so. The amount in a micropayment transaction may be too low to justify the payment using a credit card.

The major issues for micropayment are that the payment-processing cost is relatively high compared to the amount in a micropayment transaction, and the cost of implementation of existing micropayment schemes is also high. When implementing a micropayment system, one needs to consider the cost of the infrastructure support such as the communication, computation, hardware equipment, and associated software. In addition, there are other costs involved, such as the cost of customer acquisition, the cost of handling disputes and chargebacks, and the cost of customer support.

To reduce the payment-processing cost, one obvious solution is to aggregate many small micropayments into a few regular payments. The question is how can the aggregation be done. There are several ways to do the aggregation. For example, it can be performed per user session, or it can be done in different user sessions but limited to a specific online merchant. Of course, it can also be done across different merchants through a payment-service provider. Different aggregation schemes require different accounting and user transaction management approaches. Again, we encounter the cost issue for implementing the aggregation schemes for micropayment, which could be substantially high.

To handle the dispute, the customer needs to directly interact with the online merchant. In addition, the proper security measures, such as digital signatures, must be in place. In case there is a dispute, at least digital signatures can provide non-repudiation of a transaction.

To save on communication costs, it is desirable to handle the payment offline and to make the payment protocol non-interactive, for example, through an email, to reduce the number of round-trip communications between the merchant's server and the customer's browser. The offline payment can be achieved through the aggregation of authorizations and deposits. The micropayment service provider only needs to examine the value flow when necessary.

14.5 Summary

In this chapter, we have discussed the challenges and opportunities of e-payment. The major challenges for e-payment are as follows:

- **Freedom to choose an e-payment method:** giving online customers freedom to choose which e-payment method they prefer (that means, the e-payment systems/solutions need to support multiple e-payment methods).
- **Security:** how to make e-payment more secure to ensure the safety of the customers' online transactions.
- **Privacy:** how to protect the online customers' private information
- **Anonymity:** how to make the e-payment anonymous.
- **Risk:** how to reduce the online customers' risk involved in e-payment.
- **Convenience:** how to provide the online customers with convenience.
- **Cost:** how to reduce the implementation and processing costs of e-payment systems/solutions.

The opportunities are to respond to the online customers' needs and meet the challenges identified above by developing new e-payment systems/solutions.

14.6 References

[14.1]   D. Chaum (1983) Blind signature for untraceable payments. In: Advances in cryptology. Plenum Press, New York, pp. 199–203.
[14.2]   E. Mohammed, et al. (2000) A blind signature based on the discrete ElGamal signature. In: Proceedings of the 17th National Radio Science Conference, pp. C25:1–6.

[14.3]   J. L. Camenisch, J. M. Piveteau, M. A. Stadler (1994) Blind signature based on the discrete logarithm problem. In: Advances in cryptology – Eurocrypt'94, pp. 428–432.

[14.4]   R. Anderson, C. Manifavas, C. Sutherland (1996) Netcard – a practical electronic cash scheme. In: Cambridge Workshop on Security Protocols.

[14.5]   D. Chaum, S. Brands (1997) Minting electronic cash. IEEE Spectrum, February Issue.

[14.6]   D. Chaum (1992) Achieving electronic privacy. Scientific American, August Issue.

[14.7]   A. Herzberg, H. Yochai (1997) IBM-MP: charging per click on the web. In: Proceedings of the 6th WWW Conference.

[14.8]   W. Song (2000) An investigation on micropayment and its implementation. Project Report, ETI, The University of Hong Kong.

[14.9]   R. Weber (2000) Market analysis of digital payment systems. Technical Report (TUM-I9818). Institute for Informatics, Technology University of Munich.

[14.10] Z. Li, W. Kou (2002) A batch verification scheme for RSA digital signatures. Submitted for publication.

[14.11] Z. Huang, K. Chen, W. Kou (2002) A blind digital signature scheme. Submitted for publication.

[14.12] D. Zheng, W. Kou, K. Chen, Z. Gan (2002) Subliminal-free digital signature schemes in the presence of an active warden. Submitted for publication.

Glossary

Application programming interface (API)

A set of the specific methods, services, or instructions prescribed by a computer program by which a programmer writing an application program can make requests of the computer program.

Authentication

Providing assurance that the entity (user, host, and so forth) requesting access is the entity that it claims to be.

Behavioral biometric

A biometric that is characterized by a behavioral trait that is learned and acquired over time, rather than a physical or physiological characteristic (contrast with physical biometric).

Biometric system

An automated system capable of: capturing a biometric sample from an end-user; extracting biometric data from that sample; comparing the biometric data with that contained in one or more reference templates; deciding how well they match; and indicating whether or not an identification or verification of identity has been achieved.

Certificate

A digital credential in a public-key cryptography system, which contains the certificate holder's name and public key, a serial number, the expiration date of the certificate, and the digital signature of the certificate authority that issued the certificate.

Certificate authority (CA)

A trusted entity that is part of a public key infrastructure (PKI) and that creates, issues, and manages certificates for PKI users.

Certificate revocation list (CRL)

A list of certificates issued by a certification authority (CA) that are no longer valid. The CRL is maintained and published by the CA.

Chargeback

A process where the PSP requires the merchant to return funds for a disputed or cancelled payment.

Cookie

A file sent by a web server to a browser and stored by the browser. The cookie includes a destination address as a URL, possibly with wildcards. When the browser sends any request to a web server corresponding to the destination address, the browser attaches the cookie to the request. Cookies are used to identify the consumer, especially for repeat access to the same site.

Credit risk

The risk that the consumer will fail to pay the payment service provider (PSP) for aggregated payments (when the PSP charges the consumer after payments were made).

Digital cash

An electronic form of cash in a cash-like e-payment system with which a person can make online payment for goods or services purchased over the Internet.

Digital check

An electronic form of a check in a check-like e-payment system where the check can be conveyed across computer networks.

Digital signature

A digital string produced by applying a cryptographic algorithm with the private-key information on a message/document to authenticate the message/document.

Dispute resolution

A process invoked by the consumer to cancel a transaction (payment) that the consumer believes was not authorized or should be cancelled for other valid reasons.

Enrollment

The process of collecting biometric samples from a person and the subsequent preparation and storage of biometric reference templates representing that person's identity.

Enrollment time

The time a person must spend to have their biometric reference template successfully created.

Enrollment station

A workstation at which an individual's biometrics (fingerprint, voiceprint, etc.) and personal information (name, address, etc.) can be entered into a bioidentification system.

Escrow agent

A party that receives payments from the consumer and goods from the merchant, and, only when both were received properly, delivers the goods to the consumer and the payment to the merchant.

Extensible Markup Language (XML)

Universal format for structured documents and data on the Web, supporting the customized tags, enabling the definition, transmission, validation, and interpretation of data between applications and between organizations.

Extraction

The process of converting a captured biometric sample into biometric data so that it can be compared to a reference template.

False acceptance rate (FAR)

The probability that a biometric system will incorrectly identify an individual or will fail to reject an impostor. Also known as the Type II error rate.

False rejection rate (FRR)

The probability that a biometric system will fail to identify an enrollee, or verify the legitimately claimed identity of an enrollee. Also known as the Type I error rate.

HyperText Transfer Protocol (HTTP)

Standard transfer protocol used in the Internet, which defines how messages are formatted and transmitted, and what actions web servers and browsers should take in response to various commands. For example, when entering a URL in a browser, one actually sends a HTTP command to the Web server and instructs it to fetch and transmit the requested Web document.

Internet protocol security (IPSec)

A set of security functions and options available at the IP level.

Internet service provider (ISP)

A company that provides users with access to the Internet. For a monthly fee, the ISP provides users with a software package, user ID, password, and access phone number. Some ISPs also provide users with a modem to enable users to access the Internet.

Irreversible transactions

Payments that are done in such a way that the PSP cannot technically reverse them with a chargeback to the merchant, since there is no identification of the merchant.

Kerberos

In Greek mythology, the three-headed dog that guards the entrance to the underworld. In network security, Kerberos is a cryptographic authentication system that makes use of a third-party server to authenticate clients and servers. The system was developed in the Athena Project at the Massachusetts Institute of Technology (MIT).

Key

(a) A small piece of data used in conjunction with an algorithm to encrypt or decrypt messages/data of arbitrary size (see also PKI), or (b) an attribute whose value serves to identify a unique record in a database/table (e.g., employee ID number may be the primary key used to locate and identify a specific employee's personnel data, such as name, address, telephone number, salary).

Mail-order telephone (MOT)

Classification of credit card transaction performed when the credit card is not physically present for verification

Message authentication code (MAC)

A fixed-size binary code obtained by applying a shared-key cryptographic algorithm to an arbitrary amount of data to serve as an authenticator of the data.

Micropayment

A payment of small amounts, close to or below the credit card minimal fees (of about 20 US cents).

Micropayment system

A system allowing merchants to charge many payments of small amounts (micropayments) from customers over open data networks such as the Internet by using one or more payment service providers (PSPs).

Mobile agents

A computer program that represents a user and can migrate autonomously from node to node in a computer network, to perform some computation on behalf of the user.

Mobile agent host

A computer program running in a networked computer that provides an execution environment where mobile agents can execute their code and can communicate with one another.

NetBill

A payment system where the digital check is used to sell and deliver low-priced information goods.

NetCheque system

A distributed accounting service supporting the credit-debit model of payment.

Nonrepudiation

A proof that the consumer approved a particular action, typically a payment.

Octopus card

A smart card system used in Hong Kong for local transportation fare collection.

Offline payments

Payments between the consumer and the merchant which do not require communication with other parties such as the PSP.

Order information (OI)

Information included in a SET transaction to describe the transaction.

Original equipment manufacturer (OEM)

A biometric organization (manufacturer) that assembles a complete biometric system from parts, or a biometric module for integration into a complete biometric system.

Payment approval

A process where the customer agrees to a particular payment.

Payment authorization

A process where the PSP takes responsibility for a payment, in particular by indicating that there are funds to cover the payment.

Payment gateway (PG)

Entity in a SET transaction that handles credit card verification and authorization of transactions.

Payment information (PI)

Information included in a SET transaction to describe a payment (such as the credit card holder and number).

Payment order (PO)

A message indicating payment to the merchant.

Payment routing table (PRT)

A message sent by a PSP to a merchant or another PSP, indicating the terms under which the PSP sending the PRT is willing to receive payment orders issued by other PSPs.

Payment service provider (PSP)

An entity that maintains a long-term relationship with customers and merchants, receiving payments of aggregated (large) amounts from customers, and passing aggregated payments to the merchants.

Penalty payment

A payment by a merchant who has had too many disputes and/or chargebacks.

Personal identification number (PIN)

A security method whereby a (usually) four-digit number is entered by an individual to gain access to a particular system or area.

Physical/physiological biometric

A biometric that is characterized by a physical characteristic rather than a behavioral trait (contrast with behavioral biometric).

Prepayment

Requiring funds to be deposited in advance.

Private key

In public-key cryptography, this key is the secret key. It is primarily used for decryption but is also used for encryption with digital signatures.

Public key

In public-key cryptography, this key is made public to all. It is primarily used for encryption but can be used for verifying signatures.

Public-key cryptography

Cryptography based on methods involving a public key and a private key.

Public-key infrastructure (PKI)

Structure used to issue, manage, and allow verification of public-key certificates. PKI is a security framework for messages and data, based on the notion of a pair of cryptographic keys (i.e., one public and one private) and used to facilitate security, integrity, and privacy.

Radio frequency identification (RFID)

The use of radio waves to facilitate wireless (contactless) communication with a chip or device.

Record aggregation

Replacing multiple separate documents, e.g., payment orders, with a single aggregated document, e.g., a payment order.

Rejection/false rejection

When a biometric system fails to identify an enrollee or fails to verify the legitimately claimed identity of an enrollee. Also known as a Type I error.

Response time/processing time

The time period required by a biometric system to return a decision on the identification or verification of a biometric sample.

Secure electronic commerce

A form of commerce conducted via electronic means, but designed with security in mind to enable identification, authentication, authorization, or payment processing.

Secure electronic transaction (SET)

A protocol for secure payment processing over the Internet in which credit card information (e.g., Visa, MasterCard) is not read or stored by a merchant. The protocol links many parties, including the customer, merchant, acquirer, and certification authorities. The protocol is designed to emulate card-present transactions.

Secure sockets layer (SSL)

A protocol originally introduced by Netscape to secure communication between web servers and web clients, supported by most web browsers and servers; superceded by TLS.

Semi-offline payments

Payment protocol where most transactions are offline (involve only communication between the consumer and merchant, not with the PSP), but sometimes communication with the PSP is necessary.

Smart card

A plastic card with an embedded chip to enable payment processing or digital identification. A typical smart card chip includes a microprocessor or CPU, ROM (for storing operating instructions), RAM (for storing data during processing), and EPROM (or EEPROM) memory for nonvolatile storage of information.

Software agent

A computer program that acts autonomously on behalf of a person or organization to accomplish a predefined task or a series of tasks.

Stored-value card

A smart card that comes preloaded with a certain amount of value (e.g., money, phone calls, transit trips), but which cannot be reloaded.

Stored-value payments

Offline payments where the consumers have complete control over the payments, in particular they can pay any merchant without contacting the PSP.

Subscriber identification module (SIM)

SIM is for GSM digital telephony. SIM smart cards are used to provide user authentication, voice/data integrity, and confidentiality.

Symmetric cryptography

A way of keeping data secret in which the sender and receiver use the same key.

T=0/T=1 Protocols

ISO 7816 asynchronous byte (T=0) and block (T=1) transmission protocols at the data-link layer, used for communication between a smart card and a reader.

Threshold

The acceptance or rejection of biometric data is dependent on the match score falling above or below the threshold. The threshold is adjustable so that the biometric system can be more or less strict, depending on the requirements of any given biometric application.

Transmission control protocol (TCP)

Internet protocol which manages message exchanges at the transport level.

Transport-layer security (TLS)

An IETF (Internet Engineering Task Force) standard protocol to secure communication between web servers and web clients, supported by most web browsers and servers; the previous version was called SSL.

Trusted third party

An organization or entity that is impartial to both the customer and the merchant (or buyer and seller), is trusted by both, and whose testimony is accepted as valid evidence in a court of law.

URL

Uniform Resource Locator specifying the unique address of a Web document.

Validation

The process of demonstrating that the system under consideration meets in all respects the specification of that system.

Wireless application environment (WAE)

The application framework for WAP applications. WAE consists of a set of standards that collectively define a group of formats for wireless applications and downloadable content.

Wireless application protocol (WAP)

A specification that allows users to access information instantly via handheld wireless devices such as cellular phones, pagers, and personal digital assistants (PDAs) through wireless communication networks and the Internet.

Wireless datagram protocol (WDP)

A datagram protocol for non-IP wireless packet data networks. WDP specifies how different existing bearer services should be used to provide a consistent service to the upper layers of the WAP architecture framework.

Wireless markup language (WML)

An XML-based markup language for wireless handheld devices, including cellular phones, pagers, and PDAs.

Wireless session protocol (WSP)

A protocol family derived from the HTTP version 1.1 standard with extensions for wireless data applications. WSP provides WAP applications with a consistent interface for session services.

Wireless telephony applications (WTA)

A framework for integrating wireless data applications with voice networks. WTA is a collection of telephony-specific extensions for call and feature control mechanisms that make advanced mobile network services available to the mobile users.

Wireless transaction protocol (WTP)

A protocol operating on top of a secure or insecure datagram service. WTP is an extremely lightweight request-response-acknowledge transaction protocol.

Wireless transport-layer security (WTLS)

A security protocol based on SSL and adapted to wireless networks and datagram transports.

About the Editor

Weidong Kou is Associate Director of the E-Business Technology Institute (ETI) and Adjunct Professor of the Department of Computer Science and Information Systems at the University of Hong Kong.

Prof. Kou also serves as Adjunct Professor of the Department of Computer Science and Electrical Engineering at the University of Maryland in US, Shanghai Jiao Tong University, South China University of Technology, and Lan Zhou University in China, and Guest Professor of Sun Yat-Sen University, South East University, and Beijing University of Posts and Telecommunications in China. In addition, he is a member of the Advisory Committee on Computer Science and Electrical Engineering at the University of Maryland in Baltimore, Co-chair of the Technical Advisory Board of the e-Generation Technology Center at Shanghai Jiao Tong University, Deputy Director of the Academic Committee of the National Key Laboratory of the Ministry of Education of China on Computer Networking and Information Security at Xidian University, and Technology Advisor for the IBM Great China Group's University Relationship Program.

Prof. Kou was a Research Professor at Rutgers University. He served as the Industrial Co-leader of a major project of the CITR (Canadian Institute of Telecommunications Research, a Canadian National Center of Excellence), *Enabling Technology for Electronic Commerce*, for more than three years. He served as a member of American national standard committees, ANSI X9B9 (Financial Image Interchange) and ANSI X3L3 (JPEG and MPEG), for more than four years. He has also served as a Guest Editor of special issues on e-commerce for the *International Journal on Digital Libraries* and the *ACM Computing Survey*. Prof. Kou was the Founding Chair of the International Symposium on Electronic Commerce (ISEC), and from 1998 to 2001 he was the General Chair and Program Chair for the ISECs and International Workshops on Technological Challenges of Electronic Commerce.

Since joining ETI at the University of Hong Kong in August 2000, Prof. Kou has been leading the e-commerce and wireless research and development efforts. Notably, Prof. Kou and his team were awarded the Innovation and Technology Fund (ITF). The ITF exercises, being highly competitive and placing great emphasis on local relevance, select only projects with great potential for Hong Kong. Out of a total of 19 proposals submitted in January 2001 by all sectors in Hong Kong, only three projects were awarded, and two of these came from the teams led by Prof. Kou. The total funding for the two winning projects was over 17 million Hong Kong dollars for a period of two years. One of these projects focuses on payment technologies for electronic commerce.

Prof. Kou has over 12 years of industrial experience in the software development and management in North America. Prior to joining ETI, Prof. Kou was Principal Investigator at the IBM Center of Advanced Studies in Toronto, Canada, where he led R&D projects on e-commerce. From 1995 to 1997, he was an Architect of a major IBM B2B e-commerce project for a national government at the IBM Industrial Solution Development Center in Canada. Prior to joining IBM in 1995, he was the Chairman of the Imaging Committee at the AT&T Imaging Systems Division, where he led a number of financial imaging projects. Prior to joining AT&T in 1991, he was Senior Software Engineer at Siemens in Toronto, Canada, where he invented compression algorithms and implemented them in Siemens' imaging products. He received various invention achievement and technical excellence awards from IBM, AT&T, and Siemens.

Prof. Kou has authored/edited five books in the areas of e-commerce, security, and multimedia technologies, and published over 50 papers on journals and conferences, including papers in prestigious journals such as *IEEE Transactions on Communications, IEEE Transactions on Signal Processing, IEEE Transactions on Acoustics, Speech and Signal Processing*, and *International Journal of Computer and Information Science*. He has also authored nine US and Canadian issued and pending patents.

One of Prof. Kou's books, *Digital Image Compression: Algorithms and Standards*, published by Kluwer Academic Publishers in 1995, has been widely used in a variety of universities around the globe as a recommended reference book, for example in Southern Queensland University in Australia, Catalunya University in Spain, Saarland University in Germany, Glasgow University and the University of London in the UK, Chalmers University in Sweden, Bandung Technology Institute in Indonesia, Stanford University, George Mason University, Ohio State University, and Albany New York State University in the US, and Calgary University in Canada.

Prof. Kou received his Ph.D. degree in Electrical Engineering in 1985 from Xidian University, and M.S. degree in applied mathematics in 1982 from Beijing University of Posts and Telecommunications, respectively. He was a Postdoctoral Fellow at the University of Waterloo, Canada, from April 1987 to February 1989.

Prof. Kou is a Senior Member of IEEE, and a member of the Advisory Committee of W3C. He was elected as a member of the New York Academy of Sciences in 1992.

Contributors

Gordon B. Agnew received his B.Sc. and Ph.D. in Electrical Engineering from the University of Waterloo in 1978 and 1982, respectively. He joined the Department of Electrical and Computer Engineering at the University of Waterloo in 1982. In 1984 he was a visiting professor at the Swiss Federal Institute of Technology in Zurich where he started his work on cryptography. Dr. Agnew's areas of expertise include cryptography, data security, protocols and protocol analysis, electronic commerce systems, high-speed networks, wireless systems, and computer architecture. He has taught many university courses and industry-sponsored short courses in these areas, and authored many articles. In 1985, he joined the Data Encryption Group at the University of Waterloo. The work of this group led to significant advances in the area of public-key cryptographic systems including the development of a practical implementation of elliptic-curve-based cryptosystems. Dr. Agnew is a member of the Institute of Electrical and Electronics Engineers, a member of the International Association for Cryptologic Research, a Foundation Fellow of the Institute for Combinatorics and Its Applications, and a Registered Professional Engineer in the Province of Ontario. Dr. Agnew has provided consulting services to the banking, communications, and government sectors. He is also a co-founder of Certicom Corp., a world leader in public-key cryptosystem technologies.

Amitabha Das received the B.Tech. degree in Electronic and Electrical Communication Engineering from the Indian Institute of Technology, Kharagpur in 1985, and the M.S. and Ph.D. degrees in Electrical and Computer Engineering from the University of California, Santa Barbara in 1989 and 1991, respectively. He is currently an Associate Professor in the School of Computer Engineering in Nanyang Technological University, Singapore. His current research interests include mobile agents, e-commerce, mobile databases, and data mining. Dr. Das is a member of IEEE. He can be reached by email at asadas@ntu.edu.sg.

Amir Herzberg is an independent security consultant. He graduated from the Technion, Israel, in 1982, and since then has worked as an engineer and researcher, mostly in security and communication areas. After completing his D.Sc. (Computer Science) at the Technion in 1991, Dr. Herzberg joined IBM Research, filling research and management positions in New York and Israel. During 2001 he was CTO of NewGenPay, a spin-off of the IBM Micro Payments project. Since January 2002, he has been a security consultant and teaches in Tel Aviv and Bar Ilan universities. Dr. Herzberg headed the W3C MicroPayments working group and contributed to several standards, including IP-Sec and SET. He is interested, and published, in the areas of security, applied cryptography, and fault-tolerant protocols. He is writing a book on "Secure Communication and Commerce Using Cryptography" (see http://amir.beesites.co.il).

Zheng Huang received his B.S. degree and M.S. degree from Tong Ji University in 1997 and 2000, respectively. He is currently a Ph.D. student at the Department of Computer Science of Shanghai Jiao Tong University. His advisor is Prof. Kefei Chen; information security is his major. He can be reached by e-mail at huang-zheng@cs.sjtu.edu.cn.

Ed Knorr is a tenure-track instructor at the University of British Columbia (UBC). He received his Ph.D. in Computer Science from UBC. His previous degrees include an M.Sc. degree from UBC, and a B.Math. degree from the University of Waterloo. Dr. Knorr's research interests include data mining, outliers, database systems, and electronic commerce (e.g., security, privacy, usability, smart cards, and digital money).

Hui Li graduated from Fudan University in 1990 and received his Ph.D. degree from Xidian University in 1998. He is currently an Associate Professor at the School of Communication Engineering, Xidian University and Deputy Director of the Academic Department of the Key Lab for Computer Networking and Information Security. His research interest is in the area of information security.

Zichen Li received his Ph.D. degree in Signal Design and Information Processing from Beijing University of Posts and Telecommunications in 1999. From 1999 to 2002, he was a postdoctoral fellow at Tsinghua University. Dr. Li has been an Associate Professor and the Chairman of the Department of Computer Science and Technology at Jiaozuo Institute of Technology (JIT), Henan Province, China. Dr. Li is currently on leave from JIT and is working at the E-Business Technology Institute of the University of Hong Kong as a Project Manager. His research interests include information security, cryptography, and e-commerce.

Xiaodong Lin obtained his Ph.D. degree from Beijing University of Posts and Telecommunications in 1998. He subsequently spent two years at the University of Waterloo as a postdoctoral fellow. He is currently a senior security architect at Intellitactics, Inc., Canada. Dr. Lin has published more than 20 papers in journals and conferences. His research interests include network security (particularly enterprise security management, intrusion detection, performance analysis, vulnerability and exploit analysis, and penetration testing), applied cryptography, data mining, and distributed systems.

Lev Mirlas graduated in Engineering Science from the Faculty of Applied Science and Engineering at the University of Toronto in 1989, and obtained his Master's degree in Computer Engineering from the same university in 1995. He is a senior engineer at the IBM Canada Toronto Laboratory, where he has worked in the areas of trusted distributed computing and electronic commerce, including electronic procurement, insurance industry information exchange, and B2B commerce. He is a Registered Professional Engineer in the Province of Ontario.

Yi Mu received his Ph.D. from the Australian National University in 1994. Upon completion of his Ph.D., he took up a research associate position in the Centre for Computer Security Research, University of Wollongong, Australia. In 1995, Dr. Mu joined the Distributed Systems Security Research Unit in the School of Computing and IT at the University of Western Sydney (UWS), Australia, as a Postdoctoral Research Fellow. He became an Associate Lecturer in 1996 and then a Lecturer in the School of Computing and IT at UWS. He joined the Department of Computing, Macquarie University, Australia, as a Senior Lecturer, in 2001. His current research interests include electronic commerce, mobile security, access control, mobile agents, and cryptography. Dr. Mu has over 50 research publications in international journals and refereed conference proceedings. He is a regular reviewer for some major international journals and conferences. He has been a member of the Program Committee for many international conferences.

Khanh Quoc Nguyen received his Ph.D. in Secure Electronic Commerce from the University of Western Sydney, Australia, in 2000. He worked as a security engineer at the Motorola research laboratory in Australia for two years before moving to the security lab of Gemplus in Singapore in 2001. His research interests are mainly in the fields of electronic commerce security, smart-card security, and public-key cryptography. He has published a number of research papers in electronic commerce security.

Simpson Poon is Professor, Chair of Information Systems at Charles Sturt University, Australia. He has been a visiting lecturer at the University of Hong Kong. Dr. Poon earned his Ph.D in Information Systems from Monash University, Australia. He was the Founding Director of the Centre of E-Commerce and Internet Studies at Murdoch University, Australia. Dr. Poon has been an e-business consultant and has worked with both government and business organizations in Australia and Asia. He has published widely in the area of e-business in both academic and professional journals. Dr. Poon can be reached at spoon@csu.edu.au.

Vijay Varadharajan is currently the Microsoft Chair Professor at Macquarie University, Australia. He did a Ph.D. in Computer and Communication Security in the UK and has been working on various aspects of security technology over the last

19 years. He has done research in formal security models, security in distributed systems and networks, security policies, design and analysis of security protocols, design of security architectures, cryptography, secure electronic payment systems, and mobile networks security. His research work has contributed to the development of several secure systems in the commercial arena in the areas of secure distributed authentication, DCE security, distributed authorization and authorization servers, secure mobile systems, secure portable information appliances, auditing management tools for networked systems, LAN and SMDS secure network systems, secure distributed applications, and smart card systems. Prof. Varadharajan has published over 160 papers for international journals and conferences on various aspects of security technology and the applications mentioned above. He has also co-authored a book on network security and has co-edited three books on information security and one on distributed systems.

Yumin Wang is Professor at the School of Communications Engineering, Xidian University, Xi'an, P.R. China. Since the 1960s, he has conducted research in the areas of information theory, information security, and cryptology. He is a Fellow of the Chinese Institute of Electronics and the Chinese Institute of Communications. He has published several books and over 100 papers on information theory, information security, and e-business.

Johnny W. Wong received his Ph.D. degree in Computer Science from the University of California at Los Angeles in 1975. Since then, he has been with the University of Waterloo where he is currently a Professor of Computer Science. From 1989 to 1994 he was Associate Provost, Computing and Information Systems. Dr. Wong has published over 100 technical papers in the areas of information delivery systems, network resource management, performance evaluation, and distributed systems. Among his many professional roles are Editor of Wide Area Networks of IEEE Transactions on Communications (1989 to 1992), member of the Editorial Board of Performance Evaluation (1986 to 1993), member of the Editorial Board of IEEE/ACM Transactions on Networking (1997 to 2000), Technical Program Chair of IEEE INFOCOM'84, and General Chair of the 1999 International Conference on Network Protocols.

Bo Yang received his B.S. degree from Beijing University in 1986, and M.S. and Ph.D. degrees from Xidian University in 1993 and 1999, respectively. Dr. Yang is currently Associate Professor at the School of Communication Engineering, Deputy Director at the Key Lab of the Ministry of Education of China for Networking and Information Security, and Associate Dean of the School of Information Engineering in Xidian University, Shaanxi Province, P.R. China. He is a Senior Member of the Chinese Institute of Electronics (CIE), and a member of the specialist group on computer network and information security in Shaanxi Province. His research interests include information theory and e-commerce. He can be reached by email at yangbo@mail.xidian.edu.cn.

Li Yu graduated from Heilongjiang University in 1998. She received her M.S. degree in optics from Harbin Institute of Technology, Department of Physics in 2000. She is currently pursuing her Ph.D. degree in Harbin Institute of Technology, Department of Computer Science and Technology. Her research interests include image processing, biometrics, and pattern recognition. She can be reached at lyu@mbox.hit.edu.cn.

David Zhang graduated in Computer Science from Beijing University in 1974 and received his M.Sc. and Ph.D. degrees in Computer Science and Engineering from Harbin Institute of Technology (HIT) in 1983 and 1985, respectively. From 1986 to 1988, he was a postdoctoral fellow at Tsinghua University and became an Associate Professor at Academia Sinica, Beijing, China. He received his second Ph.D. in Electrical and Computer Engineering at the University of Waterloo, Ontario, Canada, in 1994. Currently, he is a Professor in the Polytechnic University of Hong Kong. He is a Founder and Director of both Biometrics Research Center in the Polytechnic University of Hong Kong and the Harbin Institute of Technology, supported by UGC/CRC, the Hong Kong Government, and the National Nature Scientific Foundation (NSFC) of China, respectively. In addition, he is a Founder and Editor-in-Chief of the International Journal of Image and Graphics, and an Associate Editor of the IEEE Trans. on Systems, Man and Cybernetics, Pattern Recognition, the International Journal of Pattern Recognition and Artificial Intelligence, Information: International Journal, the International Journal of Robotics, and Automation and Neural, Parallel and Scientific Computations. So far, he has published over 180 articles and seven books on his research areas. He can be reached at csdzhang@comp.polyu.edu.hk.

Fangguo Zhang received his B.Sc. degree from the Mathematics Department of Yantai Normal University, Shandong, China, in 1996, his M.S. degree from the Applied Mathematics Department, Tong Ji University, Shanghai, China, in 1999, and his Ph.D. degree in Cryptography from Xidian University, Shaanxi, China, in 2002. He is presently a Postdoctoral Fellow at the Cryptology and Information Security Lab, in the Information and Communications University (ICU), Taejon, Korea. His research interests are elliptic curve cryptography, hyperelliptic curve cryptography, and secure electronic commerce. He can be reached at zhfg@icu.ac.kr or fgzh@hotmail.com.

Dong Zheng received his M.S. degree in Mathematics from Shaanxi Normal University in 1985 and Ph.D. degree in Cryptography from Xidian University in 1999. From 1999 to 2001, he was a Postdoctoral Researcher at the Department of Computer Science and Engineering of Shanghai Jiao Tong University, where he is currently an Associate Professor of Computer Science. Dr. Zheng has published over 40 technical papers in the areas of mathematics, cryptography, and information security. His current research interests include cryptography, network security, and e-commerce. He can be reached at zheng-dong@cs.sjtu.edu.cn.

Index

Access control 206

Anonymity 172, 180
  Revocation 188

Audit
  Mechanism 9

Authentication 8, 32, 48, 112, 159
  CA-based 36
  Challenge-response 34
  Double-factor 34
  Password 33
  Two-stage 34

Authorization 8, 113, 205, 275
  Pre-authorization 276
  Random 275
  Threshold 275

Biometrics 71, 72
  Enrollment 311
    Time 311
    Station 311
  Extraction 312
  Facial-scan 76
  Fault access rate 86, 312
  Fault reject rate 86, 312
  Finger-scan 73
  Hand-scan 74
  Iris-scan 75
  Retina-scan 75
  System 309
  Voice-scan 78

Card acceptance devices 100

Confidentiality 8, 151

Cookie 310

Cryptanalysis 11
  Chosen-plaintext attack 11
  Cipher-only attack 11
  Correlation 11
  Known-plaintext attack 11
  Man-in-the-middle attack 11

Cryptography 9
  DNA 12
  Secret-key 13
  Public-key 17

Cryptosystem 17
  Braid group 23
  ElGamal 17
  Elliptic-curve 17, 18, 20, 225
  Hyperelliptic curve 23
  Knapsack 23
  Lucas 23
  McEliece 22
  NTRU 23
  Public-key 18
  RSA 17, 18
  Symmetric 13

Diffie-Hellman 19, 20

Digital cash 171, 246, 304, 310
  Client tracing 188
  Coin tracing 188
  Double spending 172, 179
  Fair digital cash 181
  Normal coin 178
  Signed coin 178
  Zero-knowledge proof 171

Digital check 195, 306
  Authenticity of 197
  Basic element 195
  Presentment 197

Digital signature   24, 112, 223
    Blind   27, 303
    DSA   25, 277
    ECDSA   26
    ElGamal   17
    Fail-stop   27
    Group   29
    Proxy   29
    Rabin   25
    RSA   25, 223, 277
    Undeniable   27

Dispute resolution   311

Electronic check   166, 197
    Also see digital check

Encryption 10
    AES   15
    CAST-128   16
    Cipher   10
        Block   11
        Stream   11
    Data encryption standard   13
        DES   13
        Triple DES   14
    IDEA   16
    Rivest cipher   16
        RC2   16
        RC4   17
        RC5   17
        RC6   17
    Twofish   17

Extensible markup language   311
    Also see XML

Hash algorithm   30, 262
    MD5   31
    SHA-1   31
    MAC   259, 264, 277, 313

Identification   112, 215
    Information   215

Industrial payment systems   283
    NetBill   195, 199, 310
    NetCheque   195, 207, 310
    PayPal   213, 283, 294
        Request money   295
        Send money   295
        Workflow   297
    Visa Cash   283
        PSAM   286
        Workflow   286

IP Address   213

iPIN   244, 283, 289
    Customer care   293
    Clearing and settlement   292
    Real-time accounting   292
    Transaction acquisition   289
    Transaction processing   292
    Workflow   291

IPSec   213, 312

Kerberos   206, 313

Key   313
    Credential   207
    Management   50, 115
    Private key   200, 316
    Pseudonyms   207
    Public key   200, 316
    Repository   206

Mail-order telephone   213, 313

Message
    Integrity   8
    Privacy   8

Micropayment   246, 305, 313
    Acceptability   263
    Bearer certificate   258, 261
    Centralized solution   269
    Chargeback   250, 252, 310

Click and pay 250, 263
Consumer default 252
Cookie 259
Credit risk 252, 310
Dispute 250, 252
Interoperability 268
Irreversible transaction 261, 313
Offline clearing solution 269
Offline payment 255, 275
Online payment 248, 250
Overspending 252, 254
Payment approval 247, 248, 253
Payment authorization 247, 254
Payment order 248, 250
Payment routing table 270
Payment service provider 246
Per-fee-link 258, 263
Record aggregation 251, 317
Secure payment 254
Stored value payment 276

Non-repudiation 255, 259

Octopus card 118, 124, 304
    Identification card 112, 117
    KCRC 118
    KMB 118
    MTRC 118
    HKF 118

Operational costs 266, 277

Payment 9
    Approval 247, 315
    Authorization 247, 315
    ATM 74, 110, 269
    Dispute 250
    Electronic purse 120
    Escrow agent 311
    Gateway 315
    Information 315
    P2P 290
    Privacy 301
    Service provider 316

Settlement 9
Wallet 250, 259, 263
    Local 265
    Server 265
    Multiple 266
    Third-party 266

PDA 132, 136

Pretty Good Privacy 234

Privacy-enhanced mail 60

Public-key infrastructure 40, 85, 317
    Certificate 40, 215, 309
        Authority 40, 215, 310
        Hierarchy 42
        Chain 43
        Validation 45
        Revocation list 46, 310
    Distinguished name 51
    Directory information tree 52
    LDAP 49
    Registration authority 49
    PKIX 61
    SDSI 62
    SPKI 62
    X.509 50
    X.500 51

Random number generator 31

Server security 7

SET 113, 211, 233, 318
    Acquirer CA 216
    Application layer 212
    Cardholder 215, 218
    Certificate 216
    Initial request 217
    Order information 219
    Payment card issuing CA 216
    Payment gateway 218
    Payment information 219

Performance 223
Protocol stack 212
SETCo 211
Specification 211

Smart card 95, 304, 318
   Communication interface 97
   Contact 95, 99
   Contactless 95, 99
   Java card 106
      API 108
      Converter 107
      Interpreter 107
      JCRE 107
      JCVM 107
   Memory chip 97
      EEPROM 98
      EPROM 98
      RAM 97
      ROM 98
   Reader 100
   Standards 109

Software agent 149
   CEF 155
   Code obfuscation 154
   HES 156
   Mobile agent 150, 314
   Sliding encryption 152
   SPP 164
   Trail obscuring 154

SSL 142, 214, 228, 318

TLS 146

Trusted third party 228, 230
   TTP-B 235
   TTP-M 235

WAP 134, 320
   gateway 143
   WAE 136, 320
   WBXML 136, 140
   WDP 143, 320
   WML 136, 320
   WMLScript 137
   WSP 140, 321
   WTA 139, 321
   WTAI 139
   WTLS 142, 321
   WTP 141, 321

Wireless communications 128
   AM 129
   Authentication center 130
   ASK 128
   Base station controller 130
   CBS 131
   CDMA 128
   FDMA 129
   FM 129
   FSK 128
   GPRS 129
   GSM 97, 129
   Mobile station 130
   MSC 130
   PSK 128
   PSTN 130
   SDMA 129
   SIM 101
   SMS 131
   TDMA 128
   USSD 131
   Visitor location register 130

Wireless security 144

XML 136, 311